Representation and Party Politics

COMPARATIVE POLITICS
Edited by Gillian Peele
Lady Margaret Hall, Oxford

Representation and Party Politics

A Comparative Perspective

B. D. Graham

BLACKWELL
Oxford UK & Cambridge USA

First published 1993

Blackwell Publishers
108 Cowley Road
Oxford   OX4 1JF
UK

238 Main Street
Cambridge, Massachusetts 02142
USA

British Library Cataloguing in Publication Data
A CIP catalogue record for this book is available from the British Library.

Library of Congress Cataloging-in-Publication Data
Graham, Bruce Desmond, 1931–
    Representation and party politics / B. D. Graham.
      p.   cm. — (Comparative politics)
    Includes bibliographical references and index.
    ISBN 0-631-17395-1 (acid-free paper). — ISBN 0-631-17396-X (pbk.
: acid-free paper)
    1. Political parties.   2. Representative government and representation.
3. Comparative government.   I. Title.   II. Series: Comparative politics
(Oxford, England)
JF2011.G69   1993
324.2—dc20   93-14798
                                                                 CIP

Typeset in 11 on 13 pt Sabon
by Graphicraft Typesetters Ltd, Hong Kong
Printed in Great Britain by Page Bros, Norwich

This book is printed on acid-free paper

Contents

Preface to the Series

This new series in comparative politics has been designed with three broad objectives in mind. In the first instance it is hoped that, by focusing on a number of contemporary themes and issues in comparative politics, the individual studies may cumulatively make a contribution to the subject. Comparative politics has never been an easy discipline; and the subject has become more difficult as conceptual approaches have proliferated and the weight of material available to scholars has increased. As a result there has been a certain fragmentation as the task of refining the conceptualization has become separated from the detailed studies of institutions and political processes across political systems.

This tendency for discussions of the framework of comparative politics to become divorced from the subject's empirical research agenda has certainly been debilitating for the discipline. But it has also been misleading for the student. A second aim of the series is therefore to fill a gap in the literature by providing volumes which will combine empirical and theoretical material in easily accessible form. Each study will introduce the student to the current debates between political scientists about the major issues involved in the comparative study of a particular subject. However, each study will also deploy sufficient information drawn from a range of political systems to enable the readers to evaluate those debates for themselves.

A third goal of the series is to take account of recent political developments which make it necessary to look at governmental systems in new ways. The enhanced importance of supranational institutions (such as the European Community) and the resurgence of free market doctrines are but two examples of changes in the political landscape which have major implications for the organization of government in a number of states. Therefore, in addition to the familiar canon of topics in comparative politics, the series contains studies exploring themes which are perhaps less frequently handled in a comparative manner. Thus, as well as the study of interest groups by Graham Wilson, the series already includes a study of the politics of taxation (by Guy Peters) and a study of regulation (by John Francis).

Although this series has been designed with clear goals in mind, the individual authors have been allowed to exercise their judgement about which countries they include in their discussions. The only requirement is that they should address the theoretical debates about their chosen theme and devote attention to the way the issue presents itself in the context of modern government.

The study of representation and party politics by Professor Bruce Graham is an excellent addition to the series. Political parties are essential to the functioning of a democracy; their internal practices and the pattern of their interaction with other institutions may also have profound consequences for the wider system of government. Professor Graham examines the role of political parties in a way which is distinctive and intellectually challenging. His discussion is enriched by his ability to draw on the extensive knowledge which he has of the history and politics of two very disparate systems – France and India. Although Professor Graham is alert to the significance of the internal features of parties such as factionalism, he is also interested in party types and in particular in the distinctions between formally organized parties and broad political movements.

Professor Graham's book combines an original approach to his subject matter with an enlightening discussion of the extensive literature on political parties. I am delighted to be able to include it in the series.

Gillian Peele
Lady Margaret Hall
Oxford

Preface

This book represents an attempt to fill a gap in the political science literature which I have encountered when preparing and teaching courses about parties and party systems. In this field there is no lack of general books and monographs dealing with such questions as the organization of parties, electoral and parliamentary politics, and the roles played by parties in the making of policies, for example. However, there is often a problem in providing students with material illustrating the effects of stress upon liberal democratic polities, especially when such stress results in the emergence of strong leaders or causes individual parties to undergo periods of intense political conflict. For this, one needs to turn to the specialized literature but there is often not the time available for students to come to terms with such material.

I have therefore tried here not only to provide a brief survey of the essential literature on political parties and party systems but also to discuss theories applying to leadership and to conflicts within parties. The chapters have been designed to demonstrate how the standard material on parties and party politics can be related to these theories and to provide sufficient factual information in the form of case studies to enable students to form their own views about the points at issue. The manuscript was completed in July 1992 and has been briefly updated at proof stage to take account of recent events.

I should like to thank the staff of the Library of the University of Sussex for the considerable help which they have given me in locating some of the books and articles I have needed for this work, and also Ms Helen Gray and her colleagues in the Publishing Division of Blackwell Publishers for the care which they have taken in preparing the manuscript for publication. Above all, I am indebted to those students I have taught over the years whose interest in the subject first encouraged me to undertake this project.

B. D. Graham
University of Sussex
March 1993

Part I

Theories about Party Politics

1

Representative Politics and the Advent of Organized Parties

In the late nineteenth century, representative assemblies were regarded by most liberal theorists as the best means of ensuring that the sovereignty of the people should provide the basis for government. It was generally agreed, too, that a wide suffrage and free elections would ensure that these assemblies reflected the variety of opinion within the nation. At the same time, however, sceptics were raising questions about the risks involved in basing parliaments upon a mass electorate, and a debate was taking place on the value or otherwise of political parties themselves. Some theorists argued that parties, by placing a barrier between the people and government, might undermine the whole process of representation, creating artificial divisions between groups of citizens and inhibiting the free expression of opinion. Liberals, on the other hand, took the view that well-organized parties, differentiated from each other by their programmes and by their social support could, by imposing a necessary order upon the discussion of public issues, actually increase the efficiency of government.

One of the earliest attempts to come to grips with these problems was that made by a Frenchman, Alexis de Tocqueville (1805–59), who visited the United States of America between April 1831 and March 1832 to study a democratic society in evolution. He published his findings in a book entitled *De la Démocratie en Amérique*, the first volume of which appeared in 1835 and the second in 1840. Tocqueville was convinced that European society was moving by degrees from an aristocratic to a democratic form of organization, one in which political equality would be the norm, and he wished to discover whether this process would lead to a loss of liberty. Writing with the French people in mind, he described his approach in the following terms.

> It seems to me beyond doubt that sooner or later we shall reach, like the Americans, an almost complete equality of condition. I do not conclude from this that we will necessarily be persuaded one day to draw the political conclusions which the Americans have drawn from a similar social situation. I am very far from believing that they have found the only form of government that democracy may assume; but because in the two countries the basic cause of laws and customs is the same, we have an immense interest in knowing what it has produced in each of them.[1]

His interest in the normative basis of democracy led Tocqueville to distinguish between equality of condition (*l'égalité des conditions*), by which he meant equality before the law and the absence of rigid social divisions, and the emotional desire for equality (*la passion de l'égalité*), which made people assertive and envious of others. He reached the further conclusion that equality in a democratic order tended to foster individualism and to isolate citizens from each other, a danger which the Americans had avoided, he believed, by learning to co-operate in local affairs, to form associations, to respect the laws in force and to accept the principle of majority decisions. Moreover, he considered that the frequency of their elections encouraged American citizens to work together for political purposes, and that the freedom of the press and the independence of the judiciary reinforced this tendency.

Where presidential elections were concerned, he was less optimistic and less convinced that parties would serve a constructive purpose. Andrew Jackson was President at the time of Tocqueville's visit, and it may well have been the accounts of his victory in the 1828 contest which led Tocqueville to describe electioneering at this level of the political system as an inherently unstable process:

> the parties, in the United States as elsewhere, feel the need to group themselves around a man, in order to reach the mind of the crowd more easily. In general, they therefore use the name of the presidential candidate as a symbol; they personify their theories in him. Thus, parties have a great interest in swinging the election their way, not so much to ensure the triumph of their doctrines

with the aid of the new president as to show, through his election, that these doctrines have won a majority.[2]

He claimed that, long before the actual poll, interest in the election would become all-consuming, that the incumbent president would begin to be more concerned with securing his own re-election than with governing in the interest of the country, and that citizens would find themselves divided into two camps, each identified with one of the two candidates. Tocqueville thus recognized at a very early stage the strange symbiosis between parties and candidates, and drew attention to the possibility that elections at the national level could transform a presidential nominee into a popular hero and thus convert the occasion into a plebiscite for personal rule. Moreover, he saw that the parties themselves, gambling on their ability to restore normality after the event, might court this danger in order to promote their doctrines.

In Britain, Tocqueville's ideas were taken seriously by John Stuart Mill (1806–73), the great Victorian philosopher,[3] whose own enquiries into the prospects for democratic government were centred on conditions in Britain following the implementation of the Reform Act of 1832. This had provided for a redistribution of seats and an extended franchise, thus affording more scope for the urban middle classes to challenge the political ascendancy of the landed aristocracy. Mill's most wide-ranging account of his views about democracy is to be found in his book, *Considerations on Representative Government*, which was published in 1861. His basic propositions were that best form of government was one grounded upon the sovereignty of the people and that the people should exercise their 'ultimate controlling power' through elected deputies.[4] He described the relationship which, under the British Constitution, Parliament had established with the monarchy and the Cabinet, and showed that in practice it was Parliament that decided 'which of two, or at most three, parties or bodies of men, shall furnish the executive government', the party so chosen then selecting one of its members to be Prime Minister, subject to the approval of the Queen.[5] In addition, he saw Parliament as a regulator within the institutional machinery, monitoring the performance of the ministry of the day and mediating between the executive and the people.

Mill's theory of how the parliamentary system was adapting itself to changes in British society may be inferred from a number of his comments. While he believed that representative assemblies should not be involved in public administration or the preparation of proposals for taxation and public expenditure, he attached considerable importance to the ability of the House of Commons to represent the political community in all its variety. In this respect, Parliament was:

> at once the nation's Committee of Grievances, and its Congress of Opinions; an arena in which not only the general opinion of the nation, but that of every section of it, and as far as possible of every eminent individual whom it contains, can produce itself in full light and challenge discussion; where every person in the country may count upon finding somebody who speaks his mind, as well or better than he could speak it himself – not to friends and partisans exclusively, but in the face of opponents, to be tested by adverse controversy; where those whose opinion is overruled, feel satisfied that it is heard, and set aside not by a mere act of will, but for what are thought superior reasons, and commend themselves as such to the representatives of the majority of the nation; where every party or opinion in the country can muster its strength, and be cured of any illusion concerning the number or power of its adherents; where the opinion which prevails in the nation makes itself manifest as prevailing, and marshals its hosts in the presence of the government, which is thus enabled and compelled to give way to it on the mere manifestation, without the actual employment, of its strength; where statesmen can assure themselves, far more certainly than by any other signs, what elements of opinion and power are growing, and what declining, and are enabled to shape their measures with some regard not solely to present exigencies, but to tendencies in progress.[6]

Mill valued a representative assembly as an ideal means of reproducing on a small scale the pattern of general and specific interests in society, of regulating the process of debate and confrontation, and of providing the government with clear information about the state of public opinion.

As a reformer, Mill was only too aware of the ways in which such stabilizing arrangements could be undermined and endeavoured to find conditions which would preserve those features of Parliament which he valued. While he was in favour of a suffrage wider than that granted under the 1832 Reform Act, believing that possession of the vote would serve to educate the newly enfranchised, he nevertheless advocated the use of Thomas Hare's scheme of proportional representation.[7] This, he felt, would ensure the return to Parliament not only of Liberals and Conservatives but also of minorities who enjoyed a measure of public support. In order that a wider franchise might not lead to a decline in the quality of Members of Parliament, Mill proposed various restrictions on the right to vote – literacy and numeracy tests and the exclusion from the rolls of those who paid no taxes or who received parish relief – while at the same time recommending plural votes for people with professional qualifications. Far-sighted enough to realize that a greatly extended suffrage might transform electoral politics and, at a further remove, the whole system of representation in British politics, Mill tried to envisage what might happen if the electoral process produced completely opposed blocks of opinion. In one remarkable passage he constructed a picture of a modern community divided on class lines.

> In a state of society thus composed, if the representative system could be made ideally perfect, and if it were possible to maintain it in that state, its organization must be such, that these two classes, manual labourers and their affinities on one side, employers of labour and their affinities on the other, should be, in the arrangement of the representative system, equally balanced, each influencing about an equal number of votes in Parliament: since, assuming that the majority of each class, in any difference between them, would be mainly governed by their class interests, there would be a minority of each in whom that consideration would be subordinate to reason, justice, and the good of the whole; and this minority of either, joining with the whole of the other, would turn the scale against any demands of their own majority which were not such as ought to prevail.[8]

In other words, Mill saw moderate opinion as a binding force which would maintain the stability of the system in any shift from the Liberal–Conservative dualism of his own time to a class dualism.

The problem of maintaining stability in a period of rapid change was also addressed by one of Mill's contemporaries,

Walter Bagehot (1826–77), who wrote a number of articles for *The Fortnightly* which were published together in 1867 under the title *The English Constitution*. Distinguishing between the 'dignified' and the 'efficient' parts of the constitution, he suggested that the monarchy, as the centre of the dignified element, provided a focus for the loyalty of the people and made it possible for 'our real rulers to change without heedless people knowing it'.[9] The cabinet itself he saw as the essential bond between the executive and the legislature, and he placed great faith in Parliament's ability to choose good leaders.

Although less willing than Mill to envisage changes in the existing institutional structure, Bagehot was concerned with the problem of deciding how the party system and the House of Commons would be affected by any move towards a wider suffrage. Throughout his essays, Bagehot contrasted his preferred system (one in which parties were formed in Parliament around leading personalities and regulated by an informed though restricted outside opinion) with one in which extremist politicians aroused strong popular feeling, projected this feeling into Parliament, and produced what he described as 'Constituency government'. Referring to the working of the Commons, he claimed that efficiency in an assembly:

> requires a solid mass of steady votes; and these are *collected* by a deferential attachment to particular men, or by a belief in the principles those men represent, and they are *maintaine*d by fear of those men – by the fear that if you vote against them, you may yourself soon not have a vote at all.[10]

He went on to point out that 'party organisation' was 'permanently efficient' because:

> it is not composed of warm partisans. The body is eager, but the atoms are cool. If it were otherwise, Parliamentary government would become the worst of governments – a sectarian government. The party in power would go all the lengths their orators proposed – all that their formulae enjoined, as far as they had ever said they would go. But the partisans of the English Parliament are not of such a temper. They are Whigs, or Radicals, or Tories, but they are much else too. They are common Englishmen, and, as Father Newman complains, 'hard to be worked up to the dogmatic level'. They are not eager to press the tenets of their

party to impossible conclusions. On the contrary, the way to lead them – the best and acknowledged way – is to affect a studied and illogical moderation.[11]

Bagehot drew some unfavourable comparisons between politics here and in America, poured scorn on proposals for further electoral reform in Britain, and warned of the consequences of extending the vote to the working class. He disliked the American practice of choosing the chief executive by a national constituency rather than a representative assembly. Making an exception for the presidential election of 1864, in which Abraham Lincoln had been returned for a second term, he maintained that in almost all cases 'the President is chosen by a machinery of caucuses and combinations too complicated to be perfectly known, and too familiar to require description. He is not the choice of the nation, he is the choice of the wire-pullers.'[12] Writing before the adoption of the 1867 Reform Bill, he complained that an extended male suffrage within 658 electoral districts would produce a parliament composed of representatives of the squirearchy from the agricultural areas and of 'the lowest classes' (including 'members for the public-houses') from the towns.

> The genuine representatives of the country would be men of one marked sort, and the genuine representatives for the county men of another marked sort, but very opposite: one would have the prejudices of town artisans, and the other the prejudices of county magistrates. Each class would speak a language of its own; each would be unintelligible to the other; and the only thriving class would be the immoral representatives, who were chosen by corrupt machination, and who would probably get a good profit on the capital they laid out in that corruption. If it be true that a Parliamentary government is possible only when the overwhelming majority of the representatives are men essentially moderate, of no marked varieties, free from class prejudices, this ultra-democratic Parliament could not maintain that government, for its members would be remarkable for two sorts of moral violence and one sort of immoral.[13]

In particular, he saw no justification for the representation of the working classes, which 'contribute almost nothing to our corporate public opinion, and therefore, the fact of their want of influence in Parliament does not impair the coincidence of Parliament with public opinion. They are left out in the representation, and also in the thing represented.'[14]

Despite their very different approaches to the subject, Tocqueville, Mill and Bagehot all considered representation as a means of bringing forward deputies who could stand for opinions, for local communities, and, less directly, for social groups, and they therefore took the view that parties were incidental to this process, except at the parliamentary level. However, a later generation of writers came to see that parties in a new form, as extensive extra-parliamentary organizations with roots spreading out through the localities, were likely to become the principal means of providing representation under conditions of universal adult suffrage. Such a prospect disturbed the Russian writer, Moisei Ostrogorski (1854–1919), who studied British and American politics in the 1880s and 1890s and set out his conclusions in a two-volume study, *Democracy and the Organization of Political Parties*, which was published in English in 1902. Ostrogorski believed that in both Britain and the United States the process of representation had been distorted by party organizations and that democracy had been weakened as a consequence. In the case of Britain, his empirical work was largely concerned with the efforts of the main political parties to come to terms with the expansion of the electorate, which had occurred as a result of the Second Reform Act of 1867 and the Franchise Act of 1884. He described the development of the system of local committees under the National Union of Conservative and Constitutional Associations, which had contributed to the Conservative victory in the elections of 1874, and explained how the methods of party organization applied in Birmingham by Joseph Chamberlain and Francis Schnadhorst had later been extended to other areas. The National Federation of Liberal Associations, formed in 1877, had provided the basis for the Liberals' success in the 1880 elections and its attempts to exert discipline over both candidates and Members of Parliament had given added meaning to its nickname, 'the caucus'. Equally, in his research on American politics, Ostrogorski took an interest in the devices used for binding local committees into an organizational hierarchy and paid special attention to the associated institution of the nominating convention. He also discussed the conditions which, in some parts of the United States, had seen city and state organizations converted into political machines controlled by 'bosses' who exploited to the full the opportunities for patronage and clientelism. Passing judgement on the effects these changes had had, Ostrogorski was severe. With regard to 'the caucus' in Britain, he complained that it:

> was naturally inclined, instead of bringing about an agreement of intellects, to resort to mechanical modes of rallying its forces and to keep its adherents together in an external and conventional conformity, by appealing not so much to reason, which analyzes and distinguishes, as to feeling; by preferring to stir up emotions which confuse the judgement and make a prisoner of the will.[15]

He saw this as a failure to construct something positive from the ruins of an old order.

> Blotting out independent thought and enervating the will and the personal responsibility of the voter, the Caucus ends in obliterating the individual, after having undertaken to establish his political autonomy up to the farthest limits of the extraconstitutional sphere. Attacking the old leaders as if they were an impediment to this autonomy, the Caucus has struck a blow at the leadership in general, by disparaging the qualities which constitute leadership in a healthy political community, that is, the personal superiority conferred by knowledge and character, and exalting the conventional and external qualifications enforced by stereotyped methods. In making these qualifications and methods an engine of government, the Caucus bids fair to set up a government by machine instead of a responsible government by human beings.[16]

Now that the ordinary Members of Parliament had lost so much of their former prestige, it had become possible for men such as William Gladstone, the Liberal leader, and Benjamin Disraeli (Lord Beaconsfield), the Conservative leader, to appeal over their heads to the mass of voters. Although Ostrogorski did not doubt that it had been 'the highly magnetic personalities' of these two men that had

> powerfully contributed to set up the Caesarean supremacy of the leaders, ... it was sufficiently developed by the situation ... to enable their successors, who lacked the gift of impressing the popular imagination, to obtain the usufruct of this power over the

masses. This being so, the elections have assumed the character of
personal plebiscites, each constituency voting not so much for this
or that candidate as for Mr. Gladstone or against Lord Beaconsfield or [his successor] Lord Salisbury.[17]

He saw the rule of parties as having produced similar effects
in America. Here too he felt that the relationship between the
citizens and the state had been impaired because political parties
had divided the electors into separate camps by a process which
he described as 'political formalism', thus inhibiting the spon-
taneous formation of policy demands and philosophies around
the legislature. According to Ostrogorski,

> given the manner in which the contingents of the parties sent into
> Congress by the Caucus are formed, they could not constitute
> homogeneous, closely united wholes, guided by considerations of
> general interest, and obeying a single impulse proceeding from
> common principles and aspirations. Having reduced party divisions
> to a difference in titles, the Caucus régime has arrested or per-
> verted all along the line the see-saw by which the party system is
> supposed to ensure good government or, at least, supply a tempor-
> ary remedy for misgovernment.[18]

Thus, he depicted organized parties as the culprits which had
allowed oligarchies to achieve inordinate power over elected
representatives, which had deprived the electorate of its original-
ity and its capacity to express collective opinions, and which
had repressed the process of philosophical differentiation and
development.

Other political scientists viewed the advent of organized parties in quite a different light and presented the Anglo-American
pattern – of two major parties alternating in office – as the best
means not only of forming a myriad of policy demands into
distinct programmes for government action but also of strengthening popular support for democratic regimes. In a major comparative study of the states of continental Europe, published in
1896, the American scholar, A. Lawrence Lowell (1856–1943),
effectively used the Anglo-Saxon model of two parties cutting
across class lines to evaluate the relative stability of the party systems which he encountered in France, Italy, Germany, Austria-
Hungary and Switzerland. In each case, he sought to identify factors which either were impeding or might impede the advent of

party dualism and a stable pattern of responsible government. In his account of French politics, he suggested that the acceptance of the Republic by the right would remove 'one of the chief obstacles' to the development of two large parties on Conservative and Radical lines,[19] and attributed multipartism to the requirement in French electoral law for two ballots if a contest were not decided by an absolute majority on the first round (a provision which encouraged each group to nominate a candidate knowing that the outcome of the initial ballot need not be decisive); to the effect of the Parliamentary committee system on the power of the government; and to the practice of interpellation, by which a deputy could call a minister to account and thereby challenge the administration of which the minister was a member.[20] Reflecting on the fact that the Social Democratic Party was increasing its support in German politics, he argued that so long as parties in Germany were mainly expressing class differences, the 'absolute supremacy' of the Reichstag (the lower house of the Imperial Parliament) would not 'produce true democracy'.[21] He also drew attention to the importance of sectional divisions, and suggested, for example, that the stability of the ruling party and the Government in Hungary was a function of the solidarity of the Magyars in the presence of other ethnic groups within the eastern portion of the Austro-Hungarian Empire.[22]

In another major comparative study based on research undertaken before 1914 in France, Switzerland, Canada, the United States, Australia, New Zealand and Latin America, the English diplomat and academic lawyer, James Bryce (1838–1922), adopted a similar approach, using British parliamentary practice as his standard of judgement. Although he was often critical of the way parties were behaving in particular cases, his general view was that 'party organization is a natural and probably an inevitable incident of democratic government'.[23] Far from endorsing Ostrogorski's thesis that party organizations had restricted the expression of opinion, he believed that the electorate was relatively passive and required stimulation to respond effectively to the challenge of democratic government.

Party strife is a sort of education for those willing to receive instruction, and something soaks through even into the less interested or thoughtful electors. The parties keep a nation's mind alive, as the rise and fall of the sweeping tide freshens the water of long ocean inlets. Discussion within each party, culminating before elections in the adoption of a platform, brings certain issues to the front, defines them, expresses them in formulas which, even if tricky or delusive, fix men's minds on certain points, concentrating attention and inviting criticism.[24]

For all that he saw parties as providing a stimulus to the electorate, Bryce had no illusions that the whole people of a country would ever be fully involved in its government. At one point in his book he argued that, in a democracy as in other forms of government, the actual direction of affairs was undertaken by a small number of people with the general body of citizens acting as a checking or regulating force.[25] He even suggested that democracy was no longer prized as an end in itself, that is, as an expression of liberty.

> It is now valued not for what it is, but for what it may be used to win for the masses. When the exercise of their civic rights has brought them that which they desire, and when they feel sure that what they have won will remain with them, may they not cease to care for the further use of those rights? The politicians, who in some countries have been more and more becoming a professional class, might continue to work the party machinery; but that will avail little if the nation turns its mind to other things. If the spiritual oxygen which has kept alive the attachment to Liberty and self-government in the minds of the people becomes exhausted, will not the flame burn low and perhaps flicker out?[26]

When Bryce's study was published in 1921, the Versailles settlement had restored the prospect that representative democracies could be established everywhere in Europe except in the Soviet Union. Eighteen years later, however, liberal-democratic regimes existed only on the western edge of Europe, in Scandinavia, in North America and in Australasia, while the authoritarian regimes in Germany, Italy, Japan and the USSR were aggressively asserting their strength. Despite the criticisms levelled against their policies, there were those who regarded single-party systems (whether fascist or communist) as being better able to provide strong government than could two-party or multi-party systems. The experiences of the 1920s and 1930s gave added force to the reservations which Bryce had expressed in his study and later observers shared his unease. For example, when Lawrence Lowell wrote a retrospective review of *Modern Democracies* in 1938, he combined his defence of pluralism in party politics with warnings about the dangers of competition.

> Parties have their evils; and as a friend of mine remarked long ago, the inherent defect of democracy is that it is no one's business to look after the interest of the public. Yet so long as the contending parties oscillate about the center of gravity of public opinion, the system, though irrational, works fairly well. But not when the parties are too far apart. Then one of them becomes dominant; the other irreconcilable, and therefore to be crushed, by force if necessary. In such a case the conventions on which democracy is based are undermined, and chief among them the assumption that the divergent aims of parties, though mutually repugnant, are universally tolerable. In other words, parties seeking to supplant one another in control of the state are possible in a democracy so long as all of them agree that rule by a rival is better than disorder, and any legal method of deciding who shall rule better than civil strife.[27]

Even in the decade which followed the Second World War, the importance attached to the threat of McCarthyism in the United States and doubts about whether it would be possible to re-establish competitive party politics in Germany, Italy and Japan raised further questions about the robustness and effectiveness of liberal democracy. Although valued for providing the basic freedoms of expression, association and belief, it was seen as a relatively fragile system, unable to flourish except in countries possessing a largely urban population, a well-educated middle class, independent legal institutions and a strong economy – countries in which, moreover, there was general agreement that religious, ethnic or linguistic differences should not become the basis of political divisions. Were these conditions lacking, ran the argument, liberal democracies could find themselves faced with opposed parties which had become rival communities in a state of virtual civil war, or under authoritarian rule, as a single leader, exploiting the tools of plebiscite and referendum to his own advantage, endeavoured to establish a monolithic structure of allegiance.

In our brief review of early studies of representative politics we have seen a contrast between two differing expectations about the future development of liberal democracies. One, derived from the writings of Toqueville and Mill, assumed that free elections and political competition would produce an informed public and ready consent for the practice of responsible government. A less sanguine forecast, evident in Bryce's book, saw the mass of the people placing more value on the material (as distinct from the spiritual) benefits of democracy and, by neglecting the importance of liberty, running the risk of exploitation by small elites. Judgement as to the value of parties varied in similar fashion: for an optimist, they provided the essential bonds between citizens and the government, but for a pessimist they increased the dangers of oligarchic rule and destructive competition. The experience of recent decades has produced an understanding of electoral and parliamentary politics which is more balanced and realistic than either of these early views; it is now generally accepted that party competition does serve to regulate the underlying conflicts between social groups and to represent different sectors of the community in legislatures. At a more general level, parties are seen as the most effective means of generating an acceptance of the principles that governments should be based on popular consent and that they should be held accountable for their policies to the body of citizens.

In the chapters which follow we shall briefly review, with these points in mind, some of the general approaches to the study of parties and party systems in liberal democracies. We shall then give special consideration to the processes which occur when parties come under stress, firstly, from the challenge of rallies inspired by political personalities and, secondly, from the effects of internal conflicts and divisions.

Notes

1 Alexis de Tocqueville, *De la démocratie en Amérique*, with a biography, preface and bibliography by François Furet (2 vols, Flammarion, Paris, 1981), vol. I, p. 68 (translation mine).
2 Ibid., pp. 208–9 (translation mine).
3 See J. S. Mill's review articles on *De la démocratie en Amérique* in *London Review*, II (1835), pp. 85–129, and in *The Edinburgh Review*, LXXII (1840–1), pp. 1–47. For a comprehensive account of the intellectual relationship between the two men, see H. O.

Pappé, 'Mill and Tocqueville', *Journal of the History of Ideas*, XXV, 2 (April–June 1964), pp. 217–34.

4 J. S. Mill, 'Considerations on Representative Government' (1861), in J. M. Robson (ed.), *Essays on Politics and Society by John Stuart Mill* (2 vols, University of Toronto Press, Toronto, 1977), vol. II, p. 422.

5 Ibid., pp. 427–8.

6 Ibid., p. 432.

7 See Appendix III ('Thomas Hare's Proposals') of E. Lakeman and J. D. Lambert, *Voting in Democracies: A Study of Majority and Proportional Electoral Systems* (Faber and Faber, London, 1955), pp. 245–6.

8 Mill, 'Considerations on Representative Government', in Robson (ed.), *Essays on Politics and Society by John Stuart Mill*, vol. II, p. 447.

9 W. Bagehot, *The English Constitution*, with an introduction by R. H. S. Crossman (Collins/Fontana, London, 1963), p. 97.

10 Ibid., pp. 158–9.

11 Ibid., p. 159.

12 Ibid., p. 77.

13 Ibid., pp. 161–3, quotation from p. 163.

14 Ibid., p. 176. Cf. the introduction to the second edition (1872), ibid., pp. 277–8.

15 M. Ostrogorski, *Democracy and the Organization of Political Parties*, ed. and abridged by S. M. Lipset, tr. F. Clarke (2 vols, Quadrangle Books, Chicago, 1964), vol. I, pp. 293–4.

16 Ibid., p. 304.

17 Ibid., p. 316.

18 Ibid., vol. II, p. 288.

19 A. Lawrence Lowell, *Governments and Parties in Continental Europe* (2 vols, first published in 1896, reissued in 1970 by Kennikat Press, Port Washington, NY), vol. I, p. 105.

20 Ibid., pp. 108–27.

21 Ibid., vol. II, p. 67.

22 Ibid., pp. 159–61.

23 J. Bryce, *Modern Democracies* (2 vols, Macmillan, London, 1921, reprinted 1923), vol. II, p. 28.

24 Ibid., vol. I, p. 134.

25 Ibid., vol. II, Ch. 75 ('Oligarchies within democracies'), pp. 594–604.

26 Ibid., pp. 663–4.

27 A. Lawrence Lowell, 'The future in retrospect: the evolution of democracy', *Foreign Affairs*, XVII, 1 (October 1938), pp. 30–1.

2

Theories of Party Systems

Theories about pluralist party systems offer explanations of the political process by two different means. At one level, they present historically based accounts of how parties express and influence the changing balance between groups within society; at another, more abstract level, they give an account of how parties organize debates about policy choices and compete with one another to find the best solutions for social and economic problems. This chapter concentrates on the first of these explanations and chapter 3 on the second.

The common assumption that the two-party pattern is the most stable type of party system stems from the judgement that there is a natural tendency for the division of opinion in society to be twofold; it follows, according to this theory, that the best means of capturing and expressing this duality of opinion is provided by a two-party system. Generalizations of this kind are heirs to earlier, nineteenth-century theories of political change which suggested that societies were evolving by a process of continuous struggle between the forces of progress, or movement, and the forces of reaction, or order. When the first organized parties were formed, they were seen as agents of one side or the other in this basic conflict rather than as independent bodies, capable of exerting their own influence on the formation of public opinion. As applied to the history of representative politics in Western European countries, such a theory of party origins often ran alongside a theory of class relations which attributed an interest in progress and liberalism to a rising urban bourgeoisie intent on gaining support for industry and commerce, and an interest in order and conservatism to the landed aristocracy. In this scheme of things, the divisions between philosophies, classes and parties were parallel, coeval and mutually reinforcing. When the growth of the industrial working class broke the symmetry of the pattern, the theory was used to predict a new phase in political alignments. Industrial workers were assumed to regard socialism as a way of achieving the collective control of the means of production, distribution and exchange, and the Socialist Parties which sprang up in several countries at the turn of the century were taken to be the new parties of movement. It was further assumed that liberals and conservatives would make common cause as the class conflict between capitalists and workers became the dominant one.

The actual histories of individual party systems bore enough resemblance to this general theory to be represented as evidence that its assumptions were correct, provided that awkward deviations from the predicted pattern were satisfactorily explained. In Britain, the competition between Whigs and Tories in the nineteenth century conformed to the assumed liberal–conservative dualism so long as the support which both parties drew from sections of the landed aristocracy was taken into account, just as the rise of the Labour Party could be seen as the first stage in the transition to a socialist–conservative dualism. Within the German Empire after national unification in 1871, anti-socialist laws had at first limited the activities of the Social Democratic Party (SDP) but, when these laws were allowed to lapse in 1890, the SDP rapidly increased its following amongst industrial labour; in the elections of 1912, the last before the First World War, it won 110 of the 397 seats in the Reichstag[1] and seemed set to compel the parties to its right to consolidate their forces. In France, the early years of the Third Republic (founded in 1870) had seen a conflict between Republicans and their opponents which resembled a liberal–conservative dualism, and the formation of the Radical Party in 1901, and of the unified Socialist Party in 1905 suggested that there too, as in Britain and Germany, a displacement to the right of the older parties was underway and that a socialist–conservative dualism would eventually be established.

The rise of the Socialist Parties had begun at a time when the conditions of party politics were being transformed by the introduction of universal manhood suffrage and, presented with mass audiences, parties were compelled to develop broad appeals for support. They became more concerned to gain approval for their policies and programmes; especially in Britain, where the rivalry between the Liberals and the Conservatives became increasingly intense from the 1870s onwards, elections became occasions to request a mandate, that is, an authority to introduce particular measures if returned to power. At the same time, parties were finding it increasingly necessary to adopt more elaborate forms of organization, with extensive networks of local committees and branches, a permanent administrative structure and a corps of professional managers and activists. The centre of party life was shifting away from the legislatures to the arena of public competition, and power was being transferred from the older elites, the parliamentary notables, to new professionals on the one hand and to well-known popular leaders on the other. Of course, not all parties adopted these new methods of operation; in France in particular the old style of electoral politics persisted in many regions, but the general trend was towards greater organization and integration, both inside and outside the legislatures.

In the interval between the two world wars, the liberal democracies of Western Europe were placed under considerable pressure from totalitarian movements. The Fascists established a dictatorship in Italy in 1922, the National Socialists took power in Germany in 1933, and in Spain General Franco's Nationalists finally defeated the Republican Government after a civil war which had lasted from July 1936 until March 1939. Where and when free elections and parliamentary government were maintained, pluralist party systems continued to function and, in some cases, to develop along the lines laid down earlier, despite the complications caused by the establishment of the Communist Parties in the early 1920s and by the activities of extreme right-wing groups. In Britain, the Liberal Party's support was steadily eroded as the Labour Party extended its base until what was virtually a two-party pattern was registered by the general elections of 1935.[2] In Germany and France, the multi-party rather than the two-party pattern continued to prevail. In the former, under the Weimar Republic between 1919 and 1933 the pre-war trend towards a socialist–conservative dualism was arrested; the left-wing vote was divided between the SDP and the newly formed Communist Party, while the Catholic Centre Party effectively held the balance of power between them and various conservative, liberal and regional groups before the rapid rise of the National Socialists created the conditions under which Adolf Hitler was able to take power in 1933.[3] In France, the multi-party system proved remarkably resilient and the socialist–conservative dualism which had seemed likely did not occur. The Socialist Party divided in 1920 to form a reconstructed party of the same name and a new Communist Party; the Radical Party remained firmly anchored to its position as a centre unit; and the parliamentary groups on the right of the party spectrum were still divided amongst themselves. The Socialists, Communists and Radicals won the general elections of 1936 as a Popular Front alliance and supported a sequence of governments against right-wing opposition until the latter months of 1938, when the alliance collapsed; but the dualism of 1936–8 was essentially a pattern of two blocs beneath which the various parties had preserved their separate identities.

The general theories of these and other party regimes were worked into an ambitious and striking account of the growth and diversification of party systems by the French political scientist, Maurice Duverger, whose book, *Political Parties*, published in 1951, set the terms for a debate which is still in progress. Having described the tendency for the older conservative–liberal conflict to give way to a new conservative–labour conflict, he treated as axiomatic the proposition that the two-party system (most evident in Anglo-Saxon democracies) corresponded to the twofold nature of opinion in society. Further, he maintained that the simple-majority single-ballot voting method favoured the two-party system by under-representing minor parties and inducing electors to support those candidates whose parties had well-founded hopes of taking power rather than those whose parties had no such prospects. Duverger did not exclude the possibility that a newly formed party could overcome these obstacles, as the Labour Party in Britain had done, but he claimed that the simple-majority voting method would help to preserve the two-party pattern, perhaps by forcing one of the older parties into the position of a minor unit, or by persuading it either to merge with or to form an alliance with its former rival.[4]

In accounting for the existence of the multi-party system in many Western European and Scandanavian countries, he suggested that these were partly the result of the processes of party fission, partly an effect of cross-cutting ties (that is, of lines of division on major issues which intersected each other to produce several rather than two segments of opinion) and partly a consequence of electoral methods, such as the two-ballot system or proportional representation, which he considered could reduce the natural pressures towards dualism and provide scope for the creation of new parties.[5]

To illustrate the effects of cross-cutting ties, Duverger described how various issues had influenced party- and group-alignments in French politics during the early years of the Fourth Republic (founded in 1946). One line of division in this period was that between clericals and anti-clericals, that is, between those who defended the privileges of the Church and those who favoured restrictions upon its influence, especially in the field of education; on this issue, the Communists, Socialists and Radicals were on the anti-clerical side and the progressive Christians, the Christian democratic Popular Republican Movement (MRP), the Right and the Rally for the French People (RPF) on the opposing side. However, on other questions these units were aligned differently: the Radicals, the Right and the RPF favoured economic freedom whereas the Socialists, Communists, progressive Christians and the MRP supported the principle of planning, and, where a choice between the Soviet Union and its allies (the East) and the Western powers was concerned, the Communists and the progressive Christians were inclined to the East and the remaining groups to the West.[6] His main analytic point was that the parties and groups were not organized in two mutually exclusive blocs of opinion on all issues; groups who were in agreement in one area of policy might differ in others with the result that changes in alignment were likely to occur whenever public interest or government attention moved from one question to another.

Duverger was also interested in the systematic variations in party systems which were caused by differing patterns of power relationships arising from electoral and parliamentary competition. One such pattern was that of alternation, in which first one and then another of two large parties would hold office for short periods of time, as in Britain. A second pattern was one in which the distribution of party strength remained relatively constant over a long series of elections, as in the Netherlands

under proportional representation. A third was that of domination, in which one party would acquire an apparently un-
shakeable grip on government. As a fourth kind of pattern, he
identified a tendency for a party system to shift to the left, responding to the rise of new social strata.[7] In pursuing this line
of reasoning, Duverger assumed that parties, especially if they
were relatively centralized and organized, could shape and order
as well as represent the structure of public opinion.[8]

Although Duverger's book has been subject to criticism (for
example, by Colin Leys regarding the adequacy of his account
of the relationship between electoral methods and party systems[9] and by Aaron Wildavsky regarding the soundness of his
methodology),[10] his central enterprise, an attempt to construct
a general theory of political behaviour which would respect
the relative autonomy of party systems in their relations with
governments and electorates, has continued to command the
respect of research workers in this field of scholarship.

The historical development of party systems was reconsidered
in an important essay which S. M. Lipset and Stein Rokkan
wrote as an introduction to the symposium, *Party Systems and
Voter Alignments*, which was published in 1967. Their basic
approach was to identify the extent to which major changes in
Western societies had created enduring political divisions and
had thus provided a framework within which parties could form
and develop. They identified several such divisions, one of which
concerned the conflict over whether the church or the state
should have most influence upon the moral basis of social practices. A second division was that which had arisen during the
process of nation-building, in countries where the extension of
central control and nation-wide bureaucratic structures had
caused reactions from outlying regions concerned to preserve
their own cultural traditions. The growth in the power of the
state had also added a new dimension to the tension between
secular and clerical authorities, with the former claiming the
right to manage the schooling system and the education of children while reducing if not abolishing the influence of the church
in this area of social policy. A third division was that which had
occurred because the industrial revolution and the growth in
international trade had caused an initial clash between rural
primary producers and a new urban class of merchants and

industrialists and, at a later stage a struggle between property holders and employers in one camp and tenants, labourers and workers in another. A fourth derived from the Russian revolution of 1917, which had created a division within the left between those willing to give their first loyalty to their own nation state and those who were prepared to identify themselves with an international revolutionary movement.[11] Although produced by a skilful elaboration of Talcott Parsons's pattern variables, the resultant schema stands in its own right and provides a valuable means for plotting and comparing the histories of particular party systems.

Applied to French political history, for example, it alerts us to the need to recognize the complexity of the conflict between the Republicans and the Right in the early period of the Third Republic, a conflict in which the ancient quarrel between church and state was informing the more immediate clash between the anti-clericals and their opponents over the extension of secular schooling and the widening of opportunities for entry by young people into the professions. To some extent also, it marked a tension between France's entrepreneurial and landed interests, and at the same time between those groups which favoured a parliamentary system of government and those which hoped that an opportunity would arise for them to restore either the vanished monarchical or the Bonapartist regime, depending on which they favoured. The rapid growth of the Socialist Party after 1905 can be taken to represent the strengthening of the third line of division, caused by industrialization, just as the fission of that party in 1920 can be taken to represent the appearance in France of the fourth division between the nationalist and internationalist elements of the Left.

The task of establishing a comprehensive typology of party systems was one of those undertaken by Giovanni Sartori, in the first volume of his *Parties and Party Systems*, published in 1976.[12] Where competitive party systems were concerned, Sartori placed most emphasis on the configurations formed by parties in action rather than on their actual numbers, and distinguished between the following categories:

1 *Two-party systems*, in which each of two parties aims for an absolute majority of seats in parliament, in which one of them wins sufficient seats to enable it to govern alone, and

in which the prospect of spending alternate periods in power remains a realistic one for both parties.[13] According to these criteria, the British, American, Canadian and New Zealand systems would all conform to the two-party type, as would the Australian party system at the federal level providing that the Liberal and National (formerly Country) Parties are considered as a single unit for constitutional purposes.

2 *Systems exhibiting extreme and polarized pluralism*, in which, briefly, a centre party or a group of centre parties is placed between two mutually antagonistic oppositions, including anti-system parties; in which the ideological differences between the units at either extreme are relatively wide; and in which competition tends to be centrifugal rather than centripetal (that is, it proceeds at the expense of, rather than around, the centre). Elements of this type of system were to be found in France under the Fourth Republic, in post-war Italy, in Germany under the Weimar Republic and in Chile (until September 1973).[14] The pattern was particularly clear in the case of France between 1947 and 1951, when a series of coalition governments were formed or supported by the Socialists, the Radicals, the MRP and the Conservatives (together constituting the so-called Third Force) as a means of defending the Fourth Republic both against the attacks of General de Gaulle's RPF, which wanted to alter the constitution to provide the basis for a presidential regime, and against the uncompromising opposition of the French Communist Party.

3 *Systems characterized by moderate pluralism*, in which there are three, four or five parties and in which the basic pattern is one of government by coalition with the prospect of alternative coalitions. By contrast with the pattern of polarized pluralism, there are relatively small ideological differences between the parties, there is only one source of opposition to the government in power, there are no significant anti-system parties and competition is centripetal. The examples which Sartori cites are the party systems of the Federal Republic of Germany, Belgium, Ireland, Iceland, Luxembourg, Denmark, Switzerland and the Netherlands.[15] In the case of the Federal Republic of Germany, party politics since the adoption of the Basic Law in 1949 had been characterized by competition between two evenly matched units, the combination of the

Christian Democratic Union (CDU) and the Bavarian Christian Social Union (CSU) on one side and the Social Democratic Party (SDP) on the other. Occupying the centre ground between the two rivals had been the small but robust Free Democratic Party (FDP) while various minor and splinter parties had subsisted on the margins of the electoral and parliamentary territory. The CDU/CSU formed coalition ministries with the FDP and a small German Party between 1949 and 1956 but governed without the FDP between 1956 and 1961, when election losses obliged it to arrange another coalition with its former partner. Following disagreements over financial policy, the FDP withdrew its ministers from the Government in October 1966 and in the following month the SDP combined with the CDU/CSU in a 'grand coalition'. Its gains in the 1969 elections enabled the SDP to form a coalition with the FDP. This new alliance lasted throughout the 1970s but at the end of 1982, as a result of policy disputes, the FDP changed sides once more and linked up with the CDU/CSU in a ministry under the chancellorship of Helmut Kohl. This realignment held firm for the remainder of the decade and, as a result of its victory in the first all-German elections to the Bundestag on 2 December 1990, the CDU/CSU–FDP Government took charge of the unified state. This pattern matches the analytic type of moderate pluralism in several respects: West Germany has been governed by coalition ministries for most of the time since 1949; anti-system parties have been held in check; policy differences between the major parties have not been great; and, given the willingness of the FDP to transfer allegiance, German voters have become accustomed to the idea that alternative coalitions are the most likely outcome of major changes in public opinion.

4 *Predominant party systems*, in which one party obtains an absolute majority of the seats in parliament and stays in power for at least three consecutive elections.[16] At the time Sartori was writing, the Indian party system appeared to be an exemplar of this type. The Congress Party had been in power since India had gained independence in 1947 and had won absolute majorities of the seats in the Lok Sabha (the lower house of the federal parliament), in the general elections of 1951–2, 1957, 1962 and 1967. The party had

split in 1969 but the segment led by Mrs Indira Gandhi had won a further majority in the Lok Sabha elections of 1971. However, following a brief period of emergency rule, her party lost the elections of 1977 and began a period in opposition, during which it suffered a further split. Congress (I, for Indira), Mrs Gandhi's section of the divided party, was returned to power in the elections of 1980 and, after her assassination, in those of 1984. It was defeated in the 1989 poll but was victorious in the 1991 contest, after which P. V. Narasimha Rao was able to form another Congress (I) administration. Since the late 1970s, therefore, the non-Congress groups have shown a capacity to win elections and to form coalition governments under favourable circumstances, but it remains the case that the long succession of Congress ministries from 1947 to 1977 provides an interesting illustration of a predominant party system and of the special conditions which it can generate.

Sartori's typology also included categories for one-party systems, hegemonic party systems (in which minor parties are given some limited scope for activity) and, at the other extreme, atomized systems.[17] He discussed the situations in which a party system could change from one type to another,[18] but he warned of the need to exercise caution in classifying the party systems of those Third World countries in which political structures were relatively fluid and formless.[19] His main contribution to work on party systems has been to demonstrate the importance of the centre ground, whether of opinion or of parties (as in cases of polarized pluralism), and to emphasize the necessity of distinguishing between different modes of operation (in the formation of governments and alliances) and of identifying the extent of doctrinal divergence between units in characterizing a particular party system.

A further value of Sartori's theories has been that they provide a sound basis for conducting further enquiry into the question of whether certain types of party system are related to particular kinds of social structure. One tradition of research into this relationship has assumed that parties are essentially projections into the political arena of underlying social groups and that party activities can therefore be explained in terms of, or indeed reduced to, the activities of those groups. In an extreme form, this was the approach adopted by Frederick Engels who, in the introduction which he wrote in 1895 for an edition of Karl Marx's book, *The Class Struggles in France 1848 to 1850*, maintained that:

> the materialist method has here quite often to limit itself to tracing political conflicts back to the struggles between the interests of the existing social classes and fractions of classes created by the economic development, and to prove the particular political parties to be the more or less adequate political expression of these same classes and fractions of classes.[20]

Without accepting such a degree of determinism, some political scientists, whether Marxist or non-Marxist in outlook, are prepared to take the view that the competition between social classes does indeed govern the competition between political parties, even though parties may try to win support across class lines. It was in this sense that R. M. MacIver spoke of the party system as being 'the democratic translation of the class struggle'.[21] Writing in similar terms, S. M. Lipset put this proposition even more bluntly:

> Even though many parties renounce the principle of class conflict or loyalty, an analysis of their appeals and their support suggests that they do represent the interests of different classes. On a world scale, the principal generalization which can be made is that parties are primarily based on either the lower classes or the middle and upper classes.[22]

Making a slightly different point, he also argued that:

> More than anything else the party struggle is a conflict among classes, and the most impressive single fact about political party support is that in virtually every economically developed country the lower-income groups vote mainly for parties of the left, while the higher-income groups vote mainly for parties of the right.[23]

This explanation of the social basis of party politics was accepted with few reservations by many observers of the British political system and formed the essential theme of one of the

most sophisticated and systematic accounts of electoral behaviour in the United Kingdom, *Political Change in Britain*,
published in 1969 by David Butler and Donald Stokes. Their
analysis of data derived from interviews carried out in 1963,
1964 and 1966 led them to conclude that social class continued
to provide the foundation for British parties – with the majority
of the middle class supporting the Conservatives and the majority of the working class the Labour Party – and that although
there were significant degrees of cross-class voting, the Labour
Party was still extending its support among the working class.
On the other hand, they drew attention to an apparent weakening in the intensity of class feeling which they attributed to increased affluence, a tendency for the post-1951 cohorts of voters
to be less concerned than their elders with the conflictual aspects
of class relations, and changes in the disposition of the Labour
Party, whose leadership had become more middle class in character and whose policies were growing increasingly similar to
those of the Conservative Party.[24]

Since that book was written, British party politics have
changed in certain crucial respects. The votes for the two major
parties have fluctuated unusually from election to election since
1970. In the 1970 poll the Conservatives attracted 46.4 per cent
of the votes and took office under Edward Heath while Labour's
share of the total fell to 43.0 per cent. There were two elections
in 1974, when Harold Wilson formed his second Labour Government; the Labour Party's percentage share of the vote was
37.1 in the February and 39.2 in the October contest, whereas
the Conservative Party's shares were 37.8 and 35.8 respectively.
James Callaghan succeeded Wilson as Prime Minister in 1976
but his party was defeated in the elections of 1979, after which
Margaret Thatcher came to power at the head of a Conservative
administration; on this occasion the Conservative Party's share
of the vote rose to 43.9 per cent and that of the Labour Party
fell to 37.0 per cent. The Conservatives won the subsequent
polls of 1983 and 1987 with percentage votes of 42.4 and 42.3
while Labour, having gained only 27.6 per cent of the votes in
1983, improved its position in 1987 and 1992, when it obtained
30.8 and 34.5 per cent of the votes respectively.[25] During the
same period, the share of the votes won by the minor parties
reached higher levels than had been recorded at any time since

the 1920s. This increased fluidity in party support prompted electoral analysts to re-examine the relationship between party and class. Bo Särlvik and Ivor Crewe, in their analysis of voting trends from the perspective of the 1979 elections, concluded that they were observing a process of 'partisan dealignment', in the sense that 'none of the major occupational groups now provides the same degree of solid and consistent support for one of the two major parties as was the case in the earlier post-war era'[26] but in their reinterpretation of survey data up to and including those related to the 1983 poll, Richard Rose and Ian McAllister concluded that the association between class and party was actually a weak one. As an alternative to the heavy reliance on class-bound models of voting behaviour which had restricted the scope of earlier voting studies, they proposed a 'cumulative life-time learning model' designed to take account of the influence of a number of factors, including pre-adult socialization, adult socialization, commitment to political principles, attitudes to-wards the performance of parties in Parliament, and the impact of the election campaign.[27] In the context of recent British elections, these arguments are convincing; their acceptance does not entail a denial that there is a relationship between social groups and parties but simply a recognition, to quote Michel Offerlé, 'that the connection which occurs between electors and parties is effected through multiple mediations whose full complexity is still far from clear'.[28]

In any case, the steady convergence of the two major parties with respect to public policies has made it more difficult for voters to link those parties with specific social interests and, for that very reason, has made it easier for each party to establish broad, cross-class support in regions where it was well established at the local level. Under Neil Kinnock, who succeeded Michael Foot as Labour leader soon after the 1983 elections, the Labour Party's organization was strengthened and its policies substantially revised and, as a result, Labour regained its credibility as a potential party of government. The Conservative Party was also moving towards centre ground; in November 1990, after a bitter internal struggle which culminated in the resignation of Margaret Thatcher, John Major succeeded her as party leader and Prime Minister. The two parties were evenly matched in the campaign for the general elections of 9 April

1992, which the Conservatives won by a narrow majority. Under John Smith, who took over from Neil Kinnock as party leader in July 1992, Labour has sustained its appeal to centre opinion. With convergence has come a steady increase in the combined share of the vote obtained by the two parties; this rose from 70.0 per cent in 1983 to 73.1 per cent in 1987 and to 76.4 per cent in 1992. However, the apparent trend towards another phase of dualism similar to that which obtained in the 1950s and 1960s has been accompanied by significant changes over the years in the geographical distribution of support for the two main parties, with the Conservatives registering their highest levels of support in the Midlands and the South of England and the Labour Party achieving substantial shares of the vote in northern England, the Scottish Lowlands and southern Wales.[29]

There has been considerable interest amongst American political scientists in similar changes in the geographical basis of their own party system, and this interest has produced a literature concerned with what is usually referred to as the theory of 'critical realignment'. This rests upon the assumption that the presidential and congressional elections of the periods 1892–6 and 1928–36, during which there were significant redistributions of geographical and social support for the Democratic and Republican Parties, were similar in kind, in that they expressed in political form basic changes which were occurring in American society. In abstract terms, these and comparable earlier realignments were taken to indicate that change in the American party system was not linear but cyclical in character, and that American parties, instead of adapting steadily to the development of economic and social structures, had sufficient internal strength to resist the forces bearing upon them for a considerable time; when, finally, the accumulated pressure became irresistible and they were forced to give way, went the argument, they had adjusted themselves rapidly to achieve a new equilibrium. If indeed the party system did change in this way, suddenly after long periods of relative stability, political scientists were interested in discovering what preliminary indications there might be, tremors before the earthquake as it were, which could act as a warning that a new cycle was likely to occur.

The starting point for this line of enquiry was a remarkable article by V. O. Key, 'A theory of critical elections', which was published in the *Journal of Politics* in 1955. Using aggregate polling data for towns and cities in the New England region, he showed that a decisive shift in support to the Republicans had occurred in the 1896 elections, following a period of economic unrest, and that a contrary shift towards the Democrats had taken place in the 1928 elections, when Alfred E. Smith, the Democrats' presidential candidate, had appealed strongly to Roman Catholics and to low-income voters. In Key's own words, his concept of critical elections had been developed 'to cover a type of election in which there occurs a sharp and durable electoral realignment between parties',[30] and the theory implicit in his observations was further extended in a major study by Walter Dean Burnham, published in 1970. Burnham distinguished Key's 'critical realignments' from other electoral events, such as secular realignments (that is, cumulative changes extending over a long period) and deviations (a poll in which special and short-lived factors might influence the result), and described what he took to be their essential characteristics. He argued that a critical realignment was accompanied by an extensive and rapid reorganization of the electoral groups from which the parties derived their support, and by other phenomena indicating an unusually intense level of political competition, for example, the appearance of third parties, ideological polarization within and between parties, and high voter participation rates.[31] Drawing attention to evidence that recent party votes in congressional and presidential elections were deviating from each other more than they had in the New Deal period, and also that the proportion of electors identifying with one or other of the two major parties was on the decline, he suggested that the United States might be heading towards another critical realignment of its party system. He discussed the possibility of a new party system taking shape in which the Democrats might represent an alliance of extremes, an elite which was skilled in the use of post-industrial technology making common cause with the poor, while the Republicans remained identified with white 'middle America', the peripheral regions and traditional liberal values.[32]

The periods identified as those when critical realignments had occurred (1892–6 and 1928–36), had long been recognized as times of important change in American politics. The 1890s marked the rearrangement of a pattern which had been established in the 1860s, during and after the civil war, when the newly formed Republican Party, having opposed slavery and defended the Union, had identified itself with the development of American industry, free land for farmers and the westward expansion of the frontier. Agrarian unrest in the late 1880s and the 1890s was expressed not through the Democratic Party, still on the defensive after championing states' rights and the South, but through a number of Independent and People's Parties, which gained considerable support in the prairie regions. Although the 1892 presidential election was won by a Democrat, Grover Cleveland, a People's Party (Populist) nominee headed the poll in five western states, an indication that this movement was approaching the level of strength needed to supplant one of the established parties, most probably the Democrats. During his term as President, Cleveland came into conflict with several groups which might otherwise have backed his party; his defence of the gold standard offended those western farmers (Populists included) who favoured the free coinage of silver as an inflationary measure, his decision to call in the army to put down the Pullman strike of 1894 lost him labour support, and his administration was blamed for its apparent inability to deal with the consequences of the 1893 depression. In preparing for the 1896 elections, the Democrats changed direction, choosing as their presidential nominee William J. Bryan who favoured the free coinage of silver, and instead of putting up their own man the Populists decided to join them in supporting Bryan's candidature. He was strongly attacked by the Republican contender, William McKinley, who stood for the gold standard and tariff protection and who drew support from industry, finance and labour. Building on Republican gains in the congressional elections of 1894, McKinley soundly defeated Bryan, winning 51.0 per cent of the popular vote and 217 of the 447 electoral votes (American Presidents are chosen by an electoral college, to which each state contributes a number of members equal to the combined number of its Senators and Representatives in Congress). The Republicans were now firmly in control of the industrial and established farming states of the north-east and the mid-west and, apart from a period of relative weakness following a split in their ranks in 1912, remained in a strong position in American politics until 1932.[33]

The second period of sudden change began when Alfred E. Smith, a Roman Catholic and a former Governor of New York, was nominated as the Democratic candidate for the presidential election of 1928, a choice which was taken to signify that the Democratic Party was acknowledging the importance of its urban support in north-eastern America. Although Smith was defeated by the Republican nominee, Herbert Hoover, carrying only the states in the deep South along with Massachusetts and Rhode Island in the north-east, he won 40.8 per cent of the popular vote and thus paved the way for the substantial gains made by the Democrats in the 1932 poll. In that year, Franklin D. Roosevelt, the Democrats' presidential candidate, gained the support of an electorate which had been badly shaken by the financial crash of 1929 and the onset of the great depression, and won all but a handful of north-eastern states. Roosevelt's New Deal programme – the measures he took to alleviate the distress caused by the depression and to stimulate the revival of industry and agriculture – led to his overwhelming success in the 1936 presidential election, when he won majorities in every state except Maine and Vermont and attracted 60.8 per cent of the popular vote.[34] He is credited with having formed what became known as the New Deal coalition of industrial workers, ethnic minorities, farmers and intellectuals, and with having given the Democratic Party a much more secure social and territorial basis than it had had in the period from 1896 to 1932. The variability of the party vote in presidential elections since the 1950s has often distracted attention from the underlying strength which the Democrats established in the 1930s, strength which has enabled them to win majorities in the House of Representatives and the Senate on most occasions and, given a strong candidate and favourable circumstances, to return one of their own to the White House, as they did in the 1992 poll.[35]

Whether these two periods of rapid change are indeed similar events, and whether a comparative analysis of their characteristics can provide the material for a coherent theory of partisan realignment, are questions which are still being asked. In his book, *Dynamics of the Party System*, published in 1973, James L. Sundquist argued that the 1892–6 and 1928–36 realignments could be compared with previous crises, including that which occurred in the 1850s, when the earlier dualism between the Whigs and the Democrats gave way to the modern pattern of Republicans versus Democrats. He agreed that the elections of 1896 and, in the New Deal period, those of 1932 and 1936 marked major shifts in the electoral balance of power between the two parties but warned of the need to recognize that the New Deal realignment, in the sense of definite changes of allegiance by large numbers of voters, did not take effect in some states and localities until well after the main event and that the process of delayed adjustment had still not been completed in the southern states.[36] Addressing the theoretical questions, Sundquist emphasized the effect of those divisions about major questions of public policy which were sufficiently intense and widespread to impinge upon the balance of forces within and between parties. If such an issue were to cause a division which conformed to the established line of cleavage between the parties it would simply reinforce existing alignments, but were an issue to produce a division cutting across party lines (as had happened in the debates about slavery in the 1850s, about monetary policy in the 1890s, and about the interventionist role of the state in the 1930s) the party system itself would become unstable. Whether a phase of instability would end in a critical realignment would depend on whether a group of leaders committed to radical action were formed in one party and a group of leaders strongly opposed to such action were formed in the other. If these antagonistic leadership groups (the polar forces) were to gain the ascendancy over the moderates and the conciliators in their respective parties, the pressure to shift the line of party cleavage to conform with the new division of opinion would become irresistible and the consequential social and territorial adjustments would be set in train.[37]

The problems of extending the theory of critical realignments were also the subject of a book entitled *Partisan Realignment*, published in 1980 by Jerome Clubb, William Flanigan and Nancy Zingale, who had conducted a thorough analysis of the relevant long-term trends in aggregate voting statistics and generally confirmed the historical patterns proposed by earlier writers. However, their main contribution to the discussion was to demonstrate that the completion of a partisan realignment depended significantly on whether the party taking power after a crisis could use the agencies of government to implement policies which would satisfy the newly formed electoral majority and on whether those policies could solve the problems which had caused the crisis in the first place. In making this point, they drew attention to the active role that parties had played in seizing the opportunities created by negative electoral reactions to the government in office when each crisis had occurred, and they thus rejected the view that partisan realignments were essentially electoral phenomena. Their analysis also showed that the periods between realignments consisted of a stable phase, a middle phase of minor adjustments (such as those which had taken place in 1912 and 1948) and a phase of decay.[38] Subsequently, in an article published in 1987, Stuart Macdonald and George Rabinowitz have proposed a model of structural change in which a new issue is introduced by an elite, causes a change in 'congressional ideological coalitions or in the dialogue between presidential candidates' (if the former change had taken place this would become evident in the presidential dialogue), and is finally expressed in a 'new ideological cleavage' in the party system.[39]

Interest in whether the American party system was in fact heading towards a new realignment has been subsumed in a wider enquiry as to the kinds of major changes, critical or not, which are likely to occur under various conditions. The discussion has not produced agreement and analysts differ in their judgements as to what significance should be attached to certain features of party politics in the post-war period – features such as the decline in the proportion of American voters who firmly identify themselves with either the Republican or the Democratic Party,[40] the unusual incidence of split-voting between presidential and congressional elections,[41] and the increasing ability of congressional incumbents to retain their seats. During the late 1980s, the contrast between Republican control of the presidency and Democratic control of Congress prompted a number of theoretical questions, perhaps the main one being whether the Democrats would be reduced to minority status because of their apparent inability to gain control of the executive. However, the victory of the Democratic nominee, Bill Clinton, in the presidential election of November 1992 has shown that the balance of advantage has once more shifted away from the Republicans and that a new generation of Americans has come to power.[42]

Although the predictive value of the theory of critical (or

partisan) realignment has yet to be proved, it is quite clear that the interest in it has produced a much more subtle understanding of the delicate interplay in American politics between such factors as party organization, leadership, political discourse, voters' attitudes, and the nature and effects of major issues than has been achieved in the study of other national party systems. The main relevance of this point for our present discussion is that a formal schema of party systems, or of the historical origins of those systems, does not serve political science if it restricts our interest merely to exercises in classification, or if it tempts us to equate the activity of parties with other types of activities, such as that of social classes or of supposedly autonomous elites. The great challenge of work in this field is to employ the analysis of formal and informal structure to study, firstly, how party systems function in detail in such situations as general elections, legislature debates, internal and external crises, and the choice of high officers, and, secondly, how they maintain themselves over long periods of time despite the discontinuity of so many of the institutional arrangements and political cycles which provide the context for their activity. Rather than seeing a party as a corporate entity, we have to envisage it as a loosely organized social arena in which different groups of actors endeavour to retain their relative positions and their relative freedom of manoeuvre. Making a similar point, Sundquist warned of the danger of assuming that parties correspond to the textbook model of rationality: distinguishing between a party in power and one out of power, he suggested that:

> The in-party, during periods when the president is exercising firm control, may at times approach the textbook model of rationality, but only at times. The out-party approaches that model for only a few months out of four years, between the time the presidential candidate is chosen and the election, when the candidate is setting policy. The rest of the time, an American party should be thought of not as a rational organism with some kind of collective brain making coherent strategic judgements, but as a terrain to be fought over, conquered, and controlled first by one element, then by another.[43]

Although he was writing about American parties at the rarefied national level, the points which he makes hold true for the organizational characteristics of most parties, and of the systems which they comprise.

Notes

1 See table on German election results in E. Lakeman and J. D. Lambert, *Voting in Democracies: A Study of Majority and Proportional Electoral Systems* (Faber and Faber, London, 1955), p. 184.
2 See table on British general election results from 1885 to 1951 in ibid., p. 26.
3 See table on German election results in ibid., p. 184.
4 Maurice Duverger, *Political Parties: Their Organization and Activity in the Modern State*, tr. Barbara and Robert North (Methuen, London, 1954), pp. 207–28.
5 Ibid., pp. 228–55.
6 Ibid., pp. 231–2.
7 Ibid., pp. 281–351.
8 Ibid., pp. 372–92.
9 Colin Leys, 'Models, Theories, and the Theory of Political Parties', *Political Studies*, VII, 2 (1959), pp. 127–46.
10 Aaron B. Wildavsky, 'A methodological critique of Duverger's *Political Parties*', *The Journal of Politics*, XXI, 2 (May 1959), pp. 303–18.
11 S. M. Lipset and S. Rokkan, 'Cleavage Structures, Party Systems, and Voter Alignments: An Introduction', in Lipset and Rokkan (eds), *Party Systems and Voter Alignments: Cross-National Perspectives* (The Free Press, New York, 1967), pp. 1–64. For an application and extension of this approach, see Richard Rose and Derek Urwin, 'Social Cohesion, Political Parties and Strains in Regimes', in Mattei Dogan and Rose (eds), *European Politics: A Reader* (Macmillan, London, 1971), pp. 217–37. See also Hans Daalder, 'Parties, Elites, and Political Developments in Western Europe', in Joseph LaPalombara and Myron Weiner (eds), *Political Parties and Political Development* (Princeton University Press, Princeton, 1966), pp. 67–9. For a more recent enquiry into the classification of parties by political family, see Daniel-Louis Seiler, *Partis et familles politiques* (Presses Universitaires de France, Paris, 1980), and Seiler, *De la Comparaison des Partis Politiques* (Economica, Paris, 1986).
12 Giovanni Sartori, *Parties and Party Systems: A Framework for Analysis* (Cambridge University Press, Cambridge, 1976), vol. I. For

an earlier formulation, see Sartori, 'European Political Parties: The Case of Polarized Pluralism', in LaPalombara and Weiner (eds), *Political Parties and Political Development*, pp. 137–76.

13 Sartori, *Parties and Party Systems*, pp. 185–92.
14 Ibid., pp. 131–45.
15 Ibid., pp. 173–85.
16 Ibid., pp. 192–201.
17 Ibid., pp. 125–6 and 217–43.
18 Ibid., pp. 273–323.
19 Ibid., pp. 244–72.
20 Karl Marx and Frederick Engels, *Selected Works* (2 vols, Foreign Languages Publishing House, Moscow, 1951), vol. I, p. 110.
21 R. M. MacIver, *The Web of Government* (Macmillan, New York, 1947), p. 217. See also Robert R. Alford, 'Class Voting in the Anglo-American Political Systems', in Lipset and Rokkan (eds), *Party Systems and Voter Alignments*, pp. 67–93.
22 S. M. Lipset, *Political Man: The Social Bases of Politics* (Heinemann, London, Second Edition, 1983), p. 230.
23 Ibid., p. 234.
24 See David Butler and Donald Stokes, *Political Change in Britain: Forces Shaping Electoral Choice* (Macmillan, London, 1969, reprinted 1970), pp. 65–122.
25 See table on British general election results from 1945 to 1987 in David Butler and Dennis Kavanagh, *The British General Election of 1987* (Macmillan, Basingstoke, 1988), p. 283. For the 1992 results, see *The Sunday Times* (London), 12 April 1992, II, p. 8.
26 Bo Särlvik and Ivor Crewe, *Decade of Dealignment: The Conservative Victory of 1979 and Electoral Trends in the 1970s* (Cambridge University Press, Cambridge, 1983), p. 332. See also Crewe, Särlvik and James Alt, 'Partisan Dealignment in Britain 1964–1974', *British Journal of Political Science*, VII, 2 (April 1977), pp. 129–90.
27 Richard Rose and Ian McAllister, *Voters Begin to Choose: From Closed-Class to Open Elections in Britain* (Sage, London, 1986). For a general discussion of this question, see Lipset, *Political Man*, pp. 503–21.
28 Michel Offerlé, *Les partis politiques* (Presses Universitaires de France, Paris, 1987), p. 108 (translation mine). For a discussion of the role of class in relation to survey data for the period 1964–87, see Anthony Heath et al., *Understanding Political Change: The British Voter 1964–1987* (Pergamon, Oxford, 1991), pp. 62–84.
29 See the analysis of regional electoral trends in *The Economist* (London), 12 May 1979, pp. 21–4; 18 June 1983, pp. 32–4; 20

June 1987, pp. 31–3. For the regional pattern of the 1992 election, see the *Sunday Times*, 12 April 1992, I, p. 14.

30	V. O. Key, 'A theory of critical elections', in David W. Abbott and Edward T. Rogowsky (eds), *Political Parties* (Rand McNally, Chicago, Second Edition, 1978), pp. 309–22, quotation from p. 321. (This article was first published in the *Journal of Politics* in 1955.) See also Key, 'Secular realignment and the party system', the *Journal of Politics*, XXI, 2 (May 1959), pp. 198–210, and Angus Campbell, 'A classification of the presidential elections', in Abbott and Rogowsky (eds), *Political Parties: Leadership, Organization, Linkage* (Rand McNally, Chicago, 1971), pp. 358–70.

31	Walter Dean Burnham, *Critical Elections and the Mainsprings of American Politics* (Norton, New York, 1970), pp. 6–10 and 66–70.

32	Ibid., pp. 135–74. See also Burnham, 'American politics in the 1970s: Beyond party?', in Abbott and Rogowsky (eds), *Political Parties* (1978), pp. 349–70.

33	See James L. Sundquist, *Dynamics of the Party System: Alignment and Realignment of Political Parties in the United States* (The Brookings Institution, Washington, DC, 1973), pp. 120–54. See also Everett Carll Ladd, *American Political Parties: Social Change and Political Response* (Norton, New York, 1970), pp. 169–77, and V. O. Key, *Politics, Parties, and Pressure Groups* (Crowell, New York, Fifth Edition, 1964), pp. 168–73 and 256–9.

34	See Sundquist, *Dynamics of the Party System*, pp. 183–217, and Key, *Politics, Parties, and Pressure Groups*, pp. 185–90.

35	For an excellent map showing the distribution of party support in the 1988 elections for the House of Representatives, see *Le Journal des Élections* (Paris), 5 (November–December 1988), pp. 34–5.

36	Sundquist, *Dynamics of the Party System*, pp. 218–19.

37	Ibid., pp. 275–98. See also Sundquist, 'Whither the American party system?', in Abbott and Rogowsky (eds), *Political Parties* (1978), pp. 330–48. For an enquiry into generational change as a factor in realignment, see Gerald B. Finch, 'Physical change and partisan change: The emergence of a new American electorate, 1952–1972', in Louis Maisel and Paul M. Sacks (eds), *The Future of Political Parties* (Sage, Beverly Hills, 1975), pp. 13–62.

38	Jerome M. Clubb, William H. Flanigan and Nancy H. Zingale, *Partisan Realignment: Voters, Parties, and Government in American History* (Sage, Beverly Hills, 1980).

39	Stuart Elaine Macdonald and George Rabinowitz, 'The dynamics of structural realignment', *American Political Science Review*, LXXXI, 3 (September 1987), pp. 775–96, quotations from pp. 778–9. See also Sadafumi Kawato, 'Nationalization and partisan realignment in Congressional elections', ibid., 4 (December 1987), pp. 1235–50.

40 See Helmut Norpoth and Jerrold G. Rusk, 'Partisan Dealignment in the American Electorate: Itemizing the Deductions since 1964', ibid., LXXVI, 3 (September 1982), pp. 522–37.

41 See Everett Carll Ladd with Charles D. Hadley, *Transformations of the American Party System: Political Coalitions from the New Deal to the 1970s* (Norton, New York, Second Edition, 1978), pp. 322–30.

42 See an excellent report on the election results by Alain Frachon and Jean-Pierre Langellier in *Le Monde* (Paris), 5 November 1992, pp. 1 and 4.

43 Sundquist, *Dynamics of the Party System*, p. 304.

3

Party Systems in the Abstract

Each one of the theories about party systems which we have considered in the previous chapter is the product of detailed historical enquiry and any models derived from them are necessarily very complex. They influence, and are influenced by, other more abstract theories of party and party behaviour which can be represented by relatively simply models with limited sets of variables. Whereas the former historically grounded theories enable us to ask questions about the origins and development of party systems with close reference to the cultures of the societies concerned, the more abstract theories are primarily directed towards functional and utilitarian questions regarding the general relationship of the party system to other systems in the political structure.

The latter questions provide the central themes in Joseph Schumpeter's book, *Capitalism, Socialism and Democracy*, first published in 1942. Schumpeter expressed scepticism about what he took to be the classical theory of democracy (concerning the existence of the will of the people and the representation of that will in assemblies). Instead he proposed that politics should be seen as a competition between groups of leaders, and that parties served as the means of attracting votes for such leaders and of shaping public opinion in the process: 'Party and machine politicians are simply the response to the fact that the electoral mass is incapable of action other than a stampede, and they constitute an attempt to regulate political competition exactly similar to the corresponding practices of a trade association.'[1] He argued that parties gave voters the opportunity to choose between rival elites and, taking into account the experience of modern industrial nations, he specified what he considered to be the basic conditions necessary for competition between them to work effectively: these were that party leaders should be people of 'high quality', that the areas of policy exposed to democratic decision-making should be restricted, that there should be an able and respected bureaucracy, that citizens should exercise 'Democratic Self-control' by accepting the legitimacy of existing legislation and executive orders, and that there should be 'a large measure of tolerance for difference of opinion'.[2]

These ideas were presented as part of Schumpeter's general enquiry into whether capitalism would give way to some form of socialism. While he considered that democracy, in the sense of competitive party politics, could exist within a socialist political order, it must be stressed that he attached little value to the representative functions of parties. Throughout his book, he treats them as simple and unreflective entities, serving as the instruments of elite competition, rather than as bodies of members and activists determined to advance the interests of defined constituencies. His disinclination to credit the voters with a determinate influence upon party policies stemmed from two separate though related assumptions; the first was that the ordinary voter lacked sufficient ability to observe and interpret facts and to derive rational inferences from findings, and the second was that a voter's grasp of reality and sense of responsibility diminished the further that matters for judgement were removed from the ordinary spheres of family and business life: 'the weaker the logical element in the processes of the public mind and the more complete the absence of rational criticism and of the rationalizing influence of personal experience and responsibility, the greater are the opportunities for groups with an ax to grind.'[3]

Schumpeter's attempt to build an abstract schema to account for the essential forms of representative politics was carried much further by Anthony Downs, whose book, *An Economic Theory of Democracy*, published in 1957, is one of the landmarks in the intellectual geography of modern political science. Downs constructed a predictive model in which the basic units were voters, parties and interest groups. He assumed that parties were driven by the need to attract votes, just as entrepreneurs sought profits in a market economy, and that citizens, like rational consumers, gave their votes to the party which they considered would provide them with a 'higher utility income' when in office.[4] Downs, in contrast to Schumpeter, assumed that the voters behave in a rational fashion, and that they are there-fore capable of distinguishing between alternative courses of action and of consistently choosing that course which produces the most benefits at the least cost. Responding to such rational-ity, parties seek to organize their statements of policy intentions, and to order their actions when in office, in such a way as to ap-peal to the widest possible range of voters. However, because it is impossible for parties on the one hand to obtain a complete picture of the real desires of the voters, and for voters on the other to gather precise information about what each party's real intentions might be, the electoral process takes place in a world of uncertainty. This uncertainty complicates what would other-wise be a straightforward matter of matching preferences to policy statements, and in order to reduce its effects a party adopts a number of devices, including the use of agents and intermediaries to find out more about voters' interests and the presentation of ideologies as a general indication of its policy in-tentions. For their part, voters approach elections with their own 'fixed conception of the good society' along with information which they have acquired about party policies, but they too are hampered by the problems caused by imperfect communication.[5]

In explaining his approach, Downs relied mainly on a simple framework in which voters were faced by two parties, one of which was in office, but he also envisaged a situation in which his rational voters were confronted by three or more parties and the institution of coalition governments. He pointed out that the formation of such governments would entail two stages of deci-sion; at the first stage, a voter would choose which party to sup-port in the competition for places in the legislature and at the second the parties in the legislature would negotiate to determine which of their number would provide the parliamentary majority and the members for a coalition ministry. Placed at two removes from the situation in which governments were formed, the vot-er's problem would become one of deciding not only which party to support but also one of estimating which party combinations could provide the basis for alternative coalitions, and what range of policies each alternative was likely to adopt if placed in power.[6]

In order to demonstrate the connection between structures of opinion and party systems, Downs used a spatial model in which voters and parties were distributed along a simple continuum between extreme leftist and extreme rightist positions, with moderate opinions in the centre. If the frequency distribution of voters by opinion were unimodal and symmetrical, with the majority of voters concentrated in the centre, the most likely result would be a pattern of two convergent parties with broadly similar policies. If the distribution were bimodal, with concentrations of voters at opposite ends of the continuum, the most likely outcome would be two widely separated parties in an unstable relationship with each other. To take a further example, if the distribution of voters were polymodal, with several points of concentration, the result might well prove to be a system of several parties, each with a relatively fixed ideological position but a propensity to join coalitions.[7]

In his concluding chapter, Downs demonstrates that his two central hypotheses, regarding party motivation and citizen rationality, can be used to deduce a wide range of propositions capable of being studied empirically.[8] His schema has formed the basis for further enquiry into the normative and logical aspects of democratic theory. To take one example, David Robertson has built upon Downs's approach to consider ways of studying the capacity of government to solve problems rather than restricting himself to the assumption that the process of governing 'should be seen as an activity of distributing utility to supporters';[9] and he has also suggested a number of refinements to Downs's model, extending the range of variables in the party sector so that the role of both activists and leaders can be taken into account in explaining changes in party positions, and envisaging a field of voters as a set of differentiated constituencies rather than as a single and general constituency.[10] Although Downs does consider the possibility of major contingencies (such as a change in the franchise, or an external crisis such as the Second World War, or a social revolution)[11] his model is closer to the reality of a party system working within a fairly stable domestic and international context, in other words, when the periodic election cycles are the main concerns of both voters and parties. His model is less useful for studying points in the history of a party system when unexpected events have intensified conflicts about basic values or have placed the survival of the regime itself in jeopardy.

At one level, Downs was endeavouring to meet the criticism of many economists that political scientists have been too concerned with developing normative theories of representation to pay sufficient attention to questions of how policies are made and carried into effect, and one of the consequences of his kind of model-building has been the growth in recent years of positive public-choice theory. This theory assumes that all political actors, from voters to elected representatives and administrators, are motivated by an interest in maximizing their individual utility. Thus the voter supports that candidate whose statement of policies offers him the greatest net benefit; parties and election candidates construct programmes designed to give them the best chance of winning elections; a party in power pursues policies favouring its supporters; and administrators also work in a self-interested way, for example, by increasing the size of their own organizations.[12]

An attractive feature of Downs's model is the extent to which it is based on clearly specified sets of actors and motivations and therefore avoids the limitations of earlier economic models of government, such as the 'individualistic' and the 'organismic' approaches.[13] However, another group of general theories explains the political process by analogy with the functioning of a system, in a biological or natural sense, and therefore accepts some degree of organicism, of treating the organization of government as if it were a unified body with a life of its own. The basic notion of systems theory is that any coherent pattern of related activities can be abstracted from its setting and specified as a set of independent variables existing within an environment which influences its stability and its operations. A system may be short-lived, but if it persists over time the observer may be tempted to assume that each of its constituent units serves a purpose and performs a function for the whole, as if the system were in equilibrium, with each of its parts compensating for stress and for the temporary disorientation of other parts of the whole.[14]

One of the most ambitious attempts to employ systems analysis for a general explanation of politics was that presented by David Easton in *A Framework for Political Analysis* and *A Systems Analysis of Political Life*, both published in 1965. Easton took the political system to be 'those interactions through which values are authoritatively allocated for a society'.[15] He argued that it was responsive to two categories of environmental influence, one produced by the intra-societal environment (made up of the ecological, biological, personality and social systems) and another by the extra-societal environment (consisting of international political systems, international ecological systems and international social systems). These two environments were treated as the source of inputs, in the form of the demands and support which flowed into the political system, providing both 'feedback' (that is, relevant information) for the authorities and material which could be converted into outputs (the 'authoritative allocation of values' by means of laws and formal decisions along with statements and performances associated with this process). Outputs also served the purpose of maintaining a 'feedback loop' by which the environment was given information about responses to inputs.[16]

Obviously, this scheme has a great deal in common with the concept of equilibrium in the physical sciences, especially as it uses the model of energy exchanges as a metaphor to explain the role of inputs and outputs in the process of system maintenance. In particular, the political system depends for its survival on its ability to allocate values successfully and to persuade the majority of citizens to accept such allocations. The fine working of the system is achieved by a variety of regulatory mechanisms, including the party system, and Easton took into account not only the need for the political system to deal with stress by meeting specific demands and maintaining specific sources of support but also the importance of diffuse support for the authorities, the regime and the political community.[17] Crucial to his argument was the notion that the political system required a boundary between itself and other social systems.[18] He saw his task as one of providing a broad intellectual framework in which 'partial theories of political allocation' could be related to one another:

what these allocative theories take for granted – the actual and continued existence of some kind of political system – I have here questioned and subjected to theoretical examination. How is it that a political system as such is able to persist through time? What is there in the nature of the system itself and the conditions under which it may typically find itself that would stand as a possible threat to its continued existence, whether in one form or another?[19]

The exponents of systems theory assumed that the acceptance of activities (or interactions) as the basic units of analysis would mean that political scientists could compare the politics of different countries with reference to behavioural patterns rather than to institutional structures, including legislatures, executives and parties. Easton took the view that:

> From the point of view of the analysis being developed, structure is definitely secondary, so much so that only incidentally and for illustrative purposes need discussion of structures be introduced. Certainly no attempt will be made to consider political structures in any systematic way. The assumption will be that there are certain basic political activities and processes characteristic of all political systems even though the structural forms through which they manifest themselves may and do vary considerably in each place and each age.[20]

By asserting the primacy of the behavioural rather than the structural aspects of the political process, systems theory invited the research worker to discount the importance of the roles played by institutions in particular activities (such as those of trade unions in the field of wage-bargaining) and thus to undervalue the extent to which institutions express the norms and customs of their society. In other words, the theory was cast at a level of generality far removed from the middle-level explanations of political organization which were necessarily sensitive to the effects of cultural and historical contexts upon the working of institutions.

A very similar approach to theory-building had been attempted a few years earlier by Gabriel Almond in his introductory chapter to *The Politics of the Developing Areas*, a volume published in 1960 in which a number of area specialists had sought to use a common analytic framework in their accounts of politics in several regions of the world. In a conscious attempt to promote a new set of terms which could be applied to the study of a wide range of polities, Almond substituted for 'state' the concept of 'political system', which he defined as:

that system of interactions to be found in all independent societies which performs the functions of integration and adaptation (both internally and vis-à-vis other societies) by means of the employment, or threat of employment, of more or less legitimate physical compulsion. The political system is the legitimate, order-maintaining or transforming system in the society.[21]

Faced with the problem of comparing Western polities characterized by a high degree of institutional specialization with non-Western polities in which institutions were relatively generalized and newly established, Almond specified an exhaustive set of functions required for the maintenance of any political system, whether or not that system possessed specialized institutions for each function. His basic procedure was to translate the appropriate Western institution into its essential function or task and, where parties were concerned, he described the logical steps as follows: '[t]he functions performed by political parties in Western political systems led us to the question, "How are articulated demands or interests aggregated or combined in different political systems?" or the *aggregative function*.'[22] Finally, Almond envisaged the political system as being served by four input functions (political socialization and recruitment, interest articulation, interest aggregation, and political communication) and by three output functions (rule-making, rule application and rule adjudication).[23]

He emphasized that a given structure could serve several functions and that a given function could be performed by several structures. However, in his detailed exposition of the function of interest aggregation he was drawn into a discussion of the analytic categories which had been developed within the specialist literature, and distinguished between authoritarian, dominant non-authoritarian, competitive two-party and competitive multi-party systems. He pointed out that the competitive two-party system was exemplified by the party systems of the United Kingdom, countries belonging to the old British Commonwealth, and the United States.

Here a homogeneous, secular, bargaining political culture and an effective and autonomous system of associational interest groups introduce claims into the party system, legislature, political executive, and bureaucracy which are combinable into responsive, alternative public policies. Boundary maintenance between society and polity and among the articulative, aggregative, and rule-making structures is good. The whole process tends to be overt and calculable and results in an open circulatory flow of inputs and outputs.[24]

By comparison, party politics in India were judged to have shortcomings; the boundaries between party, legislature and bureaucracy were described as 'poorly maintained by virtue of the fact that much of the aggregative function is performed within the bureaucracy in a process which does not separate aggregation, rule-making, and rule application'. In the party system proper 'the aggregative function is performed in some measure particularistically, diffusely, symbolically, and ideologically, rather than pragmatically'.[25] In this instance, Almond tended to use his analytic categories as a means of measuring a non-Western political system according to the degree of institutional differentiation and responsiveness which it had achieved, judged by Western standards.

Almond's functional categories were defined in such general terms that their use for specific comparisons was bound to present difficulties. In his contribution to *The Politics of the Developing Areas*, Myron Weiner dealt with the South Asian region and presented a detailed account of political trends in India, Pakistan and Ceylon (now Sri Lanka) in the late 1950s, but, while employing Almond's categories as a framework of reference, his most interesting comparisons of the party systems in these three countries, all of which had become independent of British rule in the late 1940s, used the specific conceptual schemes which were already familiar to political analysts at this time. Thus, Weiner showed how the Indian National Congress, under Gandhi's influence, had developed a strong nationalist philosophy, a mass organization and agitational techniques in the early 1920s whereas its main rival, the Muslim League, led by Muhammad Ali Jinnah, had not acquired a mass basis until just before the Second World War. He used this difference to explain why the Congress had been able to retain its political ascendancy in independent India while the Muslim League, which had fought so hard for the creation of Pakistan, had found considerable difficulty in establishing a widespread popular following in that state; indeed, by the time that Weiner was writing, its position had already been weakened in East Pakistan both by the rise of the Awami League, which was exploiting regional nationalism amongst the Bengali Muslims, and by the introduction of military rule in October 1958. The Ceylonese party system provided yet further contrasts; here nationalist activity before independence had been largely restricted to the English-speaking professional elites, and the parties had not acquired either the mass basis or the organizational capacity of their counterparts in India and Pakistan. Only after independence had the party system developed a popular dimension, as first the United National Party, led by D. S. Senanayake, and later the Sri Lanka Freedom Party, headed by S. W. R. D. Bandaranaike, had built up substantial support for their policies.[26] Weiner had obviously accepted the need to relate research into the party systems of particular countries to the general enterprise of constructing an adequate framework theory; but it is clear that he was just as concerned with pursuing questions of middle-level theory (such as why some of the South Asian parties developed mass organizations earlier than others, and why some were durable while others were not) as he was with the more abstract exercise of characterizing a function or process, such as interest aggregation, and making this his main field of enquiry.

The general approaches which we have reviewed in this chapter vary a great deal from each other, in both design and purpose, but they share certain significant characteristics. Firstly, they all tend to assume either that party systems do in fact act as effective agents for the state in evaluating and solving policy problems and thus in maintaining the stability and coherence of society, or that they should do so. Secondly, they all tend to assume that parties, as we understand them in the West, can exist only in countries with high levels of urbanization, literacy and numeracy and with no great social divisions. Although he does not explore this point at any length, Schumpeter appears to believe that competitive party systems are a product of bourgeois values, and that these in their turn stem from the ethics of the capitalist system; Downs's hypothesis of citizen rationality assumes a degree of literacy and understanding which could have been acquired only by a highly educated and integrated community; and one of the implicit justifications for systems theory is the claim that the difference in social and cultural conditions between Western and non-Western societies is so great that in the latter, institutions such as parties cannot be assumed to serve the same functions as their Western counterparts, thus making institutional comparisons virtually impossible.

However, the example of India does indicate that the basic elements of representative politics – frequent elections, representative assemblies, and governments derived from and responsible to those assemblies – can be understood and valued by an electorate consisting very largely of a peasantry with poor living standards, modest levels of literacy and marked status divisions. Elsewhere in the Third World the results have been less promising, and there are numerous instances of countries in which representative politics has given way to army rule, or a one-party regime, or civil disorder. It would be wrong, however, to conclude from such cases that the establishment or restoration of liberal democracy should be postponed until certain educational, social and cultural conditions have been met. Competition between groups in elections and in assemblies may well be accompanied by noise and confusion; nevertheless this competition remains the best means yet devised for ensuring that government has a popular basis and that social conflicts are settled within a process of bargaining and conciliation rather than through civil war. Rival parties of some kind tend to evolve as one of the consequences of representative politics, and though they may lack the coherence of Western models, they should be given every opportunity to develop the crucial links between government and citizens and to set out their views and programmes in open debate.

Notes

1   Joseph A. Schumpeter, *Capitalism, Socialism and Democracy* (Unwin, London, Fourth Edition, 1954, Twelfth Impression, 1970), p. 283. See also Warren J. Samuels, 'A Critique of *Capitalism, Socialism, and Democracy*', in Richard D. Coe and Charles K. Wilber (eds), *Capitalism and Democracy: Schumpeter Revisited* (University of Notre Dame Press, Notre Dame, 1985), pp. 60–119.

2 Schumpeter, *Capitalism, Socialism and Democracy*, pp. 290–5.
3 Ibid., p. 263.
4 Anthony Downs, *An Economic Theory of Democracy* (Harper and Row, New York, 1957), pp. 36–40.
5 Ibid., pp. 45–7 and 82–113.
6 Ibid., pp. 142–63.
7 Ibid., pp. 117–27.
8 Ibid., pp. 296–300.
9 See David Robertson, *A Theory of Party Competition* (Wiley, London, 1976), pp. 1–22, quotation from p. 17.
10 Ibid., pp. 23–54.
11 See, for example, Downs, *An Economic Theory of Democracy*, pp. 130–1.
12 For a succinct account, see Richard D. Coe and Charles K. Wilber, 'Schumpeter Revisited: An Overview', in Coe and Wilber (eds), *Capitalism and Democracy*, pp. 25–8.
13 Downs, *An Economic Theory of Democracy*, pp. 15–17.
14 See Morton A. Kaplan, 'Systems Theory', in James C. Charlesworth (ed.), *Contemporary Political Analysis* (The Free Press, New York, 1967), pp. 150–63; Herbert J. Spiro, 'An Evaluation of Systems Theory', in ibid., pp. 164–74; Robert E. Dowse and John A. Hughes, *Political Sociology* (Wiley, London, 1972), pp. 70–5.
15 David Easton, *A Systems Analysis of Political Life* (Wiley, New York, 1965), p. 21.
16 Easton, *A Framework for Political Analysis* (Prentice-Hall, Englewood Cliffs, NJ, 1965), pp. 108–17 and 126–7; *A Systems Analysis of Political Life*, pp. 29–33 and 352–62.
17 Easton, *A Systems Analysis of Political Life*, pp. 267–77.
18 Easton, *A Framework for Political Analysis*, pp. 59–69.
19 Easton, *A Systems Analysis of Political Life*, pp. 474–5, quotation from p. 475.
20 Easton, *A Framework for Political Analysis*, p. 49.
21 Gabriel A. Almond, 'Introduction: A functional approach to comparative politics', in Almond and James S. Coleman (eds), *The Politics of the Developing Areas* (Princeton University Press, Princeton, NJ, 1960), p. 7.
22 Ibid., p. 16.
23 Ibid., p. 17.
24 Ibid., p. 42.
25 Ibid., p. 45.
26 Myron Weiner, 'The Politics of South Asia', in ibid., pp. 185–208.

4

Parties as Organizations

The task of constructing theories of party systems has been greatly complicated by the difficulty of establishing a comparative framework for the study of the units of those systems, the parties themselves. It is no easy matter to produce a generally acceptable definition of the term 'political party'. Problems arise even if the category is restricted to those associations which participate in elections in liberal democracies with the aim of taking part in the process of government and which have a comprehensive platform, a definite philosophy and a permanent and extensive organization.[1] Parties vary considerably in structure, outlook and strength of purpose, both over time during the evolution of a party system, and over space, within the same territory. For this reason, essays in definition have almost invariably become essays in classification aimed at describing the different species which comprise the genus.

The possibility of constructing a typology of party families, based on the assumption that parties represent particular social responses in past and present divisions of the national community, has been explored by Daniel-Louis Seiler. He has used the sequence of historical cleavages set out by Lipset and Rokkan to analyse the similarities and differences between parties in the countries of Western Europe, Canada, the USA, Israel, Australia and New Zealand. His schema provides places for *class parties* which developed around the clash between property owners and workers (bourgeois parties, workers' parties, and Communist workers' parties); *clerical* and *anti-clerical parties* formed in those countries where relations between the church and the state are still a matter of contention; *centralizing* and *separatist parties* representing opposed sides in the clash between the metropolitan centre of the state and its peripheral regions; and *agrarian parties* (without urban counterparts) arising from the conflict between town and country.[2] The problem with this approach is that it places the observer in the position of a judge who must decide which goals belong to which parties in the historical scheme of things. As Michel Offerlé has pointed out:

> On what grounds can one say that the [German] CDU-CSU wears the mask (*le faux nez*) of christian democracy other than by using an *a priori* definition which neglects to state that the definition of 'true' christian democracy will be decided by political competition. Inversely, how can one agree without discussion that communist – or socialist – parties *are* workers' parties other than through a dual reification, that of the party (assumed to exist as a whole thing) and that of the cleavage of which the party is only an *expression*, whereas it is precisely the mechanisms which led to the belief that, for example, the [British] Labour Party is *indeed* the representative of the British working class which should be taken as the subject for study.[3]

The most enduring typology of parties is that which Duverger set out forty years ago in *Political Parties*. He identified four basic types of local unit – the *caucus*, the *branch*, the *cell* and the *militia* – and assumed that each expressed a distinctive organizational philosophy and a characteristic form of social action. As he saw it, the *caucus* functioned essentially as a committee of notables whose main concern was with returning candidates in elections; it was very much a product of those periods when the suffrage was limited and the management of electoral affairs was largely in the hands of the middle class. Duverger pointed out, however, that the caucus method of organization had been adapted to the demands of party politics under universal suffrage, most obviously in the case of parties in the USA and of those of the right and the centre in Europe. In an 'indirect' form, it had also been used by the British Labour Party, whose local units had included delegates from trade unions, trade councils, Socialist societies and co-operative organizations. In terms of his schema, the second type of local unit, the *branch*, was a body of fee-paying members which remained active between elections, mainly because of its interest in matters of doctrine and policy. It was generally larger than a caucus and possessed a more developed organizational structure, with a formal and differentiated hierarchy of officers. Duverger argued that the Socialist Parties had chosen the branch as the best means of organizing the working class but he noted also that the system had been favoured by other parties, with varying degrees of success. His third type, the *cell*, he regarded as being quite distinct in structure and function from the branch, in that it was a small, disciplined body with restrictive and demanding criteria of membership. Adopted by the Communist parties as the most effective method of creating cores of activists, it was designed to operate in a factory or other workplace setting. It could also be organized on a territorial basis but, unlike the branch, it was suited less to electoral and parliamentary activities than to agitation, propaganda and, if necessary, underground operations. Duverger's fourth type of unit was the *militia*, a small group of citizens organized on military lines at the local level and prepared to use force either for seizing power or for defending its party against attack. Such units had been created by the fascist parties and had been employed both by the German National Socialist Party and by the Italian Fascist Party.[4]

Duverger further assumed that these units were associated with particular types of party. Thus, he took the caucus to be the characteristic local organization of the *cadre party*, which as a national organization was weakly integrated, decentralized and dependent on the financial support of wealthy backers for the funding of its election campaigns. Having developed in political systems with a limited property franchise, it remained elitist in character. On the other hand, in Duverger's schema the branch was the distinctive local unit of the *mass party*, adapted to the conditions of universal suffrage and relying upon its income from membership subscriptions to sustain its efforts to return working-class candidates to parliament. Its organization was more centralized and more structured than that of the cadre party. Although Duverger was prepared to include both the cell-based Communist Parties and the militia-based fascist parties within the category of mass parties, he nevertheless suggested that they could be considered to be *devotee parties*, on the grounds that despite their being more open than cadre parties they were less open than mass parties, given the importance which they attached to elites (the vanguard of the proletariat in the case of the Communists and the 'order' of the most worthy in the case of the fascists.)[5] However, whereas the Socialist version of the mass party broadly corresponds to what we would now describe as a social democratic style of organization, with its acceptance of internal democracy and the continuous discussion of policy issues, the Communist version is based on the doctrine of democratic centralism (involving free discussion at the local level before a decision has been made, and disciplined acceptance of the decision once it has been taken at the central level)[6] and the fascist version relies upon unquestioning obedience to the instructions from leaders.

Subsequent enquiry confirmed the utility of Duverger's distinction between the cadre party and the mass party and also strengthened the comparative theory on which it was based. In an essay published in 1971, William Wright used the work of the 1950s and 1960s to construct contrasted models of the Rational-Efficient and Party Democracy types of party organization. Generally corresponding to Duverger's specification of the cadre party, Wright's Rational-Efficient model assumed that the main purpose of a party was to win elections and return a team of candidates to public office; it further assumed that the most efficient means of achieving this aim would be for the party to rely mainly on professional organizers and voluntary workers for the conduct of election campaigns, while respecting the rights of interest groups to promote the views of particular sections of the community and the responsibility of public officials for the determining of policies and the conduct of government. By contrast, his Party Democracy model, like Duverger's mass party, was based on the idea that party's main function was to formulate and present a comprehensive set of policies, or a programme, which was related to a distinctive doctrine; for this reason, it required a specially recruited membership working within a centralized and democratic framework to represent and develop views expressed by a broad constituency of supporters. Whereas the aim of the Rational-Efficient party was to gain office by electoral means, the principal objective of the Party Democracy association was to advance a programme, and to participate in electoral and parliamentary activity as a means of persuading the community to accept its views.[7]

As Wright suggested, these two models could be taken as the endpoints of a continuum along which actual parties could be

distributed.[8] Questions could then be asked about the relative
positions of parties on the continuum and about changes in
those positions over time. However, problems arise if an actual
party possesses a mixture of apparently contradictory features
and cannot be placed with confidence on any one part of the
scale. Some parties are highly eclectic in their choice of organizational principles: they may mimic techniques which have been
used successfully by their rivals and develop philosophies which
are highly ambiguous. There is a case, therefore, for assuming
that parties belong to a class of organization which can tolerate
and contain disparate elements for long periods of time, and one
which is not constrained, either by legal requirements or other
external pressures, to develop a coherent and consistent pattern
of structure and activity. Comparative studies have exploited this
lack of consistency by concentrating on the causes and effects of
particular structural anomalies. For example, Samuel Eldersveld's
discussion of the phenomenon of stratarchy (the degree of autonomy enjoyed by the lower 'strata' of the leadership hierarchy
within American parties) not only shows us the danger of exag-
gerating the extent to which the central leadership of a party can
control the internal affairs of its party organization but also
highlights the ability of regional and local units to develop their
own variants of their party's culture.[9] Unless a party is very centralized, it is almost bound to accept a significant degree of differentiation between its constituent territorial units, even at the
risk of finding these units developing distinctive attitudes towards the organizational ethic and policy concerns which the
central leadership has been trying to promote.

Eldersveld's explanation of the nature of stratarchy is a good
example of the way in which concentration on the specific organizational features of parties can produce interesting 'middle-
level theories' and increase the scope for comparative research. In
this way, the rich literature on the systems of clientelism in
American cities, expressed in its most specialized form in the
political machines which were so widespread in the USA in the
late nineteenth century,[10] has provided a valuable source of
theory for work on Third World countries[11] and a basis of
comparison with those West European cities which have been
affected by clientelism, as was Marseille in the 1920s and
1930s.[12] A particularly important group of 'middle-level theories'

comes from the work of Robert Michels (1876–1936), one of the earliest and most perceptive students of the European Social-ist Parties which flourished in the early years of this century. In his book, *Political Parties* (published in German in 1911 and in an English version in 1915), he argued that the leaders of democratic organizations, including parties, were always able to separate themselves from the mass of ordinary members and to become an oligarchy, controlling through bureaucratic means the organization which had given them power in the first place. Michels, a German sociologist who had studied not only in his home country but also in France and Italy, was writing on the basis of his experience as a member of the Italian Socialist Party and later of the German Social Democratic Party. His essential claim was that:

> It is indisputable that the oligarchical and bureaucratic tendency of party organization is a matter of technical and practical neces-sity. It is the inevitable product of the very principle of organ-ization. Not even the most radical wing of the various socialist parties raises any objection to this retrogressive evolution, the contention being that democracy is only a form of organization and that where it ceases to be possible to harmonize democracy with organization, it is better to abandon the former than the lat-ter. Organization, since it is the only means of attaining the ends of socialism, is considered to comprise within itself the revolution-ary content of the party, and this essential content must never be sacrificed for the sake of form.[13]

Implicit in this argument is the theory that once a Socialist Party has a mass membership, a wide range of policy concerns and difficult administrative tasks, it must build up a specialized bu-reaucracy and accept the guidance of professional elites. How-ever, instead of seeing this process as one of rational adaptation to the complexity of representative politics, Michels appraised it from a moral standpoint as a fall from grace. His strong attach-ment to the ideals of direct and equalitarian democracy and his dislike of domination in human affairs made him suspicious of professional politicians and their expertise.[14]

Michels's interest in the causes of oligarchy also alerted him to the importance of studying the Socialist Parties as distinctive systems of interaction between parliamentary groups, executives

and congresses,[15] and the special structural features of parties
has remained an important subject of enquiry. In an article
published in 1984, Joseph A. Schlesinger demonstrated the general shape that a theory of party organization might assume.
Pointing out that any organization has to deal with the problems
of maintaining itself over time, determining its main work or output, and compensating its members or participants, he set out
to discover in what respects parties differed from the business
firm, the public agency or bureau and the interest group in the
solution of these problems.

With respect to the first problem, that of self–maintenance,
Schlesinger pointed out that parties could be regarded as organizations responding to the market aspects of elections, providing
candidates and policies in return for votes, rather than as non-
market organizations which simply offered services on the basis
of public funding. However, although through the electoral market a party obtains votes and possession of office – that is, private benefits for itself and its candidates – it supplies candidates
and policies, or collective benefits, to the voters, a situation
contrasting with the economic market 'in which both sides to
a transaction give and receive private or selective goods'.[16] Despite this difference, a party is bound to the electoral market and
must learn to master its rivals by selecting candidates and policies which will give it the best chance of victory; it cannot alter
its goals without reference to the test of winning office through
the polls. For this reason, it must favour those of its candidates
who either win seats or demonstrate the potential to do so; promotion and status within its ranks are determined by this crite-
rion rather than by such considerations as seniority, length of
service or reward for special duties. Building on Mancur Olson's
work on the logic of collective action, Schlesinger pointed out
that

> in large groups, such as a political party, the increment in the
> collective good (winning the election, achieving its policies) result-
> ing from a single participant's activity is so small that it will not
> be equal to or greater that the cost of the effort to the individual,
> and therefore no rational person will participate to achieve the
> collective good.[17]

In his view, it follows that people who take part in the activity of political parties in pursuit of collective benefits are uninformed about the costs and benefits of doing so, and that most of them will tend to leave the party once experience has made them aware of the irrationality of their having joined it in the first place. As a result, a relatively high turnover of party personnel is only to be expected, although some may stay on because the work which they do for the party affords them private satisfaction. The inexperience and fluidity of a party's membership result in its affairs being run by a relatively small circle of leaders. Finally, a party compensates its members indirectly rather than directly for the time which they give to it and therefore lacks the ability to regulate their activity in detail and to command the degree of loyalty which direct compensation would provide.

Taking all these points into account, Schlesinger next considered the combination of properties which characterize the political party as an organization and noted that it 'offers collective benefits and compensates its participants indirectly, yet is market based'. However, unlike other market-based organizations, it 'is seriously deficient in its ability to discipline its participants in order to meet the ever insistent market challenges' and, unlike other groups providing collective goods, it 'is incapable of adjusting its objectives in order to maintain its tenuous supporters'.[18]

> Parties are perhaps best described as forms of organized trial and error. Thousands of individuals and interests seek to control the party's decisions. They push candidates, frame issues, recruit workers, make alliances, and devise campaigns. Among these competing forces choices are made, choices whose correctness is ultimately determined not by the party but by the electorate. Nevertheless, it is the party organization which assures that the right choices, i.e., those which win elections, are retained and the wrong ones are rejected.[19]

This account of the manner in which the imperatives of the electoral market may constrain parties to acquire certain organizational characteristics can easily be related to the model of the

'Rational-Efficient' party as specified by Wright, but the same imperatives affect the behaviour of parties which are close in form to the contrasting model of the 'Party Democracy' association. In the latter case, the most likely effect will be a tension between the formal and informal requirements of organizational activity. The constitutions of such parties are often constructed as though procedures being specified presuppose a solid corporate structure, with integrated hierarchies of executive and plenary institutions, specialized judicial bodies to settle internal disputes and an administrative structure capable of handling a variety of particular tasks. However, its need to gain power by working the electoral market may force it to develop an informal structure generally conforming to the simple pattern of a small leadership group, a relatively generalized bureaucracy, a reserve army of activists, and an unstable and constantly changing cohort of ordinary members. Certain structural consequences flow from this often quite marked divergence between formal and informal structures. For example, the leadership hierarchy of such a party is much more open and fluid than those of organizations such as trade unions, police forces, or public agencies. Although a person bidding for a leadership position in the party must demonstrate particular abilities, most obviously in the capacity to win a seat and convince a public audience that the party's policies are the best on offer, the obstacles to advancement are by no means as numerous or as formidable as they are in most organizations. Given the right opportunity, a secondary leader in the party can rise right through the ranks of more senior figures if he or she appears to have the personal qualities needed to increase or sustain the party's electoral appeal. Conversely, a primary leader whose public standing has been weakened may suddenly be deserted by former lieutenants and courtiers as they manoeuvre either to make bids of their own for the central role or to support another contender prepared to give them powerful places in a new settlement. For these reasons, a succession crisis in a party can often lead to a major organizational crisis and cause a complete rearrangement of the leadership hierarchy. The elaborate *rites de passage* and orders of rank which seal off access to high office in most organizations are either not present at all, or are there in vestigial from in a political party.

A second consequence of the probable gap between formal and informal structure in a party's organization is that the party's team of administrators will usually be much too small and too generalist to run the party's affairs in a strictly bureaucratic manner. As Samuel Eldersveld has pointed out:

> it must be recognized that parties do not possess many of the conventional attributes of the bureaucratic system. In particular, the bureaucratic prerequisites of impermeability, depersonalized human relationships, strict devotion to regulations and rule enforcement, precise allocation of obligations, duties, and roles, discipline, and sanctions, even low circulation of personnel, are found wanting in most party structures.[20]

As a result, both the leadership and the paid officers, such as the general secretary and his staff and various party agents, have to rely for intensive administrative tasks, such as running an election campaign, on the enthusiastic voluntary labour of large numbers of activists, who between such tasks resemble a dispersed body of retainers, gathered around the party's local units; it is the activists who form and maintain the culture of the party's organization, who sustain its ethic, influence the application of formal rules, and keep vigil over party policies and strategic principles which have been sanctioned by tradition. The recruitment of ordinary members is affected by their presence; admission to the party is effectively admission to one of its local units, where the *milieu* is strongly influenced by the values and attitudes of the activists. A newcomer either adapts to this *milieu* or leaves the party, and the impermeability of this activist layer, which varies in consistency from party to party, should be added to the list of factors which can cause a high turnover in the membership of the party's rank and file.

Given the undoubted tendency for the electoral process to force parties to adopt the style of operation of the 'Rational-Efficient' model, it is surprising that actual parties continue to exhibit so many variations in form and structure. One explanation for this has been offered by Angelo Panebianco, who has produced a classificatory scheme of party types which takes full account of their historical development. He has assumed that it is the struggle for position within a party in its formative stages which sets the pattern for its subsequent development. Using examples taken from the histories of West European parties, he distinguishes between an organization's genetic model (the pattern produced by a combination of factors when it was being established) and the process of institutionalization, through which it acquires a relatively stable form as it matures. Where the genetic model is concerned, Panebianco attaches great importance to whether the party originated by spreading outwards from a central core or by integrating a number of points of separate development; to whether or not the party was promoted by an internal or external sponsoring body (such as a trade union in the case of a Socialist Party or the Comintern (Communist International) in the case of a Communist Party); and to whether or not the formation of the party was aided by the presence of a charismatic leader. Once a party's organization has been formed it begins to expand in size and to develop an internal division of labour amongst its leaders, for whom its maintenance becomes an end in itself; it also attracts the loyalties of those who are to become its activists and loyal supporters. This process may produce strong institutions but it may also produce weak ones, depending upon the extent of the party's autonomy in relation to its external environment and upon the degree of its internal structural coherence.[21] These distinctions enable Panebianco to construct a typology of parties which cuts across classifications by doctrine and position on a left–right continuum, but the main value of his work is the imaginative hypothesis that a party's evolved form retains the basic characteristics of its original form.

Panebianco's interest in the historical origins of parties led him to reconsider Otto Kirchheimer's thesis that the 'mass integration parties' of the class variety, such as the Socialist Parties, were changing into 'catch-all peoples' parties' by broadening their social bases to enclose as many interests as possible while reducing their dependence on ideological appeals and committed memberships. Kirchheimer took the view that political parties in the USA were already 'catch-all' parties and that denominational mass parties (such as the Italian Christian Democrats) and the older variety of 'parties of individual representation' were being driven in that direction.[22] Examining these ideas from his perspective, Panebianco described the older form as the *mass bureaucratic party*, marked by an attachment to bureaucracy, membership, ideology and a dedicated electoral base, and the newer form as the *electoral-professional party*, distinguished by its reliance on 'professionals' (that is, staff with specialized knowledge and expertise), broad electoral support, and the promotion of issues and leaders rather than ideology. He believed that changes in the nature of society and in patterns of political communication were pushing parties away from the mass bureaucratic towards the electoral-professional model, and that this transition would entail a shift from strong to weak institutions.[23]

If parties do become more flexible, more subject to the control of professional managers and staff, and less dependent on activists and members, will they lose their role of representing social interests in the electoral and parliamentary process? A similar problem has been explored by Kay Lawson, who has analysed the ways in which parties provide connections in the chain of linkages between the citizen and the state. She has stressed the need to distinguish between the four forms of linkage which a party may assume: participatory, in which the party 'serves as an agency through which citizens can themselves participate in government'; electoral, in which the party's leaders control its elected representatives to ensure that they respond to the views of its ordinary members; clientelistic, in which the party mediates in the process whereby electors may give votes in return for favours; and directive, in which the party is employed by the government 'to maintain control over the behavior of citizens' by means of either education, or coercion or a combination of the two. Lawson points out that in practice a party will usually provide more than one of these forms of linkage, and cites as examples the representative-democratic combination (in which the main emphasis is on electoral linkage) and the authoritarian combination (in which the main emphasis is on directive linkage).[24] This framework provides a convenient means of organizing our observations of the methods used by parties to mediate between the electorate and institutions of government, and of measuring the extent of any changes in the general pattern of representative politics.

As the material reviewed in this chapter has shown, theoretical and comparative work on political parties has proceeded at many different levels of generality and from quite different starting points. At one level, parties have been analysed as distinctive organizations which, despite their differences in form and outlook, possess characteristics which distinguish them from other general categories of organization such as pressure groups, business firms and public agencies; in other words, the application of organization theory has enabled us to understand how parties as a single set vary from other types of organization. At another level, the use of ideal-type analysis has provided scope for exploring systematically the contrasting patterns of party organization and activity within that set. At both levels, imaginative efforts have been made to demonstrate how a necessarily static account of party structures can also be used to explain the dynamics of party activity over time. In the chapters which follow, we shall further explore the dynamic aspect of party behaviour, considering first the factor of leadership and then the factor of internal conflict.

Notes

1 For discussions of the problem of definition, see Anthony Downs, *An Economic Theory of Democracy* (Harper and Row, New York, 1957), pp. 24–7; Joseph A. Schlesinger, 'On the Theory of Party Organization', *The Journal of Politics*, XLVI, 2 (May 1984), pp. 373–8; Joseph LaPalombara and Myron Weiner, 'The Origin and Development of Political Parties', in LaPalombara and Weiner (eds), *Political Parties and Political Development* (Princeton University Press, Princeton, NJ, 1966), pp. 3–7; Kay Lawson, *The Comparative Study of Political Parties* (St Martin's Press, New York, 1976), pp. 2–4; Michel Offerlé, *Les Partis Politiques* (Presses Universitaires de France, Paris, 1987), pp. 18–21. See also the definition proposed in Calvin A. Woodward, *The Growth of a Party System in Ceylon* (Brown University Press, Providence, RI, 1969), p. 20. For an excellent account of the history of the term, see Giovanni Sartori, *Parties and party systems: A framework for analysis* (Cambridge University Press, Cambridge, 1976), vol. I, pp. 3–13.

2 Daniel-Louis Seiler, *Partis et familles politiques* (Presses Universitaires de France, Paris, 1980). See also Seiler, *De la comparaison des partis politiques* (Economica, Paris, 1986).

3 Offerlé, *Les partis politiques*, p. 16 (translation mine). See also

Jean Charlot, 'Political Parties: Towards a New Theoretical Synthesis', *Political Studies*, XXXVII, 3 (September 1989), pp. 353–5.

4 Maurice Duverger, *Political Parties: Their Organization and Activity in the Modern State*, tr. Barbara and Robert North (Methuen, London, 1954), pp. 17–40.

5 Ibid., pp. 63–71.

6 Ibid., pp. 57–8.

7 William E. Wright, 'Comparative Party Models: Rational-Efficient and Party Democracy', in Wright (ed.), *A Comparative Study of Party Organization* (Merrill, Columbus, Ohio, 1971), pp. 17–54.

8 Ibid., pp. 17–18.

9 Samuel J. Eldersveld, 'The Party "Stratarchy"', in David W. Abbott and Edward T. Rogowsky (eds), *Political Parties* (Rand McNally, Chicago, Second Edition, 1978), pp. 5–19.

10 See Raymond E. Wolfinger, 'Why Political Machines Have Not Withered Away and Other Revisionist Thoughts', in ibid., pp. 51–76; Leon D. Epstein, *Political Parties in Western Democracies* (Pall Mall Press, London, 1967), pp. 104–11; Howard P. Chudacoff, *The Evolution of American Urban Society* (Prentice-Hall, Englewood Cliffs, NJ, Second Edition, 1981) pp. 141–65; Edward C. Banfield and James Q. Wilson, *City Politics* (Vintage Books, Random House, New York, 1966), pp. 115–27.

11 See James C. Scott, 'Corruption, machine politics, and political change', *American Political Science Review*, LXIII, 4 (December 1969), pp. 1142–58.

12 See Paul Jankowski, *Communism and Collaboration: Simon Sabiani and Politics in Marseille, 1919–1944* (Yale University Press, New Haven, 1989); David A. L. Levy, 'From clientelism to communism: The Marseille working class and the Popular Front', in Martin S. Alexander and Helen Graham (eds), *The French and Spanish Popular Fronts: Comparative Perspectives* (Cambridge University Press, Cambridge, 1989), pp. 201–12.

13 Robert Michels, *Political Parties: A Sociological Study of the Oligarchical Tendencies of Modern Democracy* (Dover Publications, New York, 1959), p. 35.

14 See Wolfgang J. Mommsen, 'Roberto Michels and Max Weber: Moral Conviction versus the Politics of Responsibility', in Mommsen, *The Political and Social Theory of Max Weber: Collected Essays* (Polity Press, Cambridge, 1989), pp. 87–105.

15 See, for example, Michels, *Political Parties*, pp. 160–1.

16 Schlesinger, 'On the Theory of Party Organization', p. 381.

17 Ibid., pp. 385–6.

18 Ibid., p. 389.

19   Ibid., p. 390. Cf. the discussion of party organization in Epstein, *Political Parties in Western Democracies*, pp. 98–103.

20   Samuel J. Eldersveld, *Political Parties: A Behavioral Analysis* (Rand McNally, Chicago, 1964), p. 4.

21   See Angelo Panebianco, *Political Parties: Organization and Power*, tr. Marc Silver (Cambridge University Press, Cambridge, 1988), pp. 17–20 and 49–68.

22   Otto Kirchheimer, 'The Transformation of the Western European Party Systems', in LaPalombara and Weiner (eds), *Political Parties and Political Development*, pp. 177–200.

23   See Panebianco, *Political Parties*, pp. 262–7.

24   See Kay Lawson, 'When Linkage Fails', in Lawson and Peter H. Merkl (eds), *When Parties Fail: Emerging Alternative Organizations* (Princeton University Press, Princeton, NJ, 1988), pp. 16–17. Cf. Lawson, 'Political Parties and Linkage', in Lawson (ed.), *Political Parties and Linkage: A Comparative Perspective* (Yale University Press, New Haven, 1980), pp. 13–19.

Part II

Rallies and Parties

5

Exceptional Leaders and Democratic Order

Political theorists have always been interested in the changes in leadership behaviour which may occur when routine gives way to crisis politics. In such circumstances, a democracy faced with grave economic conditions, war or civil disorder, may grant special powers to a person of exceptional stature considered capable of dealing with the situation. While such authority is never given lightly, is always limited in scope, and is hedged around with safeguards to ensure that once the danger is past normal procedures will be restored, the fact that it can be given at all assumes the existence of two normative models of rule – the one generally prevailing and the other appropriate at times when the state is in peril. In this chapter, we shall consider various theories bearing on the problem of exceptional authority and propose a method of analysing the ways in which this problem has affected the behaviour of political parties.

Any community which suspends its rights in government and hands power to a leader in order that he may deal decisively with an emergency must be haunted by the fear that such a temporary grant of authority may become permanent and the normal system of law and order be set aside. During the eighteenth century the philosophers of the Enlightenment believed this to be one of the most serious problems faced by a polity based on liberty and the rule of law. As Montesquieu wrote in *The Spirit of the Laws* (1748),

> when an exorbitant authority is given suddenly to a citizen in a republic this forms a monarchy or more than a monarchy. In monarchies, the laws have protected the constitution or have been adapted to it; the principle of the government checks the monarch;

but in a republic when a citizen takes exorbitant power, the abuse of this power is greater because the laws, which have not foreseen it, have done nothing to check it.[1]

To illustrate this point, Montesquieu referred to the provisions regulating the appointment of special magistrates in the Venice of his time and in the Roman Republic of antiquity. He noted that in the latter case, Rome took the precaution of ensuring that the dictator 'was installed for only a short time' (six months in fact),

> because the people act from impetuosity and not from design. His magistracy was exercised with brilliance, as the issue was to intimidate, not to punish, the people; the dictator was created for but a single affair and had unlimited authority with regard to that affair alone because he was always created for unforeseen cases.[2]

The basic elements of later theories are already present in these observations – the recognition that a constitutional regime and its framework of law must be flexible and therefore readily adaptable to changing conditions; an acceptance of the possibility that a people may give way to impulse and, for a period, act out of character; and an acknowledgement that exceptional leadership need not become a tyranny, provided that its exercise and duration are governed by law and convention.

The development of liberal democracy in the nineteenth century provided Western states with much greater ability to respond to unexpected circumstances than Montesquieu could have imagined. Even so, questions very similar to those which had concerned him were taken up early in the twentieth century by the great German sociologist, Max Weber (1864–1920). In a treatise which he was writing in the last years of his life and which was published posthumously as *Wirtschaft und Gesellschaft: Grundriss der Verstehenden Soziologie*, he presented a broad scheme of concepts for the analysis of social, economic and political activities and, incidentally, discussed several features of Western parliamentary democracies and their general development.[3] Weber believed that the growth of industrial capitalism and the modern state had been accompanied by a constant and irreversible process of bureaucratization. The principle at work in this process was that of legal authority, whereby order was maintained by respect for rules of conduct which were derived from positive law and by the acceptance of the decisions of institutions formed within those rules. He envisaged the extension of rational-bureaucratic methods to all organizations in the modern state, among which he included not only public services but also business firms, industrial establishments, political parties, armies and churches. He saw this process as leading to the erosion of traditional authority under which a people's respect for the wisdom inherent in time-honoured custom and practice had provided a secure basis for order in the past.

In his general theory of domination outlining the forms of authority, Weber developed a schema of three ideal types – the relatively stable patterns of order associated with legal and with traditional authority, opposed by the form of exceptional authority which he described as charismatic. (For this purpose, he had taken the term 'charisma', meaning 'the gift of grace', from the doctrines of early Christianity, and had used it to signify the power to inspire devotion and enthusiasm in one's followers possessed by a person claiming to have a special vocation for spiritual, heroic or prophetic leadership.) The principle of charismatic authority was that the allegiance given by a people to a leader in whom they saw exceptional gifts of character and whose vision of the future commanded their respect could be a genuine basis for order.[4] However, Weber was at pains to emphasize that in the real world none of these three types of authority would normally exist in their pure form and that most actual organizations would exhibit a mixture of characteristics:

> the kind of terminology and classification set forth ... has in no sense the aim – indeed, it could not have it – to be exhaustive or to confine the whole of historical reality in a rigid scheme. Its usefulness is derived from the fact that in a given case it is possible to distinguish what aspects of a given organized group can legitimately be identified as falling under or approximating one or another of these categories.[5]

Where representative politics were concerned, Weber considered that charismatic authority could take the form of plebiscitary democracy, in which a modern party leader claimed to be acting on behalf of the mass of the citizens, who in their turn gave him their uncritical support, and he saw the referendum as an obvious means of legitimizing that relationship.[6] He considered that political parties, like all organizations, were affected by the three principles of domination.

> They may thus be charismatically oriented by devotion to the leader, with the plebiscite as an expression of confidence. They may be traditional with adherence based on the social prestige of the chief or of an eminent neighbor, or they may be rational with adherence to a leader and staff set up by a 'constitutional process' of election.[7]

However, as David Beetham has pointed out, Weber's analysis of democratic politics under the conditions of universal suffrage was influenced by his belief that the process of representation was shaped by small groups of leaders acting downwards, as it were, upon the mass of the electorate. 'Everywhere the principle of the small number – that is, the superior manoeuvrability of small *leading* groups – determines political activity.'[8] Weber must also have seen this principle working partly against and partly in conjunction with the principle of party bureaucratization, and Reinhard Bendix has noted that, under universal suffrage, 'tension between charismatic leadership and the imperatives of modern party organizations is a generic attribute of elections'. The electoral process offers the candidate a means of striking out alone.

> In modern electoral campaigns the quantity of oratory is ever on the increase, and it tends to lose in content what it gains in mass appeal. The aim of campaign speeches is to have an emotional impact, to give the people an image of the party's power and confidence in victory, and to convey a sense of the candidate's charismatic qualifications for leadership. Where the campaign brings to the fore the personal charisma of the leader, he can make himself independent of the party organization and may come into conflict with it.[9]

Immediately after the end of the First World War, during the constitutional debate in Germany which led to the foundation of the Weimar Republic, Weber proposed constitutional arrangements under which the president of the state would have been elected directly by the people and outside the system of Parliamentary representation. Beetham sees in his writings of this period a normative theory that, ideally, the political leader should provide not only a counterpoise to the power of the bureaucratic official but also an independent source of ideas and a means of bringing about unity in a society divided by conflicts between economic interests and social classes: 'His conception of leadership, as typified in the charismatic figure, was of a relationship of personal trust or faith in the *person* of the leader on the part of his following, which allowed him a wide range of freedom to pursue his own convictions.'[10]

The value of Weber's distinctions between legal, traditional and charismatic types of authority is that they provide an elegant means of studying the dilemmas and paradoxes posed by any social action in unexpected circumstances; in such cases the instinct to rely on experience is constantly in tension with the instinct to plan according to rational predictions and with the instinct to surrender judgement to a confident leader. However, the use of the concept of 'charisma', and its specific application to the analysis of plebiscitary democracy, invites the reader to think of exceptional leadership in religious terms and to imagine that there is a metaphysical dimension to this type of authority. In reality, the conventions and expectations associated with the exercise of exceptional authority are an integral part of the political cultures of liberal democracies. Although most citizens would prefer a regulated competition between parties as the normal basis of politics, they are also prepared to tolerate the suspension of that competition and the grant of special authority to a chief of state or some other outstanding person in an unusual or critical situation.

One of the difficulties faced by later scholars exploring the issues which Weber had raised was that the concept of charismatic leadership in a plebiscitary democracy became associated with the concepts of national leadership advanced by the Italian Fascists and the German National Socialists in the 1920s and 1930s. An understandable response to this problem was to characterize any shift from organized to fluid politics as a venture into the realm of collective irrationality. In his influential book, *Ideology and Utopia*, published in an English translation in 1936, Karl Mannheim made this point in the following terms.

Every social process may be divided into a rationalized sphere consisting of settled and routinized procedures in dealing with situations that recur in an orderly fashion, and the 'irrational' by which it is surrounded. We are, therefore, distinguishing between the 'rationalized' structure of society and the 'irrational' matrix.[11]

Fascism combined its exploitation of the irrational field in society with a blind faith in the leadership principle and therefore encouraged authoritarian rule.

In the process of transformation of modern society, there are ... periods during which the mechanisms which have been devised by the bourgeoisie for carrying on the class struggle (e.g. parliamentarianism) prove insufficient. There are periods when the evolutionary course fails for the time being and crises become acute. Class relations and class stratification become strained and distorted. The class-consciousness of the conflicting groups becomes confused. In such periods it is easy for transitory formations to emerge, and the mass comes into existence, individuals having lost or forgotten their class orientations. At such moments a dictatorship becomes possible. The fascist view of history and its intuitional approach which serves as a preparation for immediate action have changed what is no more than a partial situation into a total view of society.[12]

As in this passage, Mannheim was proposing that the process of change in industrial societies was neither continuous nor stable and that, when the provisions of the liberal-democratic state for social competition became ineffective, a complete breakdown would occur; hitherto separate classes would dissolve into an undifferentiated mass of people, intuition rather than reason would become the basis for action, and authoritarian rule would be established. Whereas Weber had envisaged charismatic authority as an integral part of the system of democratic order, and phases of plebiscitary democracy as an organic part of representative politics under universal suffrage, Mannheim saw the combination of fascist rule and mass obedience as a distinct system and as the very antithesis of class-based party politics.

The creation of Nazi Germany appeared to confirm this view. Hitler's rise to power in 1933 and the subsequent destruction of the liberal institutions of the Weimar Republic were taken to be a striking confirmation of the corrosive power of fascism and the weakness of liberal democracy. Within the space of a few months one of the most sophisticated constitutional systems of Western Europe was completely dismantled and a ruthless authoritarian state established in its place. Intellectuals were prone to interpret these events as evidence of an interaction between a people deprived of purpose and a leader adept in the construction and use of political myths. In his book, *The Myth of the State*, published posthumously in 1946, Ernst Cassirer discussed this relationship in general terms and referred to the myth-making faculty of 'modern politicians'. Like Mannheim, he regarded belief in myths as the sign of a flight, under stress, to irrationality: 'In desperate situations man will always have recourse to desperate means – and our present-day political myths have been such desperate means. If reason has failed us, there remains always the *ultima ratio*, the power of the miraculous and mysterious.'[13] Having discussed the place of myth in primitive societies, he went on to make a further point.

> The mythical organization of society seems to be superseded by a rational organization. In quiet and peaceful times, in periods of relative stability and security, this rational organization is easily maintained. It seems to be safe against all attacks. But in politics the equipoise is never completely established. What we find here is a labile rather than a static equilibrium. In politics we are always living on volcanic soil. We must be prepared for abrupt convulsions and eruptions. In all critical moments of man's social life, the rational forces that resist the rise of the old mythical conceptions are no longer sure of themselves.[14]

This reversion to irrationality requires the appropriate leader:

> The call for leadership only appears when a collective desire has reached an overwhelming strength and when, on the other hand, all hopes of fulfilling this desire, in an ordinary and normal way, have failed. At these times the desire is not only keenly felt but also personified. It stands before the eyes of man in a concrete, plastic, and individual shape. The intensity of the collective wish is embodied in the leader. The former social bonds – law, justice, and constitutions – are declared to be without any value. What alone remains is the mystical power and authority of the leader and the leader's will is supreme law.[15]

Cassirer came close to accusing 'modern politicians' of using a belief in 'social magic' to achieve power in what was otherwise a technically advanced society.

> If we admit such an historical distinction our modern political myths appear indeed as a very strange and paradoxical thing. For what we find in them is the blending of two activities that seem to exclude each other. The modern politician has had to combine in himself two entirely different and even incompatible functions. He has to act, at the same time, as both a homo magus [man the magician] and a homo faber [man the artisan]. He is the priest of a new, entirely irrational and mysterious religion.[16]

However, since the Second World War historians and political scientists have become more accustomed to the distinction between the leadership styles and techniques associated with Fascism, in which the aim is to transform state and society by appeals to romantic nationalism of an absolute intensity, and those associated with leaders and parties which ask for exceptional powers within an existing regime in order to remedy its deficiencies or to deal with an unexpected crisis. The latter process, of preservation of the state through the exercise of special authority, has been explored with reference to France in Stanley Hoffman's stimulating essay on the nature of heroic leadership.[17]

Building upon an earlier observation by Michel Crozier that organizational change in French institutions had been effected by short periods of intense crisis rather than by a regular pattern of incremental adjustments,[18] Hoffman has compared the periods in high office of three very different French heads of government who tried, each in his own way, to increase the coherence of executive authority within the state. At first glance, there may not appear to be much in common between the political outlook of Marshal Philippe Pétain, the Chief of State during the wartime Vichy regime of 1940–4, and that of Pierre Mendès-France, Prime Minister in 1954–5 under the Fourth Republic, and that of Charles de Gaulle, who was President of the Provisional Government in 1944–6 and later President of the Fifth Republic between 1959 and 1969. Hoffmann, however, draws attention to the point that they were all exceptional leaders called on by the French people to restore the integrity of a political system which had either broken down or, in the case of Mendès-France and the Fourth Republic, of a system whose functioning had been severely impaired. They therefore provided a form of leadership which Hoffmann describes as 'heroic' (preferring this to Weber's term, 'charismatic').

The analysis of any pattern of radical change, in which a system adapts to its environment by sudden bursts of activity rather than by a regular sequence of minor and incremental adjustments, requires answers to three questions – firstly, how does the system in question remain stable between crises; secondly, what conditions are necessary and sufficient to cause a crisis; and, thirdly, what types of authority are accepted as appropriate for resolving the crisis and rebuilding the system? In answering the first question, Hoffmann uses Crozier's work to specify a model of routine authority in which centrally prescribed rules provide sufficient order for the individuals within each layer of an organization to behave as though they were equals while resisting any unwarranted assertion of the rights of superior bodies or any attempt by one of their own number to assume internal leadership. The values of this system, with its stress on equality before the law, the impersonality of authority and the fullest possible participation by citizens in the making of policies and decisions, are essentially anti-aristocratic and individualistic. Hoffmann claims that:

> some of the features analyzed by Crozier in general terms are *accentuated* in the political sphere. The negative and brittle character of associations, their difficulty in cooperating and reaching compromises that do more than confirm their respective statuses, are usual features of French political parties, with the partial exception of the extreme left. Especially true of French parties and interest groups is the tendency of associations to try to obtain what they want by blackmailing higher authority (hence the resort to a frequently 'revolutionary' vocabulary [*sic*] that conceals far more limited intentions, yet reveals a general attitude toward change: all or nothing; and toward authority: a mixture of defiance and dependence). The lack of communication between strata, the distance between each stratum and higher authority, are characteristic of a political regime in which the citizens elect representatives who tend to behave as a caste of sovereign *camarades*.[19]

Hoffmann describes how, under both the Third Republic (1870–1940) and the Fourth Republic (1946–58), the pattern of routine authority was maintained by a number of mechanisms. Although both regimes were characterized by frequent changes of government and confrontations in Parliament, two factors remained constant; the bureaucracy continued to generate impersonal rules and the members of the public were generally agreed that the state should be restricted in scope and function.

> There was, among social groups and political forces, a broad consensus for a limited state, congruent with the style of authority; now, *in most circumstances* the combination of a career bureaucracy and of a parliamentary system more adept at checking than at moving that bureaucracy corresponded exactly to what was desired. Legitimacy was conditional, in the sense that for most of those groups and forces the regime was acceptable as long as its activities left intact their sphere of independence while settling conflicts to their satisfaction. But the setup was such that this was precisely what happened most of the time. The political formula produced a political class diversified enough to appease the kind of equalitarianism characteristic of the political sphere; the setup admirably divorced equalitarianism from social reform and thus pleased most groups and parties, at the same time condemning the groups and parties that wanted change to play the 'homeorhetic' game, that is, to ask for all or nothing (thus usually playing into the hands of those who wanted nothing).[20]

This system also contained special devices and procedures to deal with problems which were unusually serious. It provided for limited delegation of authority to a prime minister or head of state but it also contained redressive rules to ensure that the leader's scope for independent action was ended once the problem had been resolved. Hoffmann considered that only when the system encountered a crisis sufficiently severe to threaten its destruction would citizens revert to an aristocratic view of politics, only then would they look for an heroic leader capable of prescribing new rules for the different strata of the system and of reconstructing its framework so that normal politics could be resumed. Briefly, therefore, he saw routine authority as collapsing when a crisis placed it under unendurable strain and when the public, the political audience, believed that the compartmentalized structure within which particular concerns had been pursued was breaking down.

Hoffman outlined what he took to be the style of heroic leadership, using as his examples the behaviour of de Gaulle and of Pétain after the fall of France in 1940 and during their attempts to establish a new order – the Vichy state in the case of Pétain and the post-Liberation regime in the case of de Gaulle; the unsuccessful attempt made by Mendès-France during his premiership of 1954–5 to increase the executive efficiency within the Fourth Republic; and de Gaulle's role in establishing and maintaining the Fifth Republic. On the basis of this material, he found the heroic leader to be an outsider in relation to routine authority and a man with strongly held, even dogmatic, beliefs who, once in power, tended to punish those associated with the old order, to govern in a directive rather than a bargaining style, and to seek displays of public support for his actions.[21] The substance as distinct from the style of heroic leadership was the demonstration of prowess and exceptional competence in the conduct of internal and external affairs.[22]

The difficulty of accepting this theory in its entirety arises, firstly, in Hoffmann's choice of examples of heroic leadership and secondly, in his interpretation of French political culture. The first objection relates mainly to his pairing of de Gaulle with Pétain; although in 1940 both leaders were trying to separate themselves from the previous regime, their political objectives were fundamentally different. Whereas Pétain and his supporters thought of themselves as radical innovaters with a mission to establish a new regime which would be authoritarian, corporatist and hierarchical, de Gaulle, after a brief period of apparent indecision, presented himself as the upholder of the Republican tradition within which some strengthening of executive authority was both possible and necessary. He acted in the same spirit when he took power after the crisis of May 1958. Furthermore (and here we come to the second objection), in both 1940–6 and 1958–69 he worked with the grain of French culture, implicitly appealing to a Bonapartist tradition which had always existed alongside the Republican tradition and which had provided the French people with a notion of what could be done not only to preserve the state in the event of a crisis but also to restore the Republic once the crisis had passed. These reservations apart, Hoffmann's important essay effectively demonstrates that heroic leadership (to use his term) constituted a distinctive response to the problems of order and change within French culture and, in terms of general theory, renewed the enquiry into the conditions of plebiscitary democracy which Weber had undertaken towards the end of his life.

The crucial interdependence between Republicanism and Bonapartism had been recognized and explored on several occasions by the renowned French political scientist, André Siegfried; writing before the First World War, he said that:

There is in France a Bonapartist disposition (*tempérament*) whose seed has never been destroyed by democracy. It persists in a latent form in certain circles which we will have to determine and which, under the most diverse political labels, maintain their initial character. Then, in certain circumstances which it is possible to analyse and know about, it suddenly bursts out and spreads with such force that the whole country is temporarily transformed by it; its appearances are like eruptions.

The situation in which a Bonaparte finds his destiny is that of anarchy in government and the disrepute of parliament. At certain times, the elective assemblies seem to lose touch with the real world; they become absorbed and entangled in artificial quarrels which appear to them to be important but which are of no interest to the public; the official representatives of opinion are no longer its real representatives, and the country ceases to feel itself governed.

This is when a man who has the makings of a Caesar acquires his full stature. Over the heads of the parties (which he affects to see only as cliques), he speaks directly to the mass, not only to the active and organized electors but also to the crowd of the indifferent, the abstentionists, citizens who have not taken sides, those whom the committees have not recruited and whom he is going to make the foundation of his whole system.[23]

In a book which he published 1930, Siegfried made it clear that the relationship between Bonapartism and Republicanism was symbiotic, and that the one was the companion of the other.

Bonapartism . . . aims to establish authority within the framework of democracy. A national leader, approved by a plebiscite of all the French, who checks anarchy and silences the 'chatterboxes' of the assemblies – that is the vigorous conception of government in which equality continues to exist but in which order takes precedence over liberty and the material gains of 1789 are guaranteed against either a return to the *ancien régime* or the dangers of social revolution. Call the leader anything that you wish – emperor, consul or president – it does not matter much – he will never be a king but will always be a tribune, consolidating democracy in the name of social order.[24]

The interdependence of Bonapartism and Republicanism in France is just one special example of the duality of tradition which exists in all liberal democracies. The weight which citizens place on the virtues of equality before the law, on the impersonality of authority and on the competition between political groups is consonant with their support for representative institutions; but in a critical situation their concern to ensure the preservation of the democratic regime can persuade them to accept the necessity of a controlled autocracy. The fact that members of a liberal democracy can envisage one system of rule for normal politics and another for crisis politics allows for some variation in the *modus operandi* of their political leaders. While the majority of those leaders accommodate themselves to the demands of routine politics, making their careers within the regular framework of parties, parliament and responsible government, other more independent figures may choose to avoid being drawn into the humdrum procedures and inevitable consequences of parliamentary life; taking the long view, they call on citizens to interest themselves in major issues of internal or external policy. Should the time come when the established machinery of government fails to deal with, for example, a severe economic crisis, an outburst of violent social unrest, or war with a foreign power, an independent figure such as this rather than an established party leader may be called upon to guide the state through the emergency.

The existence of these contrasting styles of leadership is the outward sign that the free play of representative institutions generates two quite different fields of political power which we may term the party drive and the rally drive. Drawing upon the work of Weber, Siegfried and Hoffmann, we shall consider them as mutually dependent forces, each strengthening itself by reacting against the other. While the party drive arises from the demands of social groups which expect political associations to further their sectional interests, the rally drive is produced by the diffuse anxieties of groups and individuals who look to prominent personalities to accept a form of moral responsibility for the welfare of the community as a whole. The two drives do not represent different sectors of society; rather they represent aspects of that impulse which each citizen and each group must evince to some extent – the desire to make demands and to secure specific interests on the one hand and the desire to defend the unity and integrity of the community on the other.

The two drives may vary in strength from place to place and from time to time. In countries where the social groups are sufficiently differentiated to present clear and coherent sectional demands and where the structures of law and public finance are relatively secure, the party drive will usually dominate the rally drive and sustain a system of stable parties in parliament, giving a regular pattern of party government. Even where such conditions obtain, however, the destabilization of the regime by an internal or external crisis may shift the balance of forces towards the rally drive and cause the emergence of a national leader. Conversely, the rally drive will usually predominate in countries where the social structure is generalized and where the volume of sectional demands is too small to produce a set of stable and differentiated associations.

Whatever the relative strengths of the two drives, the institutions of any liberal democracy will be shaped by each of them to some extent and will therefore be two-dimensional. Parties share this quality: they not only represent specialized constituencies and the values of competition but also reflect the general concern that the regime should be preserved, if needs be by exceptional leadership, during any period of crisis. The logical extremes of these two aspects of party behaviour each constitute an ideal type, seldom if every attained in reality. On the one hand, in a situation where the party drive was absolute, each party would become nothing more than an impersonal association proposing a programme which expressed the material demands of one sector of society and seeking a mandate to carry out that programme within a fixed term. On the other hand, were the rally drive to be absolute, each party would lose its representative function and adopt a purely reflexive form, serving simply as a vehicle for the views of the exceptional leader. In the real world, neither situation would be likely to arise: even the most stable and efficient system of representation would retain some rally characteristics and the most disciplined of rally regimes would provide some scope for the functioning of representative institutions and for interaction between parties and social groups.

For as long as a crisis lasts, a successful rally both transcends and encloses the parties which comprise its community, only to release them to resume their full representational roles once the situation has returned to normal. Although a rally leader may criticize the behaviour of parties, he rarely disputes their right to exist or questions the value of liberal democratic politics. It is therefore important to distinguish rally rhetoric from the rhetoric of populism. Whereas the populist leader appeals to those sections of the community which feel that a selfish elite has deprived them of their share of the nation's wealth, the rally leader exhorts the whole community to achieve collective goals and to value solidarity above sectional aims. Again, whereas the populist stresses the line of division between elite and mass, and often between town and country, the rally leader seeks to minimize such differences; instead he emphasizes the division between those who have accepted the primacy of the national cause and those who have not. The former sees an election campaign as an occasion when established authorities may be placed on trial and justice obtained; the latter aims to transform an election into a plebiscite by means of which the people can signify their commitment to an ideal. Viewed in this light, rally politics are essentially conservative in their final effect and provide a way of concentrating loyalties on the essential core of a regime when the electorate has become disenchanted with the normal processes of parliamentary government.

For this amongst other reasons, even leaders who are convinced that the best means of expressing and resolving differences of outlook and interest is by competition between parties are generally prepared to reconcile themselves to the existence of the rally drive and to the possibility that, in certain circumstances, it may gain strength at the expense of the party drive. When it happens that the severity of a crisis creates a widespread demand for the establishment of an emergency authority and for the ritual affirmation of community solidarity, they know that the electors have expectations about the ways in which it should be met. If on a previous occasion the need for special arrangements has led to the formation of a national coalition, or to the use of emergency powers by the head of state, or to the appointment of a leader untainted by discredited policies, a similar arrangement is likely to be called for. All leaders and all parties must build such assumptions into their calculations. Of course, that does not mean that established party officers welcome the prospect of someone – perhaps even an outsider – becoming the focus of a popular rally. Experience will have taught them that their own status, and the stability of their party, may be weakened by such a development, but they will also know from experience that phases of rally politics, however intense they may be at the outset, will pass.

Notes

1 Charles de Secondat Montesquieu, *The Spirit of the Laws*, tr. and ed. by Anne M. Cohler, Basia Carolyn Miller and Harold Samuel Stone (Cambridge University Press, Cambridge, 1989), pp. 15–16.
2 Ibid., p. 16.
3 For an English translation, see Max Weber, *Economy and Society: An Outline of Interpretive Sociology*, ed. by Guenther Roth and Claus Wittich, tr. Ephraim Fischoff et al. (2 vols, University of California Press, Berkeley, Second Printing, 1978).
4 Ibid., vol. I, pp. 212–301. On ideal type analysis, see Wolfgang J. Mommsen, 'Ideal Type and Pure Type: Two Variants of Max Weber's Ideal-typical Method', in Mommsen, *The Political and Social Theory of Max Weber: Collected Essays* (Polity Press, Cambridge, 1989), pp. 121–32. See also John Gaffney, *The French Left and the Fifth Republic: The Discourses of Communism and Socialism in Contemporary France* (Macmillan, Houndmills, Basingstoke, 1989), pp. 18–19.
5 Weber, *Economy and Society*, vol. I, pp. 263–4.
6 Ibid., pp. 266–9. I should like to thank Dr Edward Page, of the Department of Politics at the University of Strathclyde, for drawing my attention to references to Weber's discussion of the concept of plebiscitary democracy.
7 Ibid., p. 286.
8 Weber, *Gesammelte Politische Schriften* (Tübingen, Second Edition, 1958), p. 336, cited by David Beetham, *Max Weber and the*

Theory of Modern Politics (Allen and Unwin, London, 1974), pp. 105–6.

9 Reinhard Bendix, *Max Weber: An Intellectual Portrait* (Methuen, London, 1966), p. 447.

10 Beetham, *Max Weber and the Theory of Modern Politics*, p. 230. See also Mommsen, *The Political and Social Theory of Max Weber*, pp. 13, 18–19 and 100–1.

11 Karl Mannheim, *Ideology and Utopia: An Introduction to the Sociology of Knowledge* (Routledge and Kegan Paul, London, 1960), p. 101.

12 Ibid., p. 127.

13 Ernst Cassirer, *The Myth of the State* (Yale University Press, New Haven, Eighth Printing, 1967), p. 279.

14 Ibid., pp. 279–80.

15 Ibid., p. 280.

16 Ibid., pp. 281–2.

17 Stanley Hoffmann, 'Heroic Leadership: The Case of Modern France', in Lewis J. Edinger (ed.), *Political Leadership in Industrialized Societies: Studies in Comparative Analysis* (Wiley, New York, 1967), pp. 108–54. See also the French version (Hoffmann, 'Le héros politique: Pétain, de Gaulle, Mendès-France', Part I, *Preuves* (June 1967), pp. 25–45; Part II, ibid. (July 1967), pp. 21–33.

18 See Michel Crozier, *The Bureaucratic Phenomenon* (University of Chicago Press, Chicago, Second Impression, 1967), pp. 286–93.

19 Hoffmann, 'Heroic Leadership', pp. 117–18.

20 Ibid., p. 120.

21 See ibid., pp. 127–39.

22 See ibid., pp. 139–52.

23 André Siegfried, *Tableau Politique de la France de l'Ouest sous la Troisième République* (Armand Colin, Paris, Second Edition, 1964), pp. 473–4 (translation mine).

24 Siegfried, *Tableau des Partis en France* (Bernard Grasset, Paris, 1930), pp. 203–4 (translation mine).

6

The Experience of Rally Politics

In each political culture, attitudes towards the party drive and the rally drive vary considerably and are strongly coloured by the mythology which underlies that culture. This chapter examines briefly some aspects of rally politics in France, Britain, the United States and India, taking note of various ways in which the phenomenon is perceived and turned to account, especially by leaders who have established some degree of independence for themselves.

In France under the Third Republic (1870–1940) the rally drive was associated with Bonapartism,[1] that is, with a set of circumstances in which a strong man appeals to the broad mass of society, uses the technique of plebiscite to obtain approval for his actions, reduces parliament to a subordinate status, and finally re-establishes order within a democratic framework. Third Republican leaders were constantly looking for signs that some right-wing politician or army leader might be following in the footsteps of Louis Napoleon, who, having been elected as President of the Second Republic in December 1848, staged a *coup d'état* on 2 December 1851, gained approval by referendum for the reshaping of the constitution, and in 1852 established a new institutional structure. Known as the Second Empire, his regime resembled that which had existed under his uncle, the first Napoleon, during the period of the Consulate and the First Empire (1799–1814); although its Constitution provided for a popular assembly elected on the basis of universal suffrage, it vested considerable powers in the office of Emperor, which Louis Napoleon promptly assumed. The Second Empire came to an end only after France's defeat in the Franco–Prussian war of 1870–1 and was succeeded by the Third Republic, whose constitution was adopted in 1875. What had so alarmed Republicans about this sequence of events was not only the ease with which Louis Napoleon had swept aside parliamentary institutions before appealing directly and successfully to the people, but also the fact that it had taken a military disaster to break his grip on power. They were at first unsure whether the parliamentary system, centred on a Chamber of Deputies and a Senate, would win the affection and respect of the citizens, but they soon found grounds for optimism. In 1877 they won a decisive encounter with Marshal MacMahon, the new regime's first President, who had dissolved the Chamber because he did not approve of its policies. However, as fresh elections produced another Republican majority, MacMahon was forced to appoint a Prime Minister who enjoyed the confidence of the Chamber.

Preserving the Republic became a matter of striking a balance between those, mainly on the right, who believed that the Chamber was a dangerously contentious body (and therefore a permanent threat to executive authority) and those, mainly on the left, who saw the principal danger to the state as being the strength of public sentiment in favour of Bonapartism. The popularity of General Georges Boulanger in the late 1880s and the support attracted by the right in the late 1890s at the time of the Dreyfus affair, showed how fragile the regime remained. Parliamentary elections were treated with a degree of caution by both sides: despite their victory in 1877, the Left still feared that elections could become the means of expressing a powerful rally drive, while the Right were uneasy that universal suffrage might strengthen the position of organized parties in the representative process. Until the turn of the century, indeed, the party content of French politics remained relatively weak; although there was a general division between the Republicans and their opponents in the country at large, the majority of election campaigns were highly localized and the groups in parliament were not strongly identified with particular regions or with particular sets of social and economic interests. While the formation of the Radical-Socialist Party in 1901 and of the united Socialist Party in 1905 provided some degree of integration in the system, the former was a weak and decentralized body by British and American standards, and the Socialist Party was viewed with a good deal of apprehension in the country as a whole, as indeed was the Communist Party, established after the Socialist split of 1920.

Parties were also treated with caution by French liberal constitutional theorists, who were inclined to advocate an ideal system of representative politics from which both the rally drive and the party drive had been excluded – a system in which nothing could interfere with the relations between deputies and electors at one level or with those between the houses of parliament and the government at another. In a book published in 1930, Louis Trotabas interspersed his account of the functioning of the 1875 Constitution with significant warnings about what might happen were a move in either direction to threaten the institutional equilibrium. In justifying the provision for the election of the President by a joint meeting of both houses of parliament, he stated that:

> The need for a neutral president requires his election by a restricted college, which has the advantage of being subdued, less costly and above all less impassioned than election by universal suffrage, which disturbs the country. Moreover, election by the people has the effect of giving the Head of State too much power in relation to other authorities, and could revive the dangers of a plebiscite, which 1852 has revealed: the presidency's lack of accountability (*irresponsabilité*) is incompatible with such power.[2]

In another section of his book dealing with the participation of citizens in the process of government, he took an equally critical view of political parties.

> In our parliamentary regime, the belief in the myth of the political party jeopardizes, unaided, the active role of the governed in the operations of government and causes all kinds of malpractice. In order for this role to be properly fulfilled, as democracy requires, parties should be reduced to a secondary activity of grouping individuals according to given problems.[3]

These scholarly views had their counterparts in the outlook of the politicians of the 1930s, who saw the balance of the regime being threatened by an incipient tendency towards rally politics and by a much more obvious tendency towards the domination of Parliament by organized parties acting in alliance. It was the former possibility which most concerned the parties of the left and the latter which worried the parties of the right. Conditions for a rally of some kind were present in 1934, when, after violent street riots in Paris on 6 February, an attempt was made to seize the Palais Bourbon, the meeting place of the Chamber of Deputies. In the wake of these events, the then Prime Minister, Edouard Daladier, resigned and his place was taken by Gaston Doumergue, a former President, who formed a government of national union (representing all parliamentary groups except the Socialists and Communists) and was authorized to govern by decree. Several months after he had taken office, Doumergue was reported to be considering the possibility of altering the Constitution in ways which would strengthen the executive in relation to Parliament, and came under fire from Léon Blum, the Socialist leader, who suspected him of wanting to build up a rally around himself. Like Trotabas, Blum saw the Parliamentary framework which had been provided by the 1875 Constitution as a barrier against Bonapartism. Alluding to the story that Doumergue was planning to convene a meeting of the members of the Chamber and the Senate in Versailles, where, acting as a National Assembly they would amend the Constitution, Blum warned:

If ever the plan that M. Doumergue has half-revealed were to be put into operation, there would no longer be a representative regime, nor even a Republic. Under what conditions are such proposals to be presented to the country? Under what conditions is M. Doumergue trying to prepare opinion before taking the houses of parliament to Versailles? Is he speaking on behalf of a united and responsible government? Has this government reached a considered decision? Not in the very least. M. Doumergue has been meditating under his plane trees, and has taken his decisions completely on his own. . . . He has hardly shared some vague confidences with his colleagues before he addresses himself directly to the country. He seeks straight away to place his ministry, then the houses of parliament, and then the National Assembly under the threat of a popular injunction which would not be a *referendum* but actually a plebiscite. For it would constitute a blank cheque secured by personal authority, without a pointed debate, without any free discussion, and without the presentation of arguments to the contrary. His way of doing things betrays his real intention, to use Bonapartist methods to effect a displacement of sovereignty. . . . And tomorrow, perhaps the blackmail of riot will be added to that of dissolution.[4]

Blum indicated in a later article that the Socialists would have preferred quite a different plan of constitutional reform.

> the abyss which separates us from M. Doumergue, his ministers and his majority is that, for us, the renovation of the state would entail the continued development of democracy, whereas for them it would entail its destruction. For authority and a strong regime (*pouvoir*) we look to the extension, expression and adaptation of popular sovereignty, whereas they look to an all-powerful individual. All their plans tend only to mutilate or annul the institutions which would balance or restrict such an individual.

Blum feared that Doumergue aimed at freeing the Prime Minister from parliamentary control.

> M. Doumergue reduces to nothing the sovereignty which was invested in parliament through the mandate, through the representation of universal suffrage, and that is precisely how *he destroys the representative regime*. But, because he takes good care to organize as compensation *the direct sovereignty* of the people, he effectively delivers sovereignty to a man, to an individual. . . . The regime which it is intended to impose upon us under the blackmail of a riot is a Consulate, a kind of fixed-term monarchy.[5]

In fact, Doumergue did not proceed with any such plans and resigned office on 8 November 1934. Nevertheless, the above passages are worth quoting at length because Blum's concern clearly reveals his understanding of the nature and mechanisms of the rally drive. It is important to note that he was not accusing Doumergue of wanting to establish an authoritarian regime; rather he was suggesting that the Prime Minister hoped to shift the balance of power within the Third Republic by making the presidency rather than the lower house the object of popular sovereignty and by using plebiscitary appeals to convert the differentiated party constituencies into a unified mass, weakening the parties in the process. Blum was disturbed by the fact that the weakness of the party drive in France had left the Republicans without a countervailing force which could be used to prevent leaders such as Doumergue from creating a rally. Writing in December 1934, he argued that:

Popular sovereignty is the principle of any republican regime. From this common mould, the Constitution of the United States, for example, and the French Constitution of 1875 derive quite different applications. But it nevertheless remains obvious that any republican constitution, any democratic constitution sets itself the aim of releasing the action of popular sovereignty. Such a release implies in practice the existence of organized parties, and political or governmental action is stable only to the extent that the parties themselves possess a certain capacity for stability. It can therefore be said that, in a democracy, there cannot be political stability without a minimum of party organization. But it happens that, by a strange contradiction, France is one of the countries in the world most resistant to the organization of parties ... while at the same time being one of the world's most fundamentally republican and democratic countries.

He claimed that governments in France had fallen one after another because they had lacked a strong basis in the form of solidly organized parties.

Parties do exist in France – indeed, there are too many of them, but in the majority of cases they manifestly lack coherence and stability. They form, lose shape and re-form according to the vicissitudes of parliamentary life; they are liable to scatter and to split up; they are prey to personal rivalries; they lack discipline, and above all they lack consistency in their positions and programmes.

The remedy, in his view, was the introduction of a system of proportional representation which would encourage the development of stable parties.[6] Just as he understood how Doumergue could have acted to harness the rally drive, so Blum knew what changes were needed in the electoral system to stimulate the party drive. In 1927 the French Parliament had agreed to the restoration of the *scrutin d'arrondissement*, by which deputies were elected to the Chamber on the basis of single member constituencies, with provision for two ballots if no candidate were to obtain an absolute majority on the first round. These arrangements had caused a dispersal of party energies as every segment of opinion sought to put forward a candidate for the first ballot. The scheme of proportional representation favoured by Blum would have entailed the creation of large, multi-member constituencies in which electors would have been forced to consider national programmes rather than local interests when deciding whom to support; at the same time, his scheme would have strengthened the position of the nation-wide, centralized parties in the selection of candidates, the presentation of issues and the control of parliamentary groups. Under such conditions, the party drive would have been sustained by powerful rising currents of opinion, freed at last from the constraining effects of localism and particularism.

A few years later, in the spring of 1938, Blum again saw the possibility that the rally drive might strengthen in response to the threat posed to French national security by the policies of Nazi Germany. On 12 March, Austria was occupied by German troops and on the following day the *anschluss* was declared. At that time, Blum was attempting to form a government following the resignation of the Chautemps administration and his intention before the international crisis had broken had been to form a conventional party coalition of some kind. The seriousness of the situation in Austria, however, forced him to think in terms of a broadly based national union. This was a path along which he was reluctant to proceed, for he realized that such a union would entail the absorption of the Popular Front (the alliance of the Communist, Radical and Socialist Parties which had won the 1936 elections) in a parliamentary bloc which contained a substantial right-wing element. He therefore tried to gain support for a two-tier system in which the right-wing groups in Parliament would be associated with the left-wing alliance in accordance with the formula, 'the rally of all Republicans around the Popular Front' (*le rassemblement du pays républicain autour du Front Populaire*).[7] However, his proposal was turned down by the right-wing groups, many of whose leaders would have preferred a straightforward national union. Blum had therefore no alternative but to form another Popular Front Government composed only of Socialists and Radicals, while conservative spokesmen continued to call for the creation of a rally. One of them, François Martin, described his feelings in the following terms:

> on all sides we hear the same call being made which, in different forms, expresses the will of public opinion that at last a

government be formed for France, not around the parties at all, but over them and, if necessary, outside them. . . .

We all rightly feel that this country would experience an immense relief if there could at last arise, to liberate it, a government of men openly and joyfully announcing the rallying of the French spirit (*le rassemblement de l'esprit français*) and possessing no other ideal than that of the homeland.[8]

Although the political context was very different, Martin's appeal for a rally was similar to that which Doumergue had made for a national union in 1934: both men wished to see French society possessed of a degree of concord which would transcend parties. The conservatives' penchant for rally politics was matched by their fear that it would soon be too late to prevent organized parties such as the Socialists and Communists from completely dominating the representative system. Blum's response to Doumergue's initiatives in 1934 and his implicit rejection of the idea of an undiluted national union in 1938 showed that he recognized that the move towards rally politics was a move against parties. Conversely, his own belief in the virtues of proportional representation was grounded in his faith that historical change could be accelerated or even forced by institutional adjustments, and that the party drive could be used to transform the diffuse electoral groupings on the Right of the political spectrum into organized national parties. What is most striking about this conflict of views is the extent to which the chief protagonists in the interwar period understood how fine was the balance between those forces which could sweep the French representative system towards a regime of organized parties and those which could sweep it in the opposite direction, towards a regime dominated by a rally leader.

In Britain, the party drive has always been stronger and more acceptable than it has in France. The phased creation of a mass electorate has been accompanied by the growth of strongly organized parties. Techniques of electoral mobilization devised by such associations as the Anti-Corn Law League in the period after the adoption of the Reform Act of 1832 were later applied by the Conservative and Liberal Parties in their efforts to control the much larger pools of voters created by the Reform Act of 1867 and the Franchise Act of 1884, and by the turn of the century these two parties had become the principal avenues for representation and political advancement. When the Labour Party displaced the Liberals as the main party of the left during the 1920s and early 1930s, it too developed efficient and comprehensive methods of local organization. The solidity and coherence of the British parties enabled their leaders to address not only an enclosed partisan audience but the people as a whole, as Gladstone did so successfully in his Midlothian campaign of 1880. This twofold nature of the leader's role was transferred to the office of Prime Minister; the head of a government was expected to be not only the leader of the majority party in the House of Commons but also something of a rally leader, acting on behalf of all citizens and of all groups in the community. To this day, when one of the major parties chooses a new leader he or she is appraised as a potential Prime Minister in both senses, that is, both as chief executive and as a person capable of commanding broad sympathies and allegiance.

Under most circumstances, the party and rally drives work in combination in Britain; both are directed through the existing major parties and channelled towards the Prime Ministership. However, in times of national emergency, the rally drive, expressed as a demand for the suspension of party competition and for the concentration of power in the executive, usually becomes much stronger. At such times there are calls not for a 'rally' in the French sense but for a 'national government'. Whether or not the call should be heeded is a matter for judgement; the prospect of a national government may cause disagreements within one or both of the major parties, and the formation of an emergency administration may be delayed or frustrated. National Governments were formed in Britain during both world wars, but only after a conventional one-party government had proved unequal to dealing with the crisis; during the First World War, the Liberal ministry headed by H. H. Asquith gave way in May 1915 to a national Government, also under Asquith, and, during the Second World War, Winston Churchill's national coalition was set up in May 1940 in succession to the National (Conservative) administration of Neville Chamberlain. The economic crisis caused by the great Depression of the early 1930s persuaded the Labour premier, J. Ramsay MacDonald, to attempt to form a national coalition with the

Conservatives in August 1931, but on this occasion the great majority of his own party went into opposition and forced a return to the two-party system. However, during the life of the two wartime coalitions, the combined parties treated the Prime Minister as a rally leader and allowed him to assume a degree of personal control over policies which would not have been tolerated under normal conditions. Lloyd George, who succeeded Asquith as leader of the earlier national coalition in December 1916, and Churchill, who headed his ministry from May 1940 until May 1945, both achieved this freedom of action; however, faced with the opposition of his own party, Ramsay MacDonald was forced to revert to the style of an ordinary Prime Minister.

The responsiveness of British parties to the rally drive has affected the configuration of their leadership groups to a significant degree. Each party has a regular hierarchy of leaders, with members of the Cabinet or, if the party is in opposition its Shadow Cabinet, at the apex, surrounded by a penumbra of relatively independent figures who provide possible foci for rally sentiments. Some of these independent figures may be former Prime Ministers or former ministers who, having lost their position at the top of the party, hold themselves somewhat apart but continue to take an active interest in those policies and programmes in which they have a special expertise. Others may be younger members of the party who have yet to make their mark but whose independence of spirit and judgement has persuaded them to leave the beaten path. This is not to say that such independent figures assume their relative isolation simply as a means of bidding for high office – they may have chosen their ground because of an attachment to principle or because they disagree strongly with a particular policy – but the effect is the same: they offer a variety of individual standpoints in public debates and generally extend the field of candidates whenever a succession crisis occurs at the level of party or of government. It is from such a group that an individual may be called to deal with exceptional circumstances which he or she has predicted in advance of the event.

Winston Churchill occupied such a position in relation to the Conservative Party throughout the 1930s. Born in 1874, he first entered the House of Commons in 1900 and gained respect as a man with deeply held though often unconventional views. As

First Lord of the Admiralty in Asquith's Liberal Cabinet when war broke out in 1914, he was held responsible for the failure of the Dardanelles expedition and resigned his post, but between 1917 and 1922 he served as a member of Lloyd George's coalition Government. Although he lost his seat in the 1922 elections he continued to be active in politics and was elected to the Commons again in 1924 as a 'Constitutionalist'. This made him enough of a Conservative for Stanley Baldwin to include him in his Cabinet as Chancellor of the Exchequer, an office which he held until Labour was returned to power under Ramsay Mac-Donald in 1929. His relationship with Baldwin then deteriorated, for the two men found themselves at odds over the Conservative Party's policies towards India. A statutory commission headed by Sir John Simon had studied conditions in that country in 1928 and 1929 and was required to submit a report to Parliament outlining proposals for the future organization of the governmental system in India. It was expected that, after the proposals based on the report had been considered by a joint committee of both houses of parliament, steps would be taken to frame a bill to replace the Government of India Act of 1919. Instead, the Labour Government decided to convene a round-table conference of British and Indian representatives in London to consider the Indian question and the possibility of the country's being accorded Dominion status. Baldwin had gone along with the change of plan and with the decision to hold such a conference and in September 1930 Churchill wrote to him urging him not to allow his friendship with Lord Irwin, the Governor-General of India,

> to affect your judgement or the action of your Party upon what, since the War, is probably the greatest question Englishmen have had to settle. Very strong currents of feeling and even passion are moving under the stagnant surface of our affairs, and I must confess myself to care more about this business than anything else in public life.[9]

Churchill also dissented from Baldwin's decision to accept tariffs on imported foodstuffs as part of the Conservative programme and continued to speak out against the new policy towards India. In January 1931, in a letter to his son, he envisaged what might happen were the Labour ministry to fall and Baldwin to form a new Conservative Government.

I have no desire to join such an administration and be saddled with all the burden of whole-hog Protection, plus unlimited doses of Irwinism for India. I shall be much more able to help the country from outside. I feel a great deal stronger since the Indian situation developed, although most people will tell you the opposite. It is a great comfort when one minds the questions one cares about far more than office or party or friendships.[10]

In the Commons on 26 January 1931, Churchill spoke out strongly against the Labour Government's resort to a round-table conference, which Baldwin continued to defend, and shortly afterwards Churchill resigned from the Conservatives' front-bench team.[11] He was not invited to join the national Government when it was formed in August 1931 and was excluded from office until 1939, first by Baldwin, who became Prime Minister again in June 1935, and later by his successor, Neville Chamberlain. Making good use of this period in the wilderness to sharpen his understanding of the military threat represented by Nazi Germany, Churchill unreservedly attacked the Munich Agreement of September 1938 and advocated firm measures to check German expansion. After the Nazi occupation of Prague in March 1939, he and a group of Conservatives brought forward a motion in parliament which called for the formation of a national government, but this initiative was not pursued when Chamberlain issued a statement guaranteeing that Britain would give Poland her full support 'in the event of any action which clearly threatened Polish independence'.[12] When war finally broke out in September 1939, Churchill's long record of opposition to fascism and his warnings against the danger of Britain's remaining in a state of military unpreparedness placed him in a strong moral position; he was immediately appointed to the Admiralty by Chamberlain and, after the latter's resignation in May 1940, was the obvious choice as Prime Minister of the wartime coalition.

Churchill's insistence on his right to judge issues on their merits and his immense faith in the collective good sense of the British people are consonant with a widespread public belief still held today that politicians should take an independent stand if the policy of their party or of the government is in conflict with their sincere convictions. His action in breaking with the Conservative Party in January 1931 and ploughing a lonely furrow was in keeping with an important British political tradition, and though during the 1930s he was treated as an outsider, his strengths were widely recognized. British political leadership in any period usually contains figures like him who (though perhaps to a lesser degree) have chosen to stand by their own policy views and to pursue a relatively independent course in Parliament. Recent examples would include Enoch Powell, Edward Heath, Margaret Thatcher and Norman Tebbit on the Conservative side, Denis Healey and Tony Benn on the side of Labour, and David Owen on the corner benches. Such personalities have their own area of expertise, a distinctive voice and a willingness to go against conventional or popular ideas; they add greatly to the vigour and colour of public debate and are valued for their independence of mind. To some extent they owe their standing to their parties but, wittingly or unwittingly, they are also sustained by the public's belief in the continued need for individual figures in the House of Commons who have intellectual courage and a broad understanding of the national interest. In other words, the status accorded to such personalities reflects the significance of the rally drive in one of the most stable party systems in the Western world.

In the United States, where universal suffrage provides the basis for both presidential and legislative elections, the rally drive has found strong expression in the presidency itself. Although the American Constitution, in keeping with the principle of the separation of powers, assigns executive power to the President, legislative power to the Congress and judicial power to the Supreme Court and the subordinate courts, the office of President has become the dominant unit of the system. The President is the country's chief executive and the Commander-in-Chief of its armed forces; it is he who makes legislative proposals to Congress; he may refuse to sign congressional bills of which he disapproves; he deals with foreign affairs, subject only to the right of the Senate to approve a treaty and to the right of the Congress as a whole to declare war (although the War Powers resolution passed by Congress in 1973 has restricted the

President's ability to use the armed forces in external crises); and his role in interpreting the law has become 'a power of quasi-legislation'.[13] In office, the President is both the leader of his party and 'a steward of the people', in the words of Theodore Roosevelt, who claimed in his autobiography to have broadened the use of executive power: 'I acted for the public welfare, I acted for the common well-being of all our people, whenever and in whatever manner was necessary, unless prevented by direct constitutional or legislative prohibition.'[14] These very different aspects of the presidency, the partisan and the monarchical, weigh heavily on the process by which the main parties, the Republican and the Democratic, choose their candidates for each presidential election. Party managers must measure each eligible contender for nomination against criteria of partisanship and the much more demanding criteria of his or her capacity to rally all sections of the community. Their task is complicated by the fact that the preliminary sorting out of aspirants takes place within a party framework, from the primary elections which begin at state level at the start of the election year to the final nominating conventions in late summer; it is only then that the eventual nominees, Democratic, Republican and, occasionally, third-party candidates embark on their essentially individual campaigns for nation-wide support. Although each candidate presents a party programme, he or she is also appealing at this stage for a non-partisan response from the electors to factors such as his or her personal qualities and breadth of vision.

Like the office of President itself, the presidential election campaign has a dual nature: it is at once an episode in a sequence of confrontations between the two main parties, given that the two-yearly cycles of the congressional elections fit into the four-yearly cycle of the presidential contests, and, at the same time, an opportunity for the creation of a rally. Should one of the candidates succeed in the latter venture, of drawing considerable support across party lines, both parties, and both houses of Congress, may find themselves dealing with a president who has taken his mandate from a massive popular vote. Recent examples of this are provided by the remarkable proportion of the total vote registered in favour of the following Presidents: Franklin D. Roosevelt (Democrat) in 1936 (60.8 per cent); Dwight D. Eisenhower (Republican) in 1956 (57.4 per cent); Lyndon B. Johnson

(Democrat) in 1964 (61.1 per cent); and of Ronald Reagan (Republican) in 1984 (58.8 per cent). The co-existence of two parallel but separate electoral processes, the congressional and the presidential, enables the latter to absorb and express the rally drive at certain times, while the power of the President's office, especially if exercised in keeping with the stewardship theory of rule, enables a secure incumbent to offer a degree of strong personal leadership inconceivable in a parliamentary regime. Franklin D. Roosevelt's ability to develop and implement the New Deal programme in the 1930s is more intelligible if the Democratic Party of that period is seen as in large part a rally, sanctioning his exceptional use of the role of chief executive to persuade Congress to accept the necessity for an extensive programme of reforms and the Supreme Court to adjust the orientation of its decisions accordingly.

Most leaders of major parties in liberal democratic countries have to come to terms with the presence of the rally drive in the political system, whether they reject it as in some sense regressive (a reversion to pre-party or plebiscitary norms) or accept it as a normal and constructive part of representative politics. In a system in which a president is elected directly on the basis of universal suffrage, as in the United States, the need to offer a degree of rally leadership is simply accepted as a routine aspect of campaigning. However, in other systems too, some leaders find rally politics more congenial than party politics and it is important to realize that not all of them are moved by anti-liberal intentions; there are those who genuinely believe that parties, by catering for special interests and offering opportunities for place-seekers and pressure groups to cluster around the institutions of government, actually inhibit the working of democracy and impede interaction between the state and the citizen. Such leaders persuade themselves that they have a special awareness of popular aspirations and, convinced that they can thus more easily produce results, they are inclined to withdraw from conventional day-to-day politics and to rely to a large extent on their ties with the masses. One of the most interesting examples of such behaviour can be seen in the career of Jawaharlal Nehru, the Prime Minister of India from 1947 until his death in 1964.

Like his father, Motilal Nehru, Jawaharlal was a member of

the Indian National Congress, which was formed in 1885 and became the most influential nationalist association in British India. It expanded its social following considerably during the inter-war period by undertaking two major agitations against British rule, the non-co-operation campaign of 1920–2 and the civil disobedience movement of 1930–3. After some hesitation (for it was reluctant to participate in the representative system set up by the British) it contested the elections of 1923 and 1926, and its success in those of 1937 allowed it to take power in several provinces. During the 1920s and 1930s the party's unofficial but very effective leader was Mohandas Gandhi, known familiarly as the Mahatma (or 'great soul'), but its direct management was in the hands of a stable core of notables, generally referred to as the 'High Command'.

Nehru did not fit easily into this hierarchy. He had been born in 1889 into a well-to-do family of Kashmiri Brahmans and educated in England at Harrow and Trinity College, Cambridge, and his first intention had been to follow a legal career in India. Drawn into Congress during the First World War, he was imprisoned for taking part in the non-co-operation movement and became part of the radical wing of the party during the late 1920s. He was Congress President for the years 1930, 1936 and 1937 and spent several periods in jail for his part in the civil disobedience movement. Although he and Gandhi disagreed at various times about Congress strategies and policies, the two men felt a deep attachment to one another and, after Motilal's death in 1931, it was to Gandhi that Nehru turned for advice.[15]

These decades of the 1920s and 1930s were the ones that shaped Nehru's attitudes towards political leadership. Then, for the first time, he had come into direct contact with the peasants of India and he felt that it was vital that the Congress should be responsive to their needs, as well as representing the ideals of the nationalist movement. In some moods he doubted his own ability to reconcile these two aims. In his autobiography, written during a period in jail in the early 1930s, he described his reaction to the statement by another Indian leader that he 'did not represent mass-feeling'.

I often wonder if I represent any one at all, and I am inclined to think that I do not, though many have kindly and friendly feelings towards me. I have become a queer mixture of the East and West, out of place everywhere, at home nowhere. Perhaps my thoughts and approach to life are more akin to what is called Western than Eastern, but India clings to me, as she does to all her children, in innumerable ways; and behind me lie, somewhere in the sub-conscious, racial memories of a hundred, or whatever the number may be, generations of Brahmans. I cannot get rid of either that past inheritance or my recent acquisitions. They are both part of me, and, though they help me in both the East and the West, they also create in me a feeling of spiritual loneliness not only in public activities but in life itself. I am a stranger and alien in the West. I cannot be of it. But in my own country also, sometimes, I have an exile's feeling.[16]

Nehru admired both Gandhi's confidence in himself and his ability to maintain his moral integrity, and in April 1938 he confessed to the older man his disillusionment with the record of the Congress provincial ministries which had been formed in the previous year:

They are adapting themselves far too much to the old order and trying to justify it. But all this, bad as it is, might be tolerated. What is far worse is that we are losing the high position that we have built up, with so much labour, in the hearts of the people. We are sinking to the level of ordinary politicians who have no principles to stand by and whose work is governed by a day-to-day opportunism.

He had decided to go abroad and went on to explain why:

For months past I have felt that I could not function effectively in India as things were going. I have carried on of course as one can always carry on. But I have felt out of place and a misfit. This was one reason (though there were others also) why I decided to go to Europe.[17]

Having returned to India in November 1938, Nehru was soon drawn into a major crisis within the Congress, during the course of which Subhas Chandra Bose, the Congress President, clashed with Gandhi and was eventually forced to resign his post. Nehru, trying unsuccessfully to act as a mediator, was once more cast into despair. In August 1939 he described his state of mind:

It is perfectly true that I have felt puzzled and perplexed. This perplexity is not due to any doubt in my own mind as to what should be done, but rather to the difficulty of inducing any considerable numbers of others to act in a particular way. When organized groups and parties within the Congress function aggressively against each other, I feel singularly out of place, as I have not been used to such functioning. It invariably happens under these circumstances that each group tries to over-reach the other, and the immediate and all-important objective seems to be to triumph over the other group. The larger good is often forgotten. Politics, seldom pleasant, become singularly unpleasant then.

I fear I am an ineffective politician at any time, and I have no taste whatever for the variety of politics that has lately developed. That is my weakness. When I cannot act effectively, I try at any rate to preserve a certain integrity of mind, and I wait for the time when I can act more effectively.[18]

The above passages reveal Nehru's mixed feelings about the nature of the relationship between the Congress Party and the Indian people. Where his own position was concerned, he had translated his private sense of belonging to two worlds into a conviction that he had a special vantage point from which he could see Congress' defects as well as its virtues; he regarded transactional politics as immoral and purposeless, and communication with the masses as the essential means of achieving economic and social democracy. Just as he saw himself as politically engaged in two different capacities, as a member of the Indian National Congress and as a man of the masses, so he saw the Congress itself as a twofold entity, an organization maintained by the myriad activities of the individuals and groups whose ambitions and interests it had come to serve and also a rally sustained by the hopes of the masses. His instinct was to identify himself with the latter, the rally, aspect of Congress and to stand aloof from its party aspect.

The same ambivalence influenced his behaviour after India achieved independence in 1947, when he became Prime Minister and, after 1951, the undisputed chief of his party. A parliamentary system of government within a federal framework was established under the Indian Constitution of 1950, and Nehru led the Congress to convincing victories in the lower houses of the federal and state legislatures in the general elections of

1951–2, 1957 and 1962, during which he undertook exacting campaign tours. He attracted large crowds wherever he went and his skill as a rally leader gave his party a decisive advantage over the several non-Congress groups which were trying to establish themselves. However, the fact remains that the Congress made sure of its electoral victories in the territorial constituencies by placing considerable financial and organizational resources at the disposal of its candidates in most regions of India. As the ruling party at the federal level, in New Delhi, and in the great majority of the states, it was an enormous dispenser of patronage, the avenue through which ambitious politicians hoped to further their careers, and the focus for the demands of pressure groups. With that side of Congress politics Nehru was never at ease; he thought in terms of programmes, plans and social commitments. Although he had been influenced by socialist ideas, he was essentially a liberal humanist with a strong belief in progress through social and economic reforms. He liked to think of Congress as being essentially a broadly-based movement and was worried by the possibility that privileged groups might take over the organization and divert it from its original purpose. In 1953, he drew his Chief Ministers' attention to the fact that members of the US House of Representatives who had visited India had found its state governments to be 'conservative in outlook and governed largely by pressure groups from landed interests and commercial groups' and he asked:

> How far is it true . . . that our Governments, Central or State, are influenced much by what might be called the conservative or vested interests in our society? We talk of the people. What are the people? The vast mass of peasants and industrial workers and landless labour appear somewhere in the background while special interests come to the front and make themselves heard. It would be a tragedy if we forgot the principal urge of the national movement that we are supposed to represent. That urge was always in favour of this vast mass of the common people and we have repeatedly declared that no private or vested interest should come in the way of progress of these people.[19]

On the other hand, he was heartened by any sign that Congress was assuming the form which he favoured, and when the party, at its 60th plenary session in January 1955, adopted a resolution in favour of 'a socialistic pattern of society', he spoke optimistically about the future:

> we have to deal with national movement. I think we are having a national movement still. Now a national movement has to move necessarily on a broad basis. During these 30 years or 40 years of my contact with the Congress, I have often, been unhappy about the slowness of the pace of the Congress. But I realised long ago that the Congress cannot function as a small sectarian movement, because it has got to carry the people with it.[20]

At times when he was depressed Nehru would consider a temporary withdrawal from office. He did so in April 1958 when he actually made such a request to the President of India; as he told the Congress Parliamentary Party, he 'was not in tune with many things, sometimes not in tune with the party but that is a small matter, but not in tune with the country, not in tune with the organization'.[21] However, despite such misgivings he carried on as Prime Minister until his death in May 1964. His most difficult period came towards the end of his life when, in October 1962, India's old ally, China, invaded her northern border regions and, after brief hostilities, withdrew on the basis of a unilaterally declared cease-fire. His spirits were lowered further when Congress lost three of four parliamentary by-elections in May 1963 and it was after this that he gave his support to an extraordinary scheme known, after the Chief Minister who had originally proposed it, as the Kamaraj Plan. Under this, all central ministers and Chief Ministers were required to submit letters of resignation to Nehru on the understanding that he would select six from each category to leave office and undertake work for the party. He explained the purpose of the plan in he following terms:

> That decision was based principally on making it clear that the Congress does not approve the people being attracted by office and the power that it brings. While all of us in the Congress should be devoted to the service of our people, the desire for office or power vitiates the desire for service.[22]

Thus, even at the end of his career Nehru still viewed personal ambition in a politician with a censorious eye, and the continual play in his speeches and writings on the conflict between humility and the lust for power, between corruption and integrity, and between competition and solidarity, seems to show deep-rooted anxieties about his own role as a political figure. His basic impulse was to offer rally leadership to the Indian people and to treat the Congress as the embodiment of their will and he was therefore reluctant to admit that, for its long-term survival, the party needed to construct a distinctive social base to enable it to compete successfully with the non-Congress parties which were already establishing themselves. Most of his energies as a party manager were absorbed in the endless routines of maintaining order within the organization, resolving conflicts between groups and steering policy proposals through the executive and plenary institutions, with the paradoxical result that Congress bosses at the state level relied on the methods of machine politics to win elections and maintain their own power. In consequence, the Congress of the 1950s and early 1960s became a combination of a rally and a machine while its party aspect, that is, those respects in which it responded effectively to a specialized constituency, remained weak and underdeveloped.

Since Nehru's death in 1964, the party has held to this pattern and it has been dependent very largely on rally leadership provided by successive members of his family. In January 1966, his daughter, Mrs Indira Gandhi, became Prime Minister and she led the party (which held office except for a brief period between March 1977 and January 1980) until her assassination on 31 October 1984, after which her son, Rajiv Gandhi, took command of the party until he too was assassinated on 21 May 1991. The Congress had suffered an electoral defeat in 1989, but it was returned to power in New Delhi in the parliamentary elections of 1991. As the new Congress Prime Minister, P. V. Narasimha Rao, took steps to liberalize the economy, his Government was faced with a serious challenge from the Bharatiya Janata Party (BJP) and other Hindu nationalist groups, whose campaign to dismantle a mosque in the northern city of Ayodhya and to build a Hindu temple in its place (to restore an ancient temple which had allegedly stood on the site before the construction of the mosque) was the cause of a great deal of social tension between Hindus and Muslims. When a crowd of Hindu nationalist activists succeeded in destroying the mosque on 6 December 1992, a wave of communal violence swept throughout

India. Direct (or President's) rule was then imposed in the four northern states controlled by the BJP, but the Congress found itself hard-pressed to command support for its traditional policy of secularism. In order to withstand the BJP's appeals to communal sentiment, the ruling party needed to be able to rely on a firm social base built up over the years by careful attention to the sectional needs of a defined constituency; however its long dependence on rally leadership as a means of winning elections has distracted it from the task of constructing such a foundation. The success of non-Congress parties such as the BJP, the Janata Dal and, in West Bengal and Kerala, the Communist Party of India (Marxist), has shown the value of developing electoral strength on the basis of detailed programmes and sectoral appeals. As a result, the Congress Party has found its field of manoeuvre much more restricted than was the case in the 1950s and 1960s.

As we have seen, leaders who have understood that representative politics can either strengthen the tendency towards a system of organized parties or foster the rally drive have been able to apply this knowledge when deciding what action to take in particular circumstances. That they could do so is an acknowledgement that representative politics have multiple dimensions and that the apparent tendency towards an organized system of parties is neither inexorable nor irreversible.

Notes

1 See above, pp. 81–3.
2 Louis Trotabas, *Constitution et Gouvernement de la France* (Armand Colin, Paris, Second Edition, 1938), p. 42 (translation mine).
3 Ibid., p. 204 (translation mine).
4 Léon Blum, 'L'homélie de M. Doumergue' (*Le Populaire*, 25 September 1934), in Blum, *L'Oeuvre de Léon Blum, 1934–1937* (Albin Michel, Paris, 1964), pp. 36–7 (translation mine).
5 Blum, 'Alerte!' (*Le Populaire*, 20 October 1934), in Blum, *L'Oeuvre de Léon Blum, 1937–1940* (Albin Michel, Paris, 1965), p. 420 (translation mine).
6 Blum, 'Pas de stabilité politique sans R.P.' (*Le Populaire*, 28 December 1934), in ibid., pp. 440–1 (translation mine).
7 From a declaration published in *Le Populaire*, 13 March 1938, in ibid., p. 76.

8 *Journal Officiel* (*Chambre des Députés*), *Débats*, 5 April 1938, p. 1072 (translation mine). Martin was a member of the Republican Federation Group.

9 Letter from W. S. Churchill to S. Baldwin, 24 September 1930, cited in Martin Gilbert, *Winston S. Churchill* (8 vols, Heinemann, London), vol. V, *1922–1939* (1976), p. 369.

10 Letter from W. S. Churchill to R. F. E. S. Churchill, 8 January 1931, cited in ibid., p. 379.

11 See ibid., pp. 380–4.

12 See ibid., pp. 1052–3.

13 Edward S. Corwin, *The President: Office and Powers, 1787–1984: History and Analysis of Practice and Opinion*, Fifth Revised Edition by Randall W. Bland, Theodore T. Hindson and Jack W. Peltason (New York University Press, New York, 1984), p. 190.

14 Theodore Roosevelt, *Autobiography*, pp. 388–9, cited in ibid., p. 175.

15 See Michael Brecher, *Nehru: A Political Biography* (Oxford University Press, London, 1959), and Sarvepalli Gopal, *Jawaharlal Nehru: A Biography* (3 vols, Jonathan Cape, London, 1975, 1979, 1984).

16 Jawaharlal Nehru, *An Autobiography, with Musings on Recent Events in India* (John Lane, London, New Edition, 1942, Reprinted 1945), p. 596.

17 Letter from Jawaharlal Nehru to Mahatma Gandhi, from Allahabad, 28 April 1938, in *A Bunch of Old Letters: Written mostly to Jawaharlal Nehru and some written by him* (Asia, London, 1960), p. 284.

18 Jawaharlal Nehru, 'Enough of It!' (18 August 1939), in Nehru, *The Unity of India: Collected Writings, 1937–1940* (Lindsay Drummond, London, Third Impression, 1948), p. 169.

19 Jawaharlal Nehru to Chief Ministers, from Srinagar, 24 May 1953, in G. Parthasarathi (ed.), *Jawaharlal Nehru: Letters to Chief Ministers, 1947–1964* (5 vols, Government of India, New Delhi), vol. III, *1952–1954* (1987), p. 309.

20 *Congress Bulletin* (New Delhi), No. 3 (April 1955), pp. 249–50.

21 Cited by Gopal, *Jawaharlal Nehru: A Biography*, vol. III, *1956–1964* (1984), p. 107. See also G. Parthasarathi (ed.), *Jawaharlal Nehru: Letters to Chief Ministers*, vol. V, *1958–1964* (1989), p. 40, n. 3.

22 Jawaharlal Nehru, speech at meeting of the Congress Working Committee on 24 August 1963, in *Congress Bulletin*, Nos. 7–8 (July–August 1963), p. 20.

7

Rally Politics in France since 1940

Although, as we have seen, the tension between the party and rally drives was already in evidence in France before the Second World War, its effect on political life has become much more pronounced during the past half century. Under the Third Republic, the lingering fear of Bonapartism amongst Republicans meant that any proposal for the granting of exceptional powers to a government was closely scrutinized by Parliament, and any Prime Minister who tried to appeal for support directly to the people was the object of mistrust – he would come under immediate pressure to acknowledge his primary responsibility to the popular assembly and to accept political parties as the main vehicle of popular representation. However, a sequence of political crises which began with the fall of France in 1940 provided ideal conditions for rally politics in which General Charles de Gaulle (1890–1970) played a prominent part. In 1958, when France under the Fourth Republic appeared to be heading towards a military *coup d'état*, he became Prime Minister and won approval by referendum for a new constitution which provided for a stronger executive and president than had previously existed. Later, in 1962 as the first President of the Fifth Republic, he secured by a further referendum a constitutional amendment which based the presidential election on universal suffrage. By so doing, he laid the foundations for the profound changes in the French system of government which have taken place in recent decades. In this chapter we shall follow the course of these changes and discuss de Gaulle's own interpretation of the events in which he was involved.

The First Gaullist Rally of 1940–1946

Charles de Gaulle, born in the northern industrial city of Lille in 1890, grew up in a staunchly Catholic family. His decision to follow a military career took him to the military academy at Saint-Cyr, and he saw active service as an officer in the First World War before being taken prisoner by the Germans. After a series of staff postings, he was appointed in 1932 to the secretariat of the Superior Council of National Defence, an agency which advised the Prime Minister on military matters, and he remained there until 1937, when he became commander of a tank regiment at Metz. During this period he wrote a number of books and two in particular, *Le fil de l'épée* (*The Edge of the Sword*), published in 1932, and *Vers l'armée de métier* (*Towards a Professional Army*), which appeared in 1934, touched on his philosophy of leadership as an aspect of military command.

Immensely proud of French military tradition, de Gaulle believed that armies contained two very different organizational drives, one directed towards the creation of a dense structure of formal hierarchies and procedural rules and the other towards fostering organic fighting units whose commanders and rank-and-file soldiers were bound together by a strong sense of common purpose. While he did not suggest that these drives were contradictory, de Gaulle was convinced that, during peacetime conditions, the bureaucratic drive had a tendency to weaken the bonding drive. He commented on the army's 'collective mistrustfulness': Formed by stability, conformism and tradition, the army instinctively dreads anything which tends to modify its structure.'[1] As he saw it:

> The army would be affected by paralysis if throughout its ranks the sense of initiative were to diminish, the taste for responsibility and the courage to speak frankly were to weaken, and the quality of leadership were to decline. Through the whole extent of the hierarchy constantly expanding grades exhaust themselves referring to higher authority matters which should be decided on the spot. Excessive regulations conflicting with a mass of minute detail and daily being modified and rectified, a pile of unworkable plans, forecasts which have already proved to be wrong, questions always under study, loads of useless advice, records prepared for

the sake of form, vain requests, this is what takes up the time of the army.[2]

De Gaulle argued that the army could come into its own in a crisis or in time of war only if it retained within its officer corps men of exceptional character and quality. It was therefore important that it should distinguish such men from conventional leaders:

> Whatever might be ... the effect on the quality of leaders of a more liberal education and a wider autonomy, the essential thing will always remain the personal and private endeavour of those who would command. For although inherited knowledge and daily routines serve to fashion the majority of our fellow men, those who are powerful form themselves. Made to leave their mark rather than to be marked, they construct within the sanctuary of their inner life the structure of their feelings, their concepts and their will. That is why, in the tragic hours when a great gust of wind sweeps away conventions and customs, they alone stand upright and are therefore needed. Nothing is more important for a state than to nurture within the officer class those exceptional individuals who will be its ultimate resort.[3]

There were close affinities between this doctrine and the social code of medieval chivalry. Like the perfect knight, the exceptional man had to accept the discipline of meditation, for by so doing he would acquire an integrated moral outlook. Secure in his own beliefs, he would then be in a position to understand the nature of the real world by a combination of reason and intuition, and to form a vision of an ideal future. To refine these qualities, the exceptional man had to learn to be self-sufficient, to rely on his own moral resources even while taking part in everyday affairs.[4]

> by remaining apart from others, the leader forgoes the pleasure of relaxation, familiarity and even friendship. He accepts the sense of solitude which is, according to Faguet, 'the burden of superior men.' Those in command cannot have that state of contentment, of inner peace, of calculated pleasure which goes by the name of happiness.[5]

Once in authority, the exceptional leader would be able to inspire the army to band together as an organic unit without losing its sense of hierarchy or relaxing its discipline. Reflecting in *Le fil de l'épée* on the condition of the French army, de Gaulle stressed its need for a moral revival:

> the development of institutions, the reorganization of equipment, and even intellectual adaptation will not be at all effective unless a moral renaissance takes place at the same time. The soldiers of today, like those of yesterday, need a faith which can draw them together, stir them and make them stand tall. A moral quality is needed to give the military order a rejuvenated ideal, to confer upon it, through the elite, a unity of outlook, to induce fervour and to enrich talent.[6]

Although de Gaulle was writing here about the organization of the army, these passages also reveal the basic elements of his political doctrine. Whether he was considering armies or regimes or political parties, he always began with the assumption that the institutional structure of each was based on a complex equilibrium of forces, and that changes in that equilibrium would bring about systematic changes in the form of the structure in question. In the case of the army, he saw the essential balance as being between those forces which tended to produce the rally or 'warrior band' form and those which tended to produce the hierarchical and bureaucratic form. In times of peace, the latter was stronger, but in times of war the prevailing tendency was towards a rally, providing that an exceptional individual was there to lead it. De Gaulle did not think in terms of revolutions or of successions in form, in which one kind of army would be replaced by another, but in terms of mixtures, the composition of which would vary as conditions changed. So also with the French state, he made no hard and fast distinction between periods of history and assumed a basic continuity between the *ancien régime* and post-revolutionary regimes. The intrinsic pattern in his reasoning was one of continuity in substance despite changes in form.

De Gaulle's experience of high politics began in June 1940, when he placed himself at the head of the Free French forces after the collapse of the French army. Earlier that year, during the battle for France, he had led the Fourth Armoured Division at Moncornet and at Laon, on the Aisne front, before joining

the ministry headed by Paul Reynaud as Under-Secretary of State
for War. He was therefore at the centre of events as the Government moved from Paris to Bordeaux and the military situation continued to deteriorate. On 16 June Reynaud resigned as
Prime Minister and was replaced by Marshal Pétain, whose preference for an armistice with the Germans was well known. De
Gaulle then flew to London and on 18 June broadcast a message
over the BBC in which he declared that French resistance to
the Germans would continue. With British support, he established himself as the virtual leader of France in exile, and he
claimed that the military and political forces which had rallied to him represented the essential will of the French nation. The Vichy regime which Pétain had established in France
he labelled as unconstitutional. In September 1941 he formed
the French National Committee (CNF) to be the executive of the
Free French movement and in 1942 was able to strengthen his
ties with the resistance organizations which had formed in metropolitan France. At first the American authorities were reluctant
to accept de Gaulle's claims to legitimacy and, after Algeria had
been liberated by allied forces at the end of 1942, it was General
Giraud whom they backed as the head of the civilian administration in North Africa. However, the two Generals eventually
agreed to form a joint executive, known as the French Committee of National Liberation (CFLN) and in October 1943 de
Gaulle became the sole head of this body. It was reorganized in
the following month to include representatives of the political
parties and the metropolitan resistance as well as members of de
Gaulle's entourage, and on 3 June 1944 it became the Provisional Government of the French Republic (GPRF). This was the
body which, after the liberation of Paris in August 1944, was to
move to the capital and assume control of the state.[7]

As its President, de Gaulle showed that he was willing to work
to restore Republican institutions. He gave leading personalities
from the various political parties important portfolios in his
ministry, worked closely with the Provisional Consultative Assembly, and agreed to hold a referendum to decide on the constitutional question. The points at issue were whether the
deputies to be returned at the general elections of 21 October
1945 should comprise a constituent assembly and be entrusted
with the task of drawing up a new constitution, or whether the

1875 Constitution should be restored, in which case they would simply become members of another Chamber of Deputies. When the referendum decided in favour of a constituent assembly, the three largest parties – the Communists, the Socialists and the Christian Democratic Popular Republican Movement (MRP) – formed a new government with de Gaulle at its head.[8]

Looking back on these events, de Gaulle had no doubt that he had created a unifying rally of the French people within the Republican tradition. In April 1947, for example, he described what had happened in the following terms:

> miraculously and fortunately, a rally of the French people was formed to achieve the liberation of the country and to win victory. . . . I had the responsibility for power so long as the rally seemed to me to be sufficient to meet national requirements.[9]

He and his entourage had been thinking in such terms as early as 1941 during their days in London. In the course of a luncheon address given in October of that year, he had referred to the formation of 'a vast French resistance' and had maintained that the essential task of the CNF was to organize and direct that resistance: 'It will do this on the authority of the people whose approval it enjoys and to whom it will be accountable. It will do this by rallying the nation to strive for liberation without excluding anyone other than those who exclude themselves.'[10] At one level this approach had simply reflected a policy of avoiding divisions within the resistance movement but at another it expressed the belief that the French people were united in their determination to free their country from foreign rule. De Gaulle alluded to these considerations at a press conference in May 1942:

> the Fighting French and the immense majority of the French in France do not at this moment want to be divided by the struggles of internal politics.
>
> The Fighting French do not belong to any party; they are made up of men of all parties, all opinions, gathered together for a single task, the liberation of France.[11]

In the face of scepticism on the part of the British and especially on the part of the American authorities, de Gaulle began to express his ideas in more romantic terms. In a speech broadcast by Brazzaville radio in September 1942, he spoke thus of the need to organize the developing national movement in France:

> When it concentrates its fury the torrent sweeps all before it. If on the other hand it allows itself to be turned aside into divergent currents, it spends all its strength in the sand. In order to seize victory and to rediscover her greatness, France must form a rally.[12]

In a letter which he sent to the American President, F. D. Roosevelt, a few weeks later, de Gaulle explained in some detail his own position:

> I was not a politician. All my life I stuck to my profession. When, before the war, I tried to interest politicians in my ideas, it was to persuade them to achieve, for the country's sake, a military objective. In the same way, at the time of Vichy's armistice, it was in a military form that I first made my call to the country. But because an increasing number of elements responded, because territories either joined or were joined to Fighting France and because I was always the only one acting in an organized way, I found that I was assuming wider responsibilities. I saw being created in France a kind of mystique, with myself at its centre uniting, bit by bit, all the elements of resistance. Thus, by force of circumstances, I have become a French moral entity. This reality creates for me duties which I feel weighing heavily upon me, and which I consider that I cannot avoid without betraying the country and without breaking faith with the hopes which the people of France place in me.[13]

By an interesting association of ideas, de Gaulle had transposed his notion of military leadership into a philosophy of political leadership. Just as he had conceived of the French army as a variable mixture of hierarchy and warrior band, so he saw the Republic as a mixture of party and rally drives. His notion of the exceptional leader in the context of the army had been translated into the more complex idea of the individual who becomes a symbol, issuing a call for the nation to gather together and preserve its unity until the ordeal is over. After the liberation of France he continued to appeal to this sense of unity[14] and enjoyed immense popularity and respect throughout his term as President of the GPRF. A series of opinion polls in which people were asked whom they would like to see as president of the government during the drafting of the constitution produced percentages in favour of de Gaulle of 71 in July 1945, 64 in September, 65 in October and 75 in November.[15]

From de Gaulle's point of view, the first rally was to end badly. The Government which he had formed in November 1945 was soon in conflict with the Constituent Assembly over issues of current policy and there was a bitter dispute over the defence budget at the end of December. De Gaulle's own freedom of manoeuvre as President had already been restricted by the strength of the three main parties in the Assembly and in his Government and finally, on 20 January 1946, he resigned office. In the ministerial crisis which followed, the parties quickly regrouped and formed another tripartite government headed by the Socialist, Félix Gouin. De Gaulle claimed later that he had had to chose between the following alternatives:

[I had] either to join in the game of parties, which I believe would have reduced without any profit the kind of national capital which I had come to represent in the course of events, and rapidly compromised what was essential. Or [I had] to allow the parties to carry out their experiment, having [myself] already ensured that the people themselves would have the right to decide, by means of a referendum, which regime would be established.[16]

The draft constitution produced by the first Constituent Assembly provided for a parliamentary system in which the lower house, the National Assembly, would have the dominant role. It was supported only by the Communist and Socialist Parties and was rejected in the referendum of 5 May 1946 by 53 per cent of the valid votes. Arrangements were then set in train for the formation of a second Constituent Assembly and the elections for this body, held on 2 June 1946, again created a house dominated by the Communists, the Socialists and the MRP. Although the MRP had opposed the first constitution bill, it shared the view of its two allies that the Republic needed a parliamentary system, and that the instability which had marked party politics under the pre-war regime might be avoided if the French party system were to consist of centralized parties with strong roots in the constituencies. Stability, the argument ran, would be fostered by the introduction of the electoral method of proportional representation, for this was expected to shift the attention of voters from local to national issues and thus enable the parties to form longer-lasting alliances, whether in government or in opposition. It now seemed certain that the three large parties would settle their differences and prepare a constitution designed to favour the party drive within a parliamentary rather than a presidential framework. This was not de Gaulle's view of what was required and on 16 June 1946, in a speech at Bayeux in Normandy, he outlined his own preference for a regime in which the President would enjoy considerable powers, including those of appointing the Prime Minister and other ministers, and of acting as an arbiter in political contingencies.[17] Soon afterwards, one of his supporters, René Capitant, founded the Gaullist Union for the Fourth Republic to advance these ideas.[18]

Despite these moves, the large parties stuck to their task. On 23 June 1946 another tripartite government was formed under the presidency of Georges Bidault, the MRP leader, and the second Constituent Assembly produced another draft constitution which was approved by referendum on 13 October 1946 by 53 per cent of the valid votes. In its final form, the new constitution provided for a bicameral legislature composed of a strong National Assembly and a weak Council of the Republic, and for a President with limited powers who was to be elected by the two houses of parliament. A separate law provided for the election of the National Assembly by a system of proportional representation involving competition between lists of candidates within departments (the basic administrative districts), or sub-divisions of departments, and using the highest-average method for the allocation of any seats remaining after the application of the quotient method. De Gaulle had spoken against the draft constitution on several occasions and candidates of the Gaullist Union contested the first elections to the National Assembly in November 1946, but the tide was now running strongly against him. The three large parties once again won a majority of the seats and in January 1947, after an interim ministry led by the Socialist leader, Léon Blum, had dealt with routine business, Paul Ramadier formed another tripartite government and Vincent Auriol became President of the Republic. Both men were Socialists.

De Gaulle's challenge to the new regime was not long delayed.

In a speech at Strasbourg on 7 April 1947, he attacked the parties for working upon the divisions in society and threatening the unity of the state. Scorning the new constitution, he outlined the economic, social, imperial and external policies which he considered were necessary and stressed the immensity of the task which lay ahead: 'The time has come for the formation and organization of the Rally of the French People which, within the framework of the law, will promote and bring to fruition, despite differences of opinion, a great effort to achieve common security and a basic reform of the state.'[19] As he had done during his wartime rally, so now de Gaulle claimed that he was providing an outlet for a sentiment which was already in existence and which was essentially national and trans-party in character. At a press conference on 24 April, he spoke of the difficulties and anxieties which were affecting both national life and the lives of individuals, and he claimed that 'a common spirit and a common sentiment' had arisen among those French men and women who were concerned about their country:

> this common sentiment lacks a framework which would enable it to find expression and become a force capable not only of establishing in our country an atmosphere without which nothing will be achieved but also of providing the basis for a resolute policy ... in France such as it is, the parties such as they are cannot provide the necessary framework for this common sentiment. Their nature is to represent and set in opposition to each other our divisions and our differences.[20]

De Gaulle made it clear that the Rally of the French People (RPF) would not be a party in the ordinary sense, that he did not intend it to become the only political association within a dictatorship, and that it would take part in elections. While underlining the need for unified action in the major fields of policy, he did not deny the importance of representative politics: 'In a democracy, nothing is more natural than the existence of parties. They express our reciprocal oppositions. But when public security is at stake, and it is, there is a field of activity which is beyond them.'[21]

The party leaders were well aware that de Gaulle's basic objective was to produce a rally drive, and incidentally to weaken their own position. They therefore counter-attacked vigorously. In preparing its activists to meet this new challenge, the Socialist Party's secretariat maintained that, whereas a political party might be expected to accept a class attachment, to mirror class consciousness, and to possess a clearly specified ideology and a programme of constructive action, the RPF was intended to group together the discontented, the disoriented, the ambitious and the reactionary, while advancing the idea (which the Socialists saw as leading inevitably to a personal dictatorship) that a social movement could be incarnate in a 'chief'.[22] Such attacks employed emotive language, but they did represent a genuine understanding of the relationship between the party and the rally drives, and an appreciation of how they could work against each other if they were expressed, as on this occasion, by separate associations.

Rally rhetoric is at its most effective when it can play on particular anxieties – that the nation is faced with a deadly external enemy, that groups within the nation are in sympathy with that enemy, and that the state, the organizational expression of the nation, is not capable of dealing with the situation. In de Gaulle's first rally of 1940–5, these themes were easily developed; Nazi Germany was the external enemy, the Vichy regime its internal accomplice, and the institutions of the Third Republic the cause of the weakness of the state in 1940. The struggle against Germany and Vichy was therefore linked to the task of reconstructing the state, which de Gaulle felt that he had accomplished in 1944 and 1945. During his second rally, begun in 1947, however, it was the Soviet Union which he portrayed as the external enemy, and the French Communist Party as its internal ally. When the RPF was formed, the Cold War between the Western powers and the Soviet Union was still in its early stages and Communist ministers were still members of the French Government; then, in May 1947 the Prime Minister, Paul Ramadier, relieved them of their posts after they had voted with other members of their parliamentary group against a motion of confidence in the National Assembly. At the time this had not been seen as a definite break, but the Communists gradually moved into a position of outright opposition to the Government, supporting the industrial strikes which occurred during the summer of 1947. These events enabled de Gaulle to intensify the anti-Communist themes in his addresses, and in a speech at Rennes in Brittany on 27 July 1947 he drew a comparison between the circumstances of the first and second rallies:

> Although national unity was maintained in spite of those who had accepted Hitler's law, everyone feels that today it is once more in peril. I say that it is in peril because of a grouping of men whose leaders place service to a foreign state above all else.[23]

He explained how, after liberation, he had tried to involve the Communists in the government of the country, but to no avail:

> on our soil, in our midst, some men have vowed obedience to a foreign enterprise of domination, directed by masters of a large Slav power. Their aim is to bring about a dictatorship here, as those like them have succeeded in doing elsewhere with the support of that power.[24]

Calling on the French people to rally against this new threat, he emphasized the need to reorganize the institutions of government:

> Let us rally, above all, to reform the republican State, to rescue it from the absurd confusion of powers in which it is floundering, to make it capable of maintaining the unity of the nation and that of the French Union, to direct the effort of renewal of the one and the other, to uphold clearly and firmly the interest of the country against outsiders and to provide for its eventual defence.[25]

The intensification of the Cold War over the next four years gave added point to his warnings. The Communist take-over in Czechoslovakia in February 1948 was followed a few months later by the Berlin blockade and in 1949 by the formation of the North Atlantic Treaty Organization (NATO) as a defensive military alliance against the Soviet Union. There was another wave of strikes in France in 1948, and her economic difficulties continued despite the economic and financial assistance which the country received from the USA under the Marshall Aid programme. In June 1950, the outbreak of the Korean War further worsened an already critical international situation. By this stage, de Gaulle was drawing a clear parallel between these events and those which had led to the Second World War. Speaking at

Lille on 11 December 1950, shortly after Chinese troops had entered the Far Eastern conflict on the side of North Korea, he stressed the need for France to build up its armed forces and to collaborate with other Western powers in the defence of Europe:

> It is again necessary that France should do her duty. She must have a strong state and a united people so that she can acquire the framework without which she would run the strong risk of being first neglected by her allies and then invaded by her adversaries, so that she can play her part and not be dragged along, and so that she can come into her own again and win outside recognition.[26]

Compared with his Rennes speech, this was a much harsher and more assertive condemnation of the constitutional regime and of the role that parties were playing in its affairs.

> The parties well know that the system which they practise amongst themselves cannot inspire, lead and defend the nation in the crisis which has begun and which threatens to become the most serious that the world has known. However worthy their men and however they group themselves, they can only juxtapose differences and thus cause contradictions in which the people have no faith. What blindness, or perhaps what despair, makes them cling to this game? Why, thus scorching the earth, must we go from bad to worse, until a crisis sweeps everything away?[27]

He was now talking much more in terms of a government under his control rather than of the RPF's forming the core of a future rally.

> As for me, I am quite ready. It is necessary, absolutely necessary that the plan and the framework should be changed. It is necessary to form a government which would be above the parties and would reach the soul of France. It is necessary to rally the people to defend their native land.[28]

Although de Gaulle was at pains to stress that the RPF was not a party, its structure was designed to sustain a wide range of activities at both the local and the national level of politics. Its organization was described as 'a framework of volunteers established for joint, united and disinterested action', and its rank-and-file were known as 'companions' (*compagnons*) rather than as members. Its formal rules and procedures envisaged three principles of recruitment: by territory, with the basic unit at the level of the administrative department; by economic sector or occupation (*groupements professionnels*), such as workers, civil servants, teachers, members of the liberal professions, businessmen and farmers; and by social category, such as war veterans, intellectuals and youth. Although there were provisions for the election of representative bodies and for plenary meetings at all levels of the organization, all three pillars of the movement (territorial, sectoral and social) were controlled by delegates who were responsible to the central leadership. As its founding President, de Gaulle was at the centre of the RPF, authorized to form an Executive Committee which was, in its turn, to appoint a General Secretariat. In a directive issued on 13 November 1947, de Gaulle set down procedures which entitled him to establish not only the Executive Committee but also the General Secretariat, and to assign particular tasks to certain members of the Executive Committee. His virtual control of the executive institutions and, indirectly, of the system of delegates, ensured that his ability to direct the work of the organization would be considerable, and that the apparent checks to his power, the National Council and the National Congress, would remain essentially consultative bodies.[29]

The RPF's first electoral trial came in the municipal elections of October 1947, when it won 38 per cent of the votes, gaining control of Bordeaux, Rennes and Strasbourg amongst the larger cities.[30] However, the intergroup which it formed in the National Assembly failed to attract many members and it won only 58 of the 320 seats in the contest for the Council of the Republic in November 1948.[31] By this stage, the parties of the Centre Right and the Centre Left were operating as a third force, defending the Fourth Republic against the Communists on one side and the RPF on the other, and on this basis they formed a succession of Governments. Before the 1951 general elections, the electoral law was changed to enable parties to present their candidate lists as part of a common set (a method known as *apparentement*) in all constituencies other than those in Paris. Another change in the law provided that, if either a single list or a combination of allied lists were to win an absolute majority of the votes, it would be allocated all the seats for the constituency concerned.

Both these factors worked to the advantage of the third-force parties and to the disadvantage of the Communist Party and the RPF, the latter making matters worse for itself by refusing, except in a few cases, to join allied lists. In the event, at the 1951 polls the RPF won 22.51 per cent of the votes but only 19.14 per cent of the seats (120 of 627).[32] In 1953, after further setbacks at the parliamentary level, de Gaulle finally abandoned his venture, leaving those Gaullist deputies who remained to carry on under the title of Social Republicans.[33]

De Gaulle had probably never expected that the RPF would win power as a pseudo-party; his main objective had been to create a rally to which people could belong without altogether abandoning their party allegiance. At one point, early in 1948, its membership had in fact passed the million mark[34] but it had appealed less to the ranks of workers, civil servants and farmers, and to Communist and Socialist voters, than de Gaulle would have wished.[35] Hemmed in by party pressures which were more powerful than those with which he had had to contend in 1944 or 1945, de Gaulle himself never regained, during the RPF period, the degree of popular support which he had enjoyed during his first rally. Replies to the frequent IFOP question 'Do you want de Gaulle to return to power?' provide some indication of the extent of his personal standing between February 1946 and July 1949, but even the most favourable result (*Yes*: 40 per cent; *No*: 45 per cent; *No Opinion*: 15 per cent; returned in April 1948) is well below the level of popularity which he had enjoyed in 1945.[36] De Gaulle's own interpretation of what had happened shows that he attributed the failure of the enterprise to the unwillingness of first the Left and then the Right to give him their backing. Speaking in May 1953 of the period preceding the formation of the RPF in 1947, he said:

While the weakness of the state prevented our recovery, a new peril appeared. The Communist menace arose without and within. I then called upon the French people to unite once more. There was, in fact, the beginnings of a rally. The Right, whether traditionalist, or secularist, or economic, at first took an important part in this. But the danger seemed to lessen. Thanks to the Rally, the Communists had drawn back. Furthermore, the Americans, by coming up with the Marshall Plan and the Atlantic Treaty, created the impression that some security had been provided. Thus reassured, the Right, which was in any case opposed to my intention to carry out social reform, and influenced, moreover, by the financial and press barons, unrepentant Vichyites and foreign agencies, then turned against me as well.[37]

Having abandoned the RPF experiment, de Gaulle took refuge in the village of Colombey-les-deux-Églises; but his persistent advocacy of the presidential style of government, and the object lesson he had given of how it might work in the post-liberation period, had forced even his harshest critics to think seriously about the nature of executive power. He had shown that a strong president, authorized to act as arbitrator or use emergency powers, was a more effective agent in dealing with crises than the resort, in Third Republican fashion, to a national union (a temporary alliance of all parties except those on the Left) or to a sacred union (a national coalition similar to that formed at the beginning of the First World War). He had also shown that his call for a rally had been made within the existing framework of the state, and that he had no interest in either Bonapartist or Caesarist forms of leadership. By 1953 these distinctions had been generally accepted and his kind of rally politics was no longer regarded as a cloak for personal ambition but as a form of representation compatible with Republican tradition.[38]

Although the parties of the Third Force had successfully upheld the 1946 Constitution in their contest with the RPF, they had not taken adequate stock of how the new institutions were working, especially at the level of the executive. In fact, during the first legislature of the new regime, the parliamentary groups of the Republican mainstream had reverted to the practices which had caused the chronic ministerial instability of the interwar period; governments were forced to resign on relatively minor issues, groups insisted on being consulted about the choice of ministers and the allocation of portfolios, and alliances within successive majorities were conditional and fragile. Under such circumstances, the powers of the Prime Minister became steadily weakened, his ability to undertake policy initiatives was restricted by the preferences of the parliamentary groups, he was virtually obliged to share out cabinet places amongst those groups which had voted for his investiture, and even in constructing his core-group of senior ministers he had to consider the rights of notables who had held key portfolios in previous administrations, as well as the claims of party leaders that certain of their colleagues should be given particular responsibilities.[39] As a result, governments tended to lack coherence, and while this did not prevent them dealing effectively with routine policy matters, it did reduce the ability of the executive to solve major problems, such as those presented by the protracted war in Indo-China. The only way in which a Prime Minister could obtain the leeway to deal with a pressing difficulty was by appealing beyond the parties to public opinion, as Antoine Pinay did in his efforts to check inflation in 1952. Nevertheless, once the immediate crisis had passed, the parliamentary groups were adept at reasserting their control.

Apart from de Gaulle, the only Prime Minister of the Fourth Republic who was prepared to test the limited powers of his office to their furthest extent within the law was Pierre Mendès-France. Where he most resembled de Gaulle was in his belief that it was possible to break out of the endless cycle of short-term policies and lay the foundations of a modern and dynamic France. Born in Paris in 1907, Mendès-France had served in Léon Blum's Government of March–April 1938 as Under-Secretary for the Treasury, and had been with the Free French Air Force during the war. In de Gaulle's provisional Government he held the post of Minister for National Economy but resigned in April 1945 after a dispute over financial policy. Under the Fourth Republic he became one of the most respected leaders of the Radical Party, and gained a reputation for his independent views on economic and foreign policy. He made his first bid to form a government during the long ministerial crisis of May–June 1953, but failed to obtain the absolute majority of all the deputies in the National Assembly specified under the Constitution as necessary to secure appointment as Prime Minister. However he was widely recognized as being a man not only with his own programme for obtaining peace in Indo-China but also with a policy for reducing defence expenditure and applying the resources thus saved to the task of strengthening the French economy.[40] In June 1954, shortly after the defeat of the Laniel Government over its Indo-China policy, the President called on Mendès-France to bid for office again, and on this occasion he obtained the necessary majority on the investiture vote. Having taken office, he assembled a compact and relatively young team of ministers, whom he had chosen on the basis of their competence rather than on considerations of seniority or the claims of the parliamentary groups.

Using his executive authority to the full, Mendès-France first devoted his energies to the international discussions on Indo-China being held in Geneva and, as he had promised, obtained a settlement by 20 July. He then flew to Tunis, where he announced measures intended to provide Tunisia with internal autonomy, that is, greater freedom for its institutions within the relationship with France. In domestic affairs, he obtained special powers from the National Assembly to pursue his financial proposals. His most intractable problem proved to be that of defining French policy for the defence of Western Europe, but even here he made progress; French opinion had been sharply divided over the scheme for a European Defence Community (EDC) and, finding that no compromise was possible, he allowed the Assembly to debate the subject without guidance from the Government. This resulted in the EDC Treaty's being rejected on 30 August, and the way cleared for a fresh approach to the subject. Further discussions led to the Paris Agreements under which Germany and Italy were brought into the West European Union and the creation of a German army within the framework of NATO became possible.

In the meantime, Mendès-France and his style of government had attracted considerable support; has radio broadcasts on Saturday evenings had become popular, and his sheer energy and professionalism were compared favourably with the cautious circumspection of his predecessors. His declared intention had been to clear away the accumulated problems and then to embark on a sustained programme which would strengthen the French economy and restore the country's international standing. Although he would have rejected the idea, he had become a rally leader and his rally, like de Gaulle's, cut across party boundaries. A poll taken in the late summer of 1954 revealed that, amongst voters, 78 per cent of the Socialists, 85 per cent of the Radicals, 60 per cent of the Gaullists, 60 per cent of MRP supporters, 40 per cent of the Communists, and 63 per cent of the Conservatives were satisfied with him.[41] Unlike de Gaulle, Mendès-France did not think in terms of two flows of representation, one leading to the chief executive and the other to Parliament, however; he wanted to work within the Constitution, strengthening the links between the executive and the people by working through Parliament rather than against it.[42] Nevertheless it was virtually impossible for him to build up a parliamentary majority of deputies willing to place loyalty to him as an individual above loyalty to their parties, and even at the height of his popularity the majorities which he obtained were as much the result of group decisions to accept a certain policy as of direct support from their members. Moreover, once the group leaders felt that he could be crossed with impunity, they were prepared to work against him and, on 5 February 1955, he was defeated in the Assembly on a vote of confidence on his Government's North African policy and he resigned as Prime Minister.[43]

After this reverse, Mendès-France's only way forward was to try to convert the Radical Party into a unified organization under his control and to drive for an electoral victory with a secure majority in another assembly. While he and his followers were making some progress in their campaign to restructure the Radical Party, they were taken by surprise at the end of 1955 when a sudden dissolution of the Assembly precipitated a general election campaign several months earlier than had been expected. Even so, the parties associated with Mendès-France in a Republican Front alliance improved their positions in the ballot, the Radicals increasing their share of the vote from 7.69 per cent of enrolments in 1951 to 12.06 per cent on this occasion.[44] Mendès-France accepted a post in the Government then formed by the Socialist leader, Guy Mollet, but he resigned from the Cabinet in May 1956 and one year later, in May 1957, faced with divisions in the Radicals' parliamentary group and with the increasing isolation of his own supporters within the party organization, he resigned from his positions of responsibility within the party.[45]

The familiar comparison of this venture with de Gaulle's rallies seems fully justified. Like de Gaulle, Mendès-France had claimed personal authority, defined a mission, challenged the position of the established parties, and attracted a public following which transcended party divisions. Each man had been sustained by an organization and by an informal fellowship – de Gaulle's inherited from his Free French period and Mendès-France's drawn from young professional people who had been

attracted by his vision of a modern France. Both men had demonstrated that it was possible to envisage forms of executive
action which could ensure effective government within the Republican tradition. Although both de Gaulle's RPF venture of
1947–53 and that of Mendès-France in 1954–5 were ultimately
contained by the system which they had challenged,[46] they had
alerted the French people to new methods of expressing popular
sovereignty.

Each of the three rallies which we have discussed had been
formed to meet a major crisis – that caused by the military
defeat of France in 1940, that produced by the onset of the Cold
War in 1947, and that arising from the deterioration of the
French military situation in Indo-China in 1954. It was therefore
not surprising that the intensification of French difficulties in ·
Algeria in the summer of 1958 caused another rally movement to
build up around de Gaulle. The Algerian uprising, which had
begun as a revolt in the Aurès mountains in November 1954,
had grown rapidly in scale in the years which followed, both in
its dimension as a guerilla movement in the countryside and in
its aspect as a conflict touching the whole of North Africa,
signified by the presence of a large Algerian army in Tunisia. The
Front for National Liberation (FLN) claimed to represent the
Muslims of Algeria and called on their behalf for political independence from France. The possibility that the war could soon
extend beyond Algeria's boundaries became an immediate issue
when, on 8 February, French aircraft bombed the Tunisian village of Sakhiet, causing many civilian casualties. The French
Prime Minister, Félix Gaillard, was obliged to accept the offer of
a 'good offices' mission from the British and American Governments as a means of restoring relations between Tunisia and
France, but when the first proposals from this mission were considered on 15 April, his ministry was defeated in the Assembly.
Gaillard resigned from office and for some time negotiations to
form a new government proved fruitless. Early in May, hopes
that a ministry could be put together to negotiate directly with
the FLN and prepare the ground for a peaceful settlement were
encouraged by the choice of the liberal-minded Pierre Pflimlin
(MRP) as a candidate for the Prime Ministership. This produced
a hostile reaction amongst die-hard civilians and military men in
Algiers, however, and there was an uprising in that city on 13

May. The rioters seized control of Government House and formed a Committee of Public Safety, all with the apparent connivance of a section of the French army. Civil war now seemed likely, and though Pflimlin was at last able to form a government in Paris, the continued tension persuaded the majority of deputies that de Gaulle should be recalled to power. On 1 June, he was invested as Prime Minister by a vote of the National Assembly and the following day he obtained full powers for his ministry to govern the country for a period of six months. A small committee then prepared a draft constitution providing for a strong president (who was to be elected by a restricted college of notables for a seven-year term) and for a bicameral legislature, consisting of a national assembly and a senate. This document was approved as a new Constitution by a referendum held on 28 September, with 79.25 per cent of the voters supporting it. Then, elections held on 23 and 30 November (under the two-ballot, single-member system rather than under proportional representation) resulted in a striking victory for a party entitled the Union for the New Republic (UNR). It won 206 seats in a house of 578 on the claim that it was the group most strongly identified with de Gaulle and his mission. In December, the General was elected to the office of President, and in January 1959 he appointed Michel Debré to be the first Prime Minister of the Fifth Republic.[47]

For the third time, a rally had formed around de Gaulle, and on this occasion he used his power to make changes in the regime which would restrict the ability of the parties to regain control once the rally had subsided; in effect, he changed the constitutional rules to increase the authority of the presidency. The association he had belatedly accepted was sufficiently like a regular party to pass muster in the rough-and-tumble of elections and parliamentary affairs, but he was now installed in a permanent executive office, instead of being the head of a provisional Government as in 1944–6. The massive majority for the new constitution had in one sense been a plebiscite in his favour and was taken as proof that the French people considered him to be the only person of sufficient stature to restore the supremacy of civil rule and bring the Algerian war to an end. Nevertheless, he had once more respected the Republican tradition: there were still limits to his freedom of action, the Constitution which he had fostered still provided for the basic principles of liberal democracy (including that of the responsibility of the Government to Parliament), and the seasoned parties of the Fourth Republic, though weakened, were still strong enough to move against him once the Algerian problem had been solved.

It took four and a half years for de Gaulle to obtain a settlement in Algeria and during that time he defeated two serious challenges to his rule from sections of the French army – the first in January 1960, when some elements in the army showed sympathy for a further European uprising in Algiers, and the second in April 1961, when General Challe and certain of his fellow officers attempted to stage a coup. When, in March 1962, de Gaulle concluded the Évian agreement with the FLN and secured its ratification in a referendum in April by a majority of 90.7 per cent of the votes, some party leaders felt that the time had come to reassert the rights of the political parties and to use Parliament as a means of restricting the authority of the presidency. However, de Gaulle moved against them by proposing that the Constitution should be amended to provide for the election of the President by universal suffrage and further, that this change should be approved by referendum. His plan was supported by the UNR but opposed by most of the older parties, which moved a censure motion against the Government (now headed by Georges Pompidou) when the referendum procedure was considered by the National Assembly. De Gaulle saw the conflict as being one between two quite different political outlooks: 'Basically it was a clash between two Republics, the Republic of yesterday whose hopes of a re-birth were discernible behind the bitter diatribes of the partisans, and the Republic of today which was personified by me and whose survival I was endeavoring [sic] to ensure.'[48]

Although the Assembly did adopt the censure motion, de Gaulle invited his Prime Minister to remain in office and dissolved the lower house. The referendum was held on 28 October and in it 61.8 per cent of the voters registered approval for the constitutional amendment. In the subsequent general elections of 18 and 25 November 1962, the UNR increased its total of seats to 233 in a house of 482, thus placing the Government in an almost unassailable position.[49]

Three years later, in December 1965, de Gaulle was re-elected President under the new provision, and from that time onwards the presidency has been regarded as the most important prize to be won in political competition, the true centre of power in France. In April 1969 de Gaulle resigned from office after the rejection of his proposals for a measure of decentralization and the reform of the Senate in a referendum, but as Georges Pompidou replaced him as President after the poll of June 1969, Gaullist control of the state continued for another few years. After Pompidou's death in office in 1974, however, the subsequent presidential election produced a victory for Valéry Giscard d'Éstaing, from the Republican Independent or liberal wing of the ruling majority. Then, standing as a Socialist, François Mitterrand won the contest of 1981 and was re-elected for a second seven-year term in 1988.

The major political parties – the Socialists on the Left and the neo-Gaullist Rally for the Republic (RPR) and the liberal Union for French Democracy (UDF) on the Right – now generally accept the scope of presidential power established by de Gaulle, including the exercise of the President's right, under Article 5 of the Constitution, to act as an arbiter and thus to ensure 'the regular functioning of the public authorities' and the continuity of the state. The President has the constitutional right to appoint the Prime Minister, to dissolve the National Assembly (after having consulted the Prime Minister and the Presidents of the two houses of parliament), and to assume exceptional powers in an emergency. Each of the large parties now devotes a great deal of time to the task of identifying and nurturing potential presidential candidates – individuals whom they consider capable of appealing well beyond the boundaries of the party's traditional constituency and of becoming, in effect, a rally leader. Since the 1965 contest, the presidential election campaign has been marked by the determined attempts of each of the main contenders to create a surge of opinion in his own favour, rather than simply consolidating the party's traditional vote. The five-yearly elections for the National Assembly still provide the principal arena for party competition, but even these have been affected by the tidal pulls of the presidential contests. This is especially the case when (as happened in 1981 and 1988) an incoming president has called for the sudden dissolution of the lower house in an attempt to create a 'presidential majority' by snap elections to that body.

It is not only their electoral tactics which the parties have

adapted, but they have also altered their rhetoric to meet the
demands of rally politics around the presidency. John Gaffney,
in his book *The French Left and the Fifth Ripublic*, has argued
convincingly that the necessity to compete for presidential power
has profoundly changed the political discourse of both the Communist and the Socialist Parties. By analysing specific texts, he
has demonstrated that the apparent liberalization of the Communist Party which occurred in the 1970s was related to the
tendency of its General Secretary, Georges Marchais, to present
himself as a political personality to an audience wider than that
usually addressed by Communist leaders, and to lessen the doctrinal constraints which had previously restricted their ability
to do so. Similarly, he has shown that the Socialist Party's
acceptance of François Mitterrand as a presidential candidate
rather than simply as First Secretary of the party in the 1970s
was accompanied by greater flexibility in its use of traditional
symbols; for example, it placed much more emphasis than its
predecessor, the SFIO, had done on the importance of Socialist
heroes such as Jean Jaurès and Léon Blum, in providing a personal focus for social and political loyalty. Gaffney also stresses
the interaction between presidentialism and personalism, and
underlines the extent to which the latter process 'exploits the
features pertaining to representation within the republican
tradition'.[50]

Under the Fifth Republic, the French people have become accustomed to the exercise of power by a strong chief executive
within the parliamentary system and, at the electoral level, to
the interaction between the rally drive and the party drive. The
French pattern of representative politics now resembles the
American to the extent that the rally drive is directed mainly
towards the presidency and the party drive mainly towards the
legislature. However, whereas in America the equilibrium between the two drives is regulated by a whole series of mechanisms – most obviously by the use of primaries in the selection of
Legislative candidates and by the strict division of constitutional
responsibilities between the Congress and the President – in
France the separation of the institutions is much less clear-cut.
The constant preoccupation with the choice of candidates for the
presidency tends to weaken the coherence of the parties, and the
President's ability to dominate the government has reduced that
body's responsiveness to the legislature.

Charles de Gaulle died in 1970, but the legacy of his ventures into rally politics remains with his successors. His understanding of the phenomenon was remarkable for, although closely involved in the tumultous events of his time, he was still able to take the long view, judge what was possible and what was not, and ensure that his rallying calls to the French people were made within the broad framework of the Republican tradition rather than in opposition to it. As a result, he expanded the public understanding of the nature of representative politics and left his country with a regime which, for all its ambiguities and lacunae, is much more flexible and responsive to popular pressures than those which preceded it.

Notes

1 Charles de Gaulle, *Vers l'Armée de Métier* (Berger-Levrault, Paris, 1934, reprinted in 1963 in Presses Pocket), p. 180 (translation mine).

2 De Gaulle, *Le Fil de l'Épée* (Berger-Levrault, Paris, 1944, reissued 1962, reprinted in 1964 in Le monde en 10/18), p. 68 (translation mine).

3 De Gaulle, *Vers l'Armée de Métier*, pp. 177–8 (translation mine).

4 De Gaulle, *Le Fil de l'Épée*, pp. 26–7, 37–8, 53–4 and 57.

5 Ibid., p. 89 (translation mine).

6 Ibid., p. 52 (translation mine).

7 On his career between 1940 and 1944, see de Gaulle, *Mémoires de Guerre*, vol. I, *L'Appel 1940–1942* (Plon, Paris, 1954); ibid., vol. II, *L'Unité 1942–1944* (Plon, Paris, 1956).

8 For his own account of this period, see ibid., vol. III, *Le Salut 1944–1946* (Plon, Paris, 1959), pp. 1–276. See also Jean Lacouture, *de Gaulle*, vol. II, *Le politique 1944–1959* (Seuil, Paris, 1985), pp. 11–224.

9 Press conference, Paris, 24 April 1947, in de Gaulle, *Discours et Messages*, vol. II, *Dans l'Attente Février 1946–Avril 1958* (Plon, Paris, 1970), p. 66 (translation mine).

10 Speech in London at a luncheon organized by the international press corps, 2 October 1941, in ibid., vol. I, *Pendant la Guerre Juin 1940–Janvier 1946* (Plon, Paris, 1970), p. 112 (translation mine).

11 Press conference, London, 27 May 1942, in ibid., p. 191 (translation mine).

12 Radio broadcast, Brazzaville, 21 September 1942, in ibid., p. 225 (translation mine).

13 Letter from Charles de Gaulle to F. D. Roosevelt, from London, 26 October 1942, in de Gaulle, *Mémoires de Guerre*, vol. II, *L'Unité*, p. 383 (translation mine). On the background to this letter, see Jacques Soustelle, *Envers et contre tout*, vol. I, *De Londres à Alger: Souvenirs et documents sur la France Libre 1940–1942* (Robert Laffont, Paris, 1947), pp. 368–73.

14 See, for example, his speech at the Palais de Chaillot, Paris, 12 September 1944, in de Gaulle, *Mémoires de Guerre*, vol. III, *Le Salut*, p. 306; radio broadcast, 14 October 1944, ibid., pp. 405–6; speech to the Provisional Consultative Assembly, 2 March 1945, ibid., p. 457.

15 Institut Français d'Opinion Publique (IFOP), *Les Français et de Gaulle* (with presentation and commentary by Jean Charlot) (Plon, Paris, 1971), p. 194.

16 Speech at Strasbourg, 7 April 1947, in de Gaulle, *Discours et Messages*, vol. II, *Dans l'Attente*, p. 50 (translation mine).

17 For the text of the Bayeux speech, see de Gaulle, *Mémoires de Guerre*, vol. III, *Le Salut*, pp. 647–52.

18 See Christian Purtschet, *Le Rassemblement du Peuple Français 1947–1953* (Cujas, Paris, 1965), pp. 43–50.

19 Speech at Strasbourg, 7 April 1947, in de Gaulle, *Discours et Messages*, vol. II, *Dans l'Attente*, p. 55 (translation mine).

20 Press conference, Paris, 24 April 1947, in ibid., p. 56 (translation mine).

21 Ibid., p. 66 (translation mine). On the formation of the RPR, see Lacouture, *de Gaulle*, vol. II, *Le politique*, pp. 286–311; Purtschet, *Le Rassemblement du Peuple Francais*, pp. 53–67; Jean Charlot, *Le Gaullisme d'opposition 1946–1958: Histoire politique du Gaullisme* (Fayard, Paris, 1983), pp. 69–79.

22 'Le R. P. F. est-il un Parti?', in Parti Socialiste (SFIO), *Arguments et ripostes*, No. 26 (December 1947), A.6, pp. 1–3.

23 Speech at Rennes, 27 July 1947, in de Gaulle, *Discours et Messages*, vol. II, *Dans l'Attente*, p. 98 (translation mine).

24 Ibid., p. 99 (translation mine).

25 Ibid., p. 103 (translation mine).

26 Speech at Lille, 11 December 1950, in ibid., p. 397 (translation mine).

27 Ibid. (translation mine).

28 Ibid., pp. 397–8 (translation mine).

29 The original *statuts* of the RPF are given in Purtschet, *Le Rassemblement du Peuple Français*, pp. 68–9. These were extended by two additional documents, namely, 'Instruction sur l'organisation du Rassemblement du Peuple Français', signed by de Gaulle on 13

November 1947 (ibid., pp. 375–8), and 'Règlement concernant l'organisation et le fonctionnement des groupements', signed by de Gaulle on 20 February 1948 (ibid., pp. 379–86). On the general dispositions, see ibid., pp. 67–104, and Philip M. Williams, *Crisis and Compromise: Politics in the Fourth Republic* (Longmans, London, 1964), pp. 137–9. Note that the Executive Committee became the Conseil de Direction in June 1949.

30   Jean-Pierre Rioux, *The Fourth Republic, 1944–1958*, tr. Godfrey Rogers (Cambridge University Press, Cambridge, 1987), p. 128; Purtschet, *Le Rassemblement du Peuple Français*, pp. 291–301.

31   Rioux, *The Fourth Republic*, p. 157; Purtschet, *Le Rassemblement du Peuple Français*, pp. 301–7.

32   On the change in the electoral law, see Williams, *Crisis and Compromise*, Appendix VI, pp. 504–8, and for the election results see ibid., Appendix V, pp. 502–3. See also Lacouture, *de Gaulle*, vol. II, *Le politique*, pp. 364–75.

33   See Lacouture, *de Gaulle*, vol. II, *Le politique*, pp. 376–99. See also Purtschet, *Le Rassemblement du Peuple Français*, pp. 331–69; Roy Pierce, 'De Gaulle and the RPF-a post-mortem', *Journal of Politics*, XVI, 1 (February 1954), pp. 96–119; Robert G. Neumann, 'Formation and Transformation of Gaullism in France', *Western Political Quarterly*, VI, 2 (June 1953), pp. 250–74.

34   Rioux, *The Fourth Republic*, p. 156.

35   See the details of an IFOP survey of 18–26 April 1947 in IFOP, *Les Français et de Gaulle*, p. 176, and the analysis of a later IFOP survey of March 1952 in Purtschet, *Le Rassemblement du Peuple Français*, pp. 323–9.

36   See IFOP, *Les Français et de Gaulle*, pp. 199 (data) and 200 (diagram). Cf. the data and diagram relating to 1945 in ibid., pp. 194–5.

37   Statement, 6 May 1953, in de Gaulle, *Discours et Messages*, vol. II, *Dans l'Attente*, p. 581.

38   On the problem of relating presidentialism to the Republican tradition, see John Gaffney, *The French Left and the Fifth Republic: The Discourses of Communism and Socialism in Contemporary France* (Macmillan, Houndmills, Basingstoke, 1989), pp. 1–11.

39   See Williams, *Crisis and Compromise*, pp. 404–27.

40   On the defeat of Mendès-France in 1953, see Jean Lacouture, *Pierre Mendès France* (Seuil, Paris, 1981), pp. 205–12; Alexander Werth, *The Strange History of Pierre Mendès-France and the Great Conflict over French North Africa* (Barrie, London, 1957), pp. 74–7; Jacques Fauvet, *La IVᵉ République* (Arthème Fayard, Paris, 1959), pp. 237–9; Philip M. Williams, 'Pierre Mendès-France and the

revolt against conservatism', in Williams, *French Politicians and Elections 1951–1969* (Cambridge University Press, Cambridge, 1970), pp. 27–33.

41 From *Sondages*, 4, 1954, cited by Rioux, *The Fourth Republic*, p. 230.

42 See Pierre Rouanet, *Mendès France au Pouvoir (18 juin 1954–6 février 1955)* (Robert Laffont, Paris, 1965), pp. 153–5.

43 On the rise and fall of the Mendès-France Government, see Lacouture, *Pierre Mendès France*, pp. 225–393; Fauvet, *La IVᵉ République*, pp. 249–87; Rioux, *The Fourth Republic*, pp. 224–40; Werth, *The Strange History of Pierre Mendès-France*, pp. 87–177; Duncan MacRae, *Parliament, Parties, and Society in France 1946–1958* (St Martin's Press, New York, 1967), pp. 125–9.

44 Calculated from data given in a table in François Goguel, Alain Lancelot and Jean Ranger, 'Analyse des résultats', in Mattei Dogan et al., *L'établissement de la Cinquième République: Le référendum de Septembre et les Élections de Novembre 1958* (Armand Colin, Paris, 1960), p. 298.

45 See Luther A. Allen, 'The Renovation that failed: Mendès-France and the Radical Party', *Western Political Quarterly*, XIII, 2 (June 1960), pp. 445–63; Francis de Tarr, *The French Radical Party: From Herriot to Mendès-France* (Oxford University Press, London, 1961), pp. 186–234.

46 On this point, see MacRae, *Parliament, Parties, and Society in France*, pp. 313–19.

47 See Lacouture, *de Gaulle*, vol. II, *Le politique*, pp. 400–689.

48 Charles de Gaulle, *Memoirs of Hope: Renewal 1958–62: Endeavour 1962–*, tr. Terence Kilmartin (Weidenfeld and Nicolson, London, 1971), p. 320.

49 On these events, see Philip M. Williams and Martin Harrison, *Politics and Society in de Gaulle's Republic* (Longman, London, 1971), pp. 24–41. On the character of the UNR, see Jean Charlot, *The Gaullist Phenomenon: The Gaullist Movement in the Fifth Republic*, tr. Monica Charlot and Marianne Neighbour (Allen and Unwin, London, 1971), pp. 63–84. Cf. Angelo Panebianco, *Political parties: organization and power*, tr. Marc Silver (Cambridge University Press, Cambridge, 1988), pp. 147–55.

50 Gaffney, *The French Left and the Fifth Republic*, p. 209.

Part III

Politics within Parties

8

Conflict and Competition within Parties

The internal politics of parties are generated by the cycle of their routine activities – the conduct of organizational elections, the discussion of policy issues at regional and national conferences, the preparation for local or general elections, and the work of the parliamentary group in the life of the legislature and of government – activities which involve varying degrees of co-operation and competition between members, officers, deputies and the leaders of the party. Most parties in liberal democracies accept the need for debate, for the expression of differences of opinion and for some degree of dissent in the conduct of their affairs, and rely on devices such as the taking of a vote to resolve any difficulties or disagreements. Party members generally respect the normative rules which define the boundaries of approved behaviour, but there are times when they claim the right to form combinations to intervene in the internal politics of their organization or to establish informal groups to advance particular interests.

Political scientists have long been interested in the character and activities of such intra-party groups and in the circumstances under which intra-party conflict spirals out of control and endangers the unity of the party itself. In this chapter we shall briefly review some of the writings on this subject before discussing an analytic model designed to provide a basis for further research in this field.

I

The first major post-war enquiry into the behaviour of party factions was reported in V. O. Key, *Southern Politics in State and Nation* (1949), which contained case studies of the internal politics of the Democratic Party in the eleven states of the American South. Although the Republican Party had established itself successfully in a few areas, the Democrats were completely dominant throughout the region and were therefore able to tolerate a considerable degree of competition among those within their ranks who sought nomination as the party's candidates for public office. (The huge black population of the South was poorly represented, not only in the membership of the Democratic Party but in the body of qualified electors also, with the result that it was virtually excluded from direct participation in party politics.)

By the 1930s and 1940s the Democratic Party organizations in the southern states were using 'primaries', or preliminary ballots of party members, to decide who should be the party's nominees in the four-yearly contests for the state governorship, and in the contests to elect Senators and Representatives to the Congress in Washington. Although Key took the Congressional primaries into account, it was the primaries for the governorship which he saw as the best means of estimating degrees of competition within the party. In two of the eleven states, Virginia and Tennessee, the primary election for the governorship consisted of a single ballot but in the remaining states there were provisions for two ballots – first, a preliminary round in which all the candidates who had survived a screening process could stand and then a final round (or 'run-off') for the contenders who had obtained the first and second place in the first ballot. Key found that there were significant variations in the number of serious candidates who contested these primaries; by taking 5 per cent of the vote as the measure of significance, he found some instances in which the race was essentially between two candidates and others in which the nomination was being disputed by three or more.

Key assumed that serious candidatures in these contests indicated the existence of factions, and he defined a faction as 'any combination, clique, or grouping of voters and political leaders who unite at a particular time in support of a candidate'.[1] He distinguished between 'bifactionalism', where there were only two serious candidates, and 'multifactionalism', where three or more were in contention, and offered various explanations for this variation. In three states, Virginia, North Carolina and

Tennessee, he found a long-standing bifactional pattern; in six, South Carolina, Alabama, Mississippi, Arkansas, Texas and Florida, the pattern was predominantly multifactional; and in the remaining two, Georgia and Louisiana, he found that a semblance of bifactionalism had been created by the ability of a powerful leader to establish a cohesive group around himself in the face of a disparate and fluctuating opposition.

When his case studies are examined closely, it becomes clear that Key was working with a much more complicated theory of internal party politics than these findings may at first suggest, and that he had used the term 'faction' generically, to cover several types of intra-party group, just as he had stretched the term 'factionalism' to cover different types of conflict. To take an example, the dominant unit of the bifactional systems was usually an 'organization' (in the sense of a machine) through which an oligarchy of politicians had, by means of nepotism, clientelism and the selective allocation of public funds and resources, been able to build up a reliable pool of voters. Faced with such a machine, the various opposition elements within the party had found it better, rather than offering resistance separately, to combine to produce unified minorities, and over successive primaries this had created the impression of a binary pattern. Such was the case in Virginia where the organization headed by Senator Harry F. Byrd was in control, in Tennessee where the Memphis-based machine of E. H. Crump operated, and in North Carolina where an earlier 'Simmons machine' had been succeeded by an equally strong 'Shelby dynasty', whose leading figure was Max Gardner of Shelby in Cleveland County.[2] Less cohesive machines existed in other states, and it is evident that the methods of building and directing an organization were well understood throughout the region. The essential rules were to gain control of the state legislature and its main financial and service committees with a view to allocating public resources on a preferential basis, to establish chains of patronage which led down from the state capital to the main cities and counties and beyond them to the local level, and at the same time, to ensure that the machine controlled access to the main public posts and that only those candidates willing to work with the organization were allowed to stand for election.

Key further demonstrated that a Democratic leader could also build up a substantial personal following amongst party members by the skilful use of populist rhetoric aimed at showing that elite interests were exploiting the 'little people' (that is, the poor white farmers and country townspeople) of the state. The original People's Parties of the 1890s had attracted a good deal of support in the rural areas of the South, and the neo-populists of the 1920s and 1930s were often appealing to the values of this older tradition. The most successful of the neo-populists was Huey Long, who was elected as Governor of Louisiana in 1928. He challenged the powerful urban and corporate interests which had dominated the Democratic Party in his state through a machine based in New Orleans. Claiming that the interests of poor farmers had been neglected, Long raised taxes and increased public expenditure on education, health and social services generally. He was assassinated in 1935 but at the time that Key was writing this book the Long machine was strong and still using neo-populist appeals in its contests with the party's liberal wing.[3] In Mississippi, Theodore Bilbo, who was elected Governor in 1915 and later became a Senator, had adopted a similar approach, identifying himself with the 'redneck' views of the hill farmers of the eastern counties and playing on their antipathy towards the planter aristocracy of the delta regions.[4]

In his analysis of voting patterns throughout the region, Key referred to the influence of various factors such as 'localism' (the tendency for a candidate to attract the majority of votes in his home county or town) and 'sectionalism' (the tendency for voters to divide on regional lines). Examples of the latter were seen in Alabama, where there was a cleavage between the small-farmer regions of the south-east and north, and the so-called 'black belt' which enclosed counties containing large proportions of blacks and the cities of Birmingham and Mobile,[5] and in South Carolina, where there was a division between the coastal plain and the inland Piedmont region.[6] Some conflicts reflected differences of outlook. Although Key noted with dismay the general lack of interest in policy issues which he found among southern Democrats, he described a period in the history of Texas in which intra-party disputes had been strongly affected by matters of general principle. Between 1944 and 1948 the Texas Democrats had tended to divide into liberal and conservative camps, the liberals signifying their support for the New Deal programme by their backing of President Franklin D. Roosevelt and, after his death, of politicians identified with President Harry S. Truman.[7] In his detailed narratives, Key also drew attention to the intervention in the primary campaigns of a variety of pressure groups, including local units of the American Federation of Labor and of the Congress of Industrial Organizations (which were then separate trade unions), networks of returned servicemen, civil rights associations, and financial and industrial corporations, and he showed that factions were able to attract support from organized interests.

As these comments make clear, there are two levels of analysis in the case studies which he presented in *Southern Politics*. At one level, he was interested in the generalized systems of competition produced by factions and in the external variables (such as the size of the Republican minority in the state and the relative proportion of blacks in the state's population) which decided whether a bifactional or multifactional pattern would form. At another level, however, he was interested in the relative weight of various principles of organization in determining the specific characteristics of each system. He therefore took care to distinguish and analyse the various processes of group formation and action such as machine-building, populism, sectionalism and localism which were at work within the party. Thus, in the case of Louisiana, he showed how Long and his successors had matched their populism to a sectional interest (the poor agrarian parishes in the north-western part of the state)[8] while at the same time constructing a machine to develop their use of patronage. In some cases, he found that one factor was predominant (for example, localism in the case of Florida)[9] but in most cases he considered the factional system to have been affected by a combination of factors.

Later researchers in this field have shown much more interest in Key's general theory of intra-party factionalism than in his second-order theories about such phenomena as localism, sectionalism, machine-building and interest-group pressure. This is understandable; the main emphasis in his book is on the difference between a political party, in the sense of an association which bids openly for electoral support on the basis of a public programme of policy objectives, and an intra-party group which tries to control its parent body while avoiding being accountable to the outside community. However, the relative neglect of second-order theories has tempted analysts to reduce the diversity of processes involved in intra-party conflict to a simple set of propositions about the covert nature of 'factions' and their instrumental use of beliefs, interests and resources. Influenced by a parallel debate in Social Anthropology, political scientists have often assumed that factionalism in parties resembles factionalism in local communities and other bodies; that factions in general are characterized by a particular style of leadership and recruitment, in which a leader or a clique of leaders recruits followers with diverse interests or backgrounds, and in which relationships are vertical, as between patron and client, rather than horizontal.[10] This model has been reinforced by the use which some researchers have made of another theoretical concept regarding the nature of the dyadic tie, a term employed by social anthropologists to refer to relationships which arise, not from kinship and lineage roles but independently of them, sometimes cutting across social divisions. These dyadic relationships involve a bond of reciprocity between two individuals of unequal status, the more influential of whom provides benefits and protection for the weaker in exchange for deference or perhaps a vote or some form of service. The bond between patron and client is taken to be a special type of dyadic tie.[11]

Although the use of such extended models of factionalism has produced some extremely interesting case studies,[12] there has been a tendency for researchers to concentrate on the clientelist and power-seeking aspects of factions and to neglect their other equally important aspects. This bias has been sustained in several ways: firstly, writers have been inclined to adopt a 'hard-boiled' and cynical theory of political motivation, implying that even when faction leaders are appealing for support on the basis of a doctrine or a policy they are basically interested in power for its own sake, their use of ideas being purely instrumental; secondly, they have been prone to assume that leader–follower bonds in factions have a material rather than a moral foundation and that factions are therefore rather like a raiding group – held together by the anticipation of a successful coup and the subsequent distribution of booty. The danger of this approach is that intra-party conflicts caused by philosophical, doctrinal or policy differences may not be analysed systematically or, worse still, may simply be reduced to the 'power-game', clientelist model of factionalism.

The case for keeping the theory of factionalism open was strongly argued by Raphael Zariski in an article published in 1960. Having surveyed early work in the field, he proposed an unrestrictive definition of the term 'faction', which he took to mean: 'any intra-party combination, clique, or grouping whose members share a sense of common identity and common purpose and are organized to act collectively – as a distinct bloc within the party – to achieve their goals'.[13] Most importantly, Zariski allowed that factions thus defined might have a wide range of goals, including not only the acquisition of patronage but also the realization of local, regional or group interests, influence on the strategy of the party and of the government, and the promotion of a discrete set of values.[14] He further reasoned that factions would differ from each other in behaviour and organizational characteristics, and outlined a provisional typology of faction forms, while warning that his categories were not mutually exclusive.[15]

Later surveys have revealed the tension between the relatively open and the relatively closed 'power-game' model of factionalism. Reporting in 1972 on his study of the literature, Norman K. Nicholson defined a factional system as:

> a political system (or subsystem) characterized by the informal competition of a plurality of amorphous segments (factions) operating within a cultural context which places a high value on diffuse and unrestrained personal power and led by an elite whose orientations are self-centred and instrumental.[16]

While Nicholson, in this definition, attached some value to the 'power-game' model of factional behaviour, he went on to suggest that the formation of groups in intra-party conflict could involve relatively complex principles of affiliation. For example, he considered that the factional leader could attract support by means of three types of relationship:

> In the first, personal magnetism or charisma seems to be the basis of the faction, and the leader has immense normative influence over his followers . . . In the second, the authority of the leader is merely an expression of the solidarity of a social segment or community and its preference for a personal link to the outside world

rather than an organizational one. Finally, the faction may represent an incidence of the classic patron–client relationship in which
individuals may see the need for intermediaries between themselves and the 'powers' or the advantages of patrons to assist them
in the advancement of their political careers. . . . These traditional
and institutionalized social relationships (guru–student, patron–
client) nurture and feed the factional system, which depends upon
them because the factions themselves are intermittent composite
groups . . . organized for specific political purposes in particular
circumstances.[17]

Nicholson thus drew attention to the roles which factions could
fulfil in the expression of normative and sectional conflicts as
well as in the pursuit of clientelist objectives.[18]

Other writers have moved further in this direction. In an
article published in 1964, Richard Rose explored the possibility
of constructing a model of intra-party politics which took full
account of the extent to which informal groups could arise out
of conflicts over party philosophy, programme or policy. Drawing his material mainly from the parliamentary groups and national organizations of British parties, he distinguished between
a faction (defined as a group of individuals 'based on representatives in Parliament who seek to further a broad range of policies
through consciously organized political activity'), a tendency ('a
body of attitudes expressed in Parliament about a broad range
of problems; the attitudes are held together by a more or less
coherent political ideology') and a position of non-alignment,
occupied by those party members identified with policy positions supported by the electoral party as a whole, rather than
with factions or tendencies.[19] As Rose made clear in his detailed
examples (he saw the Labour Party as being more prone to
factionalism and the Conservative Party as more disposed to
tendencies), factions and tendencies were differentiated, firstly,
by their relative durability and, secondly, by their use of ideas.
Whereas a faction such as the Bevanite group in the Labour
Party in the 1950s had a coherent membership, regular cycles of
activity, and an interest in advancing a distinctive programme, a
tendency was a relatively ephemeral group suited to the expression or defence of attitudes already accepted by a party and
justified by its general philosophy. With regard to the Conservative Party, he envisaged three possible pivots for tendencies –

attitudes sanctioning reaction, those expressing approval of the status quo, and those associated with the principles of amelioration and reform.[20]

Rose's ideas on this subject have been applied and developed by a number of writers, including David Hine, who, in 1982, published an article about factionalism in Western European parties.[21] While accepting the value of the distinction between faction and tendency, Hine suggested that the typology could be extended to include groups formed within a party to promote a single issue rather than, for example, a programme or piece of legislation affecting a number of issues. He argued that intra-party conflict involved three dimensions of behaviour – the extent of organization, the degree of 'coverage' caused by the conflict (that is, its penetration of the various layers of the party structure), and the degree of concern with matters of policy, ideology and party strategy. Like Zariski and Nicholson, Hine drew attention to the varied sources of factionalism, distinguishing between a conflict arising from 'genuine disagreements over strategy, policy or ideology' and one which 'really represents a personal struggle for power between different leaders and their respective followers'.[22] He also discussed the effect of the 'representation inside a party of various types of sectional group or interest'.[23]

Both Rose and Hine developed their theories of factionalism within defined cultural areas in which comparisons between parties could assume a reasonable correspondence between colloquial terms (such as 'tendency') and analytic categories. However, the problem of establishing a set of terms and analytic procedures for world-wide comparisons remained a daunting one. Frank P. Belloni and Dennis C. Beller followed up an admirable survey of work on this problem[24] by organizing a symposium, published in 1978 under the title of *Faction Politics*, which brought together contributions from researchers who had worked on factionalism in parties in a wide variety of countries including the USA, China, the USSR, Japan, India, Israel, France, Italy, West Germany, Britain, the Philippines, Columbia, Uruguay, Bolivia and Chile.[25] This volume contains case studies and theoretical discussions of considerable interest, including a review by Zariski which discusses the extent to which empirical research carried out since the publication of his article in 1960 had contributed to the development of 'a theory of party factionalism'.[26] As Belloni and Beller point out, the case studies in their symposium raise three basic questions, about the degree of organization in factional structure, the functions served by factions for parties, party systems and polities, and finally, the causes of factionalism.[27] In their concluding chapter they offer a definition of faction as: *'any relatively organized group that exists within the context of some other group and which* (as a *political* faction) *competes with rivals for power advantages within the larger group of which it is a part'*.[28] At the same time, in reviewing the responses to their initial questions concerning the structure, functions and causes of factions, they emphasize that the form of factionalism may vary by content and political level; and finally they examine some possible methods of classification, including a subdivision of the field into cliques or tendencies, clienteles related to a particular patron, and institutionalized or organizational factions.[29]

The actual case studies in this symposium demonstrate also a continuing interest in the second-order theories which Key had employed so effectively in *Southern Politics*. For example, researchers have taken much further the task of producing a general definition of a 'machine' as a highly organized system of patronage, in which a single but powerful patron or an oligarchy of patrons work through a hierarchy of subordinate leaders to supply benefits to large numbers of clients within a territory in return for esteem, votes and other forms of support,[30] and several contributors to *Faction Politics* make use of this concept. Thus, in his article on factionalism in party politics in the Philippines, K. G. Machado shows that whereas one of his areas of research, the small town of Dumalag (in an inland sector of the island of Capiz, now called Panay) still displayed the features of traditional factional rivalry revealed by Landé's earlier work, the city of Batangas (to the south of Manila on the main island of Luzon) had become the setting for machine politics.[31] Belloni himself contributes an account of internal conflict within two Italian parties, the Christian Democrats (DC) and the Socialists (PSI), and shows that it had arisen from a variety of causes. Earlier studies of factionalism in the DC had demonstrated the manner in which the traditional clientelism of agrarian society, in which landlord and tenant were also patron and client respectively, had been changed into 'party-directed patronage'[32] as the DC used its control of public agencies and utilities to build up groups of clients on an unprecedented scale, and how the party had divided into several vertical segments, each tied to a particular national leader and linked by chains of descending patron–client ties to the provincial and local levels of the state. However, Belloni draws attention to the point that clientelism was not the only factor contributing to this result. He emphasizes that the factional system had evolved through several stages at the national level: when the DC, under the leadership of Alcide de Gasperi, first established itself as the party of government in the late 1940s its internal groups were essentially teams of activists bound to particular leaders, but after Amintore Fanfani began to organize his own supporters very systematically in the late 1950s, the factions developed into more elaborate structures. Competition between them for positions in the party was further formalized in 1964, when a change in the party rules required the publication of the list of candidates for party offices at an early stage in the annual cycle of business, before the provincial congresses. Belloni also describes how the factional system was influenced by interest groups, most notably by the various 'collateral' organizations of the party such as Catholic Action, the Christian Association of Italian Workers (ACLI), the Italian Confederation of Workers' Unions (CISL), and the National Confederation of Direct Cultivators. He shows that the factions differed over questions of party strategy, for example over whether the party should work with the parties of the centre right or with those of the centre left including the Socialists, and over more fundamental philosophical issues, and he concludes that 'in both the DC and the PSI, ideology and clientelism are amply present as bases of factions'.[33]

As one might expect, the contributors to *Faction Politics* differ amongst themselves as to the meanings which should be attached to the central concepts of 'factionalism' and 'faction'. Some have employed definitions which are specific and restrictive and others use ones which are general and easily extendible. Many of the case studies illustrate the difficulty of distinguishing 'factionalism' within the welter of activities and conflicts taking place in the system under observation. The comparative study of political parties has always had to face the fact that groups which

identify themselves by a general term such as 'political party' or
'port authority' or 'peasants' union' will rarely correspond to an
abstract model of the thing in question, but the problem takes
a particularly acute form in the comparative analysis of intra-
party conflicts and the groups which this process generates. This
is so mainly because informal competition within parties is often
strongly influenced by notions of social conflict within the community as a whole, and intra-party groups are identified as the
functional equivalents of groups which occur within families or
villages. In a very real sense, the boundary between party and
society is critically weakened once the formal organization has
failed to contain intra-party conflict within acceptable limits.
Matters tend to be settled according to the conventions of
the society in question and the whole process becomes cultur-
ally specific. Such a state of affairs emphasizes the difficulty of
assuming that universal categories can be applied in social science despite cultural variations between country and country or
between region and region.

II

What, then, are the most pertinent avenues for theoretical work
and empirical research where intra-party conflict is concerned?
My own preference would be to divide the field into two parts
and develop analytic terms for each, recognizing that there must
be some overlap between them. The first sub-field would be
intra-party conflict at the level of the legislature (the national
level in a unitary state, and the central and regional levels in a
federal state) and the second, intra-party conflict at levels below
the legislature (especially common during election campaigns, the
preparation for central conferences of the party, and the allocation of resources by local authorities under the control of the
party). Such a division of the field recognizes the greater sensitivity of party groups at the level of the legislature to issues of
grand strategy, government policy and political doctrine and, in
so doing, would facilitate the study of some of the more difficult
empirical questions regarding the relationships between belief
and action which have bedevilled work in this area. At what we
may call the legislature level, the party's institutions most closely
resemble its ideal picture of itself as a corporate body; the

members of its parliamentary group are obliged to work together over long periods of time and to deal in common with a constant stream of legislative and administrative measures; even the delegates at plenary conferences and national councils of the party organization have been taken away from their local communities for short periods of intense discussion and rounds of decision-making. Conflicts at this level affect the very core of the party and threaten its integrity, touching as they often do on fundamental questions of identity, doctrine, strategy and policy. It is better to study such conflicts within their own confined arenas using analytic methods which take full account of the range and complexity of the factors affecting the process.

At what we may call sub-legislature levels, in the districts, cities and localities, the main interest remains the interaction between intra-party disputes and the social and economic conflicts in the community. Where horizontal divisions in society, such as those between social classes or ethnic layers, are either absent or weak, it is likely that conflict groups within the party will construct separate chains of patron–client links which run parallel to each other right down to the local level, a pattern which held in the Philippines before the declaration of martial law in 1972. By providing an adequate flow of particularistic rewards, such links weaken the pressure for the allocation of benefits by category. Where horizontal divisions do exist, conflict groups cannot rely exclusively on clientelism to win support. In India, for example, with its heavily stratified social structure, competing factions within the same party combine patronage directed towards individuals with patronage directed towards the local caste units. In all such instances, the researcher cannot avoid analysing the means by which parties maintain their presence at the local level: in some situations, a party may decide to establish an enclosed unit and to exercise a firm control over its activities, thereby ensuring that its affairs are governed by party rules and conventions; in other cases, it may decide to allow local units to accommodate themselves to the host community, settling any disputes in accordance with prevailing customs.

A subdivision of the field in this way should not reduce our ability to study those situations in which conflict fractures move through the whole party, whether upwards or downwards. Indeed, our understanding of how this process works should be improved once we have accepted that the systematic differences between levels, such as that between the relatively closed and integrated institutions at the legislature level and the relatively open and permeable units at the local level, present variable conditions for the expression of conflict as it spreads from layer to layer.

In looking at the internal politics of parties at the legislature level, it seems useful to analyse actual cases with reference to three ideal types of intra-party conflict, which we may term sectarian, sectional and factional conflict respectively.[34] We shall look at each of these ideal types in turn, identifying its basic organizing principle.

A sectarian conflict may be described as one in which the opposing sides are in disagreement about the moral values which should form the basis of the party's organization and activity.[35] An intra-party sect may believe that the party should redefine its basic objectives, perhaps by revising an existing doctrine or reviving a neglected tradition or even by adopting new ideas more suited to the party's circumstances. It aims at counteracting mistaken attitudes within the party, but places a high value on party solidarity – a sect sees no enemies within the party, merely the secular equivalent of backsliders, members who have forsaken their own vision and that of the collectivity. The leader of a sect must therefore be able not only to inspire its core membership with faith in the ideals for which it stands, but also to win other members to its cause.

At one level, the sect assumes that its membership is potentially coterminous with the membership of the party and that all within its fold are susceptible to its appeals, but in practice its active membership consists of those who are convinced of the truth of its interpretation of party philosophy and of the importance of its mission. Structurally, the sect resembles a religious congregation: all its active members are equal in their role as true believers; they signify their belief by periodic rituals, and they expect nothing from each other or from their leader other than fellowship and reassurance.

The second type of conflict, sectionalism, arises when a group within a party seeks to make that party the instrument of an outside section of society – perhaps of a social class, a regional community, or a religious, ethnic or linguistic grouping. As a principle of organization, taken to its logical extreme, sectionalism entails the party's becoming the projection into organized politics of the section's values, outlook and judgement of policy matters. For example, an extra-parliamentary organization representing a peasant movement may try to insist that those deputies representing the movement within a parliamentary party should form a coherent group; that this group should then aim to dominate the party, determining its philosophy, its doctrines and its policies; and that deputies unwilling to adopt peasant values should either accept subordinate status or leave the party. An organization claiming to represent a nationalist movement could act in a similar way. In order to be successful, therefore, the leader of a sectional group must epitomize the virtues and life-style of the section concerned, dressing and speaking in the appropriate manner, and he must be prepared to invite conflict with individuals or groups representing rival sections, and to challenge anyone claiming that the party's task is to represent the political community in all its variety. Unlike a sect, which accepts the party's moral authority, a sectional group feels no compulsion to do so, claiming that it is from the underlying section that the party has acquired its *raison d'être*.

The scope for sectionalism depends on the extent to which the political community as a whole has been divided into broad social categories. Where this process of categorization has just begun, the extra-parliamentary associations acting on the basis of a shared economic, ethnic, linguistic or religious interest may be relatively small and localized; over time and given the right conditions, they may be expected to link up and form more widespread and more generalized associations. In an interesting account of this process, Carl Landé has described the first generation of these associations as 'trait groups' and has distinguished them from what he calls 'trait associations', which have a broader spectrum of aims and a greater concern to maintain collective action.[36] Landé suggests that the latter associations tend to expand 'through the broadening of categories, and the "nesting" of narrower trait associations within more comprehensive ones'.[37]

Where a liberal democracy provides for the allocation of resources to and the levying of taxes and dues from specified categories of the population by impersonal criteria, and where

interest groups can claim, with good reason, to be advancing the
collective demands of such categories (farmers, merchants, industrial workers or the inhabitants of a particular region, for example), the stage is set for political parties to come under direct
sectional pressures, and for sectionalism to become one of the
sources of conflict within those parties. A perverse form of this
process occurs if a political party secures the control of those
agencies by means of which resources and benefits are distributed, and uses this control to reward favoured individuals or
groups in return for services – most often votes. By establishing
vertical chains of patron–client ties, the leaders of such parties
are able to penetrate downwards through the levels of the political system and to deal with specific sets of clients rather than
with categoric groups. In doing so, they inhibit the development
of horizontal associations and postpone the evolution of sectional politics.[38]

The third type of conflict is factionalism, not factionalism in
the very general sense in which this term has been used in much
of the literature, but in the more restricted sense recommended
by F. G. Bailey in his book, *Stratagems and Spoils*.[39] Following
his approach, one can define intra-party factionalism as a conflict
caused by an informal attempt to capture high office in a party,
that is, by an attempt which disregards the party's established
rules governing succession to that office. To succeed in such an
enterprise the faction leader must, avoiding all issues of doctrine
or programme, concentrate on demonstrating that the would-be
office holder (who may well be himself) would be a more worthy
custodian of the office than the actual incumbent or than rival
candidates. In addition, he must be able to convince a sufficient
number of party members that the enterprise will succeed, and
that the benefits to be gained from it warrant taking action
outside the party's rules of appointment. This process depends
above all on personal commitment, and for this reason recruitment to a faction takes the form of a series of one-to-one
engagements between individuals: in its simplest form, therefore,
a faction consists of a leader and a diversity of followers, each
of whom has formed a vertical tie with him and offers him
personal loyalty in return for some specific promise of future
recompense. As a set, given the particularist mode of its recruitment, the members of a faction will come from a variety

of backgrounds. Moreover, the lines of communication within
it will follow the lines of recruitment, and its structure will
be segmentary and liable to fission. Unlike intra-party groups
with sectarian and sectional orientations, factional groups (in the
sense used here) place themselves on the difficult boundary between private understandings, which party authorities may be
prepared to tolerate, and conspiracies which they will not. They
therefore run the risk of being suppressed and must depend
upon something akin to a smugglers' code involving private
understandings and promises to honour one's word and to meet
personal obligations even when to do so may incur penalties.
Factional struggles, by their very nature, must be settled quickly.
A pure faction therefore has a short life – either its leader suc-
ceeds in his bid for office, in which case his followers are
rewarded and the faction has served its purpose, or he fails and
his followers drift away from him.

As set out above, these may be taken to be the three ideal
types of intra-party conflict at legislature level. In fact, of course,
most actual conflicts are mixtures of all three types, and the
groups which come into conflict also possess a mixture of characteristics. Given that the three modes of conflict are based on
very different organizing principles, we should expect to find that
conflict groups follow very uneven paths of development, responding first to one form of conflict and then to another with
quite rapid changes of identity, orientation and style of operation. If, for example, in a particular party an electoral defeat
were to produce a doctrinal dispute, conflict groups might be
constrained to behave like sects. Even so, the groups would
preserve some capacity to respond to other aspects of the conflict, which would almost certainly raise issues concerning the
party's relationship with its various constituencies, and the competence of its leadership; conflict groups would therefore maintain their own links with sympathetic sections and their leaders
would have some latitude to explore the possibility of an informal bid for high office within the party. Suppose that this crisis
were then to be followed by another of a quite different nature,
precipitated by the introduction of legislation affecting one of the
party's supporting sections; one conflict group might offer to act
as a mediator between the section concerned and the party leadership while others attempted to represent the interests of other

sections. Proving their credentials for such a role would force the groups to alter their behaviour and form, but it would still be possible for them to signify *sotto voce* that they were interested in doctrinal matters and in the party's leadership affairs. Finally, suppose that, after these events, one of the party's top officials were to resign from his post; if a leader of a group were then to challenge the designated successor and to begin to recruit factional support to that end, the challenger's group might find itself in disarray with some of its members joining him and some claiming that he had sacrificed his principles for the sake of power. In none of these three examples would either the conflict or the conflict groups have become absolute; one type of conflict would predominate, but elements of the other two would also be present. Unlike a party which, given its degree of formal organization and the extent of its formal commitments finds great difficulty in making rapid changes in form and behaviour, an intra-party conflict group is able, chameleon-like, to make sudden changes in its colour to match alterations in its background.

A party's central leadership is always concerned to ensure that the organization's internal conflicts are settled by established procedures and in this aim they generally have the support of the majority of the party's activists. In his discussion of this aspect of party life, Panebianco has suggested that those whom he defines as believers ('whose participation depends primarily on collective incentives of identity') are in a majority amongst party activists, and that those whom he defines as careerists ('whose participation depends primarily on selective, material and/or status-oriented incentives')[40] are in the minority.

> This explains why, even in the parties divided into factions, one can find a great many sectors of activists who do not participate in factionistic games. The believer, by definition, identifies with the party (and not with one sector of the party) – to which he is highly loyal – unless the leaders demonstrate that they don't take seriously the official organizational goals upon which his personal identity depends. The fact that in many cases most activists are of the believer rather than of the careerist type, explains why there is always a sort of natural majority supporting the leadership in power.[41]

Whatever their differences, conflict groups have a common interest in wearing down the regulatory powers at the disposal of the central leadership and thereby giving themselves the maximum scope for manoeuvre. If they succeed, the party is converted from a unitary body into a kind of federation, and effective power devolves to its constituent groups. Paradoxically, this is most likely to happen to a party which has achieved a commanding position in the party system, as had the Democratic Party in the American South at the time of Key's survey of its internal politics. Once the party's central authority has weakened beyond a certain point, it becomes possible for the sub-groups to strengthen their own organizations and to establish their own direct external links with the constituencies, either through pressure groups or through patron–client systems extending into the surrounding society. These points can best be explored by reference to detailed examples, and in the three chapters which follow we shall discuss cases of intra-party conflict which present interesting contrasts and points of comparison. In each case, the focus will be on the specific structure, traditions and context of the party concerned, and on the ways in which these have influenced the form and content of its internal conflicts.

Notes

1 V. O. Key with the assistance of Alexander Heard, *Southern Politics in State and Nation* (Alfred A. Knopf, New York, 1949), p. 16, n. 1.
2 See ibid., pp. 19–35, 58–81 and 205–28 for accounts of Democratic Party affairs in Virginia, Tennessee and North Carolina respectively.
3 Ibid., pp. 156–82.
4 Ibid., pp. 229–53
5 Ibid., pp. 36–57.
6 Ibid., pp. 130–55.
7 Ibid., pp. 254–71.
8 Ibid., pp. 178–9.
9 Ibid., pp. 82–105.
10 See Ralph W. Nicholas, 'Factions: A Comparative Analysis', in Michael Banton (ed.), *Political Systems and the Distribution of Power* (Tavistock, London, 1965), pp. 21–61.
11 See S. N. Eisenstadt and Louis Roniger, 'Patron–Client Relations as a Model of Structuring Social Exchange', *Comparative Studies in Society and History*, XXII (1980), pp. 42–77. See also Christopher

Clapham, 'Clientelism and the state', in Clapham (ed.), *Private Patronage and Public Power: Political Clientelism in the Modern State* (Frances Pinter, London, 1982), pp. 1–35; Luigi Graziano, 'Patron–Client Relationships in Southern Italy', *European Journal of Political Research*, I, 1 (April 1973), pp. 3–34; Graziano, 'A Conceptual Framework for the Study of Clientelistic Behavior', ibid., IV, 2 (1976), pp. 149–74; Graziano (ed.), *Political Clientelism and Comparative Perspectives,* being *International Political Science Review*, IV, 4 (October 1983); James C. Scott, 'Patron–Client Politics and Political Change in Southeast Asia', *American Political Science Review*, LXVI, 1 (March 1972), pp. 91–113 (see especially definition on p. 92); Carl H. Landé, 'Networks and Groups in Southeast Asia: Some Observations on the Group Theory of Politics', ibid., LXVII, 1 (March 1973), pp. 103–27.

12   For example, Carl H. Landé, *Leaders, Factions, and Parties: The Structure of Philippine Politics* (Yale University Southeast Asia Studies, New Haven, 1965); Alan S. Zuckerman, *The Politics of Faction: Christian Democratic Rule in Italy* (Yale University Press, New Haven, 1979).

13   Raphael Zariski, 'Party Factions and Comparative Politics: Some Preliminary Observations', *Midwest Journal of Political Science*, IV, 1 (February 1960), p. 33.

14   Ibid.

15   Ibid., pp. 34–6.

16   Norman K. Nicholson, 'The Factional Model and the Study of Politics', *Comparative Political Studies*, V, 3 (October 1972), p. 292.

17   Ibid., pp. 297–8.

18   For other surveys published at this time, see J. A. A. Stockwin, 'A Comparison of Political Factionalism in Japan and India', *The Australian Journal of Politics and History*, XVI, 3 (December 1970), pp. 361–74; Richard Sandbrook, 'Patrons, Clients, and Factions: New Dimensions of Conflict Analysis in Africa', *Canadian Journal of Political Science*, V, 1 (March 1972), pp. 104–19.

19   Richard Rose, 'Parties, Factions and Tendencies in Britain', *Political Studies*, XII, 1 (1964), pp. 37–8.

20   Ibid., pp. 38–40. For a later statement of his theory, see Rose, *The Problem of Party Government* (Penguin Books, Harmondsworth, Middlesex, 1976), pp. 312–28.

21   David Hine, 'Factionalism in West European Parties: A framework for analysis', *West European Politics*, V, 1 (January 1982), pp. 36–53.

22   Ibid., p. 41.

23   Ibid., p. 46.

24 Frank P. Belloni and Dennis C. Beller, 'The Study of Party Factions as Competitive Political Organizations', *The Western Political Quarterly*, XXIX, 4 (December 1976), pp. 531–49. See also Giovanni Sartori, *Parties and Party Systems: A Framework for Analysis* (Cambridge University Press, Cambridge, 1976), vol. I, pp. 71–115.

25 Frank P. Belloni and Dennis C. Beller (eds), *Faction Politics: Political Parties and Factionalism in Comparative Perspective* (ABC-Clio, Santa Barbara, California, 1978).

26 Zariski, 'Party Factions and Comparative Politics: Some Empirical Findings', in ibid., pp. 19–38, quotation from p. 19.

27 Beller and Belloni, 'The Study of Factions', in ibid., pp. 3–17.

28 Beller and Belloni, 'Party and Faction: Modes of Political Competition', in ibid., p. 419.

29 Ibid., pp. 419–22.

30 See James C. Scott, 'Corruption, Machine Politics, and Political Change', *American Political Science Review*, LXIII, 4 (December 1969), pp. 1142–58.

31 See K. G. Machado, 'Continuity and Change in Philippine Factionalism', in Belloni and Beller (eds), *Faction Politics*, pp. 193–217.

32 On this distinction, see Graziano, 'Patron–Client Relationships in Southern Italy', pp. 19–25.

33 Belloni, 'Factionalism, the Party System, and Italian Politics', in Belloni and Beller (eds), *Faction Politics*, pp. 73–108, quotation from p. 98.

34 For an earlier application of this schema, see B. D. Graham, 'The play of tendencies: internal politics in the SFIO before and after the Second World War', in David S. Bell (ed.), *Contemporary French Political Parties* (Croom Helm, London, 1982), pp. 138–64.

35 Cf. the use of the notion of the *secte* to explore tensions within Hindu nationalism in Christophe Jaffrelot, 'La place de l'état dans l'idéologie nationaliste hindoue: Éléments pour l'étude de l' "invention de la tradition politique"', *Revue Française de Science Politique*, XXXIX, 6 (December 1989), pp. 829–50, especially 836–9.

36 Landé, 'Networks and Groups in Southeast Asia', pp. 120–6.

37 Ibid., p. 125.

38 This paragraph is derived from the points made by Landé in ibid. and in Appendix II ('Group politics and dyadic politics: notes for a theory') in his *Leaders, Factions, and Parties*, pp. 141–8.

39 F. G. Bailey, *Stratagems and Spoils: A Social Anthropology of Politics* (Basil Blackwell, Oxford, 1969), especially pp. 51–5.

40 See Angelo Panebianco, *Political parties: organization and power*, tr. Marc Silver (Cambridge University Press, Cambridge, 1988), pp. 25–30, quotations from p. 26.
41 Ibid., p. 30. Cf. Rose's discussion of the phenomenon of 'non-aligned partisans' in his 'Parties, Factions and Tendencies in Britain', p. 38.

9

Conflict within the
French Socialist Parties

The history of the internal politics of the French Socialist Parties provides some interesting examples of sectarian conflict and its consequences. As we shall see, there have been several occasions on which the tendency of the French Socialists to divide over issues of doctrine and strategy has threatened the stability of the party and caused bitter disputes. Socialist leaders have not found it easy to deal with this disorder. Partly as a consequence of the intensity of sectarian differences, they have had an uphill struggle trying to construct loyal majorities amongst the membership and to build up direct and reliable ties with sectional groups within the party's general constituency. In order to understand these issues of conflict and control, we must look at certain developments which took place from 1930 onwards within the Section Française de l'Internationale Ouvrière (SFIO) and its successor, the Parti Socialiste de France (PS).[1]

I

The SFIO was formed in 1905 by the fusion of several left-wing groups, including the highly disciplined Parti Socialiste de France and the Parti Socialiste Français. The respective leaders of these two groups, Jules Guesde and Jean Jaurès, were men who held very different views about party strategy. Whereas Jaurès was in favour of the Socialists playing a full part in the politics of the Third French Republic and, under certain circumstances, co-operating with the centre party, the Radical Socialists, Guesde believed that the SFIO should remain independent and foster a revolutionary outlook. The party's founding document, the Charter of 1905, was predominantly Guesdist in content and referred to the SFIO as a party of the class struggle and of 'fundamental and irreducible opposition to the whole of the bourgeois class and to the State', which it saw as the instrument of that class.[2]

Organized on the basis of federations of local branches within each Department (the main administrative unit in France), and with its policy co-ordinated by a system of national congresses of delegates, the SFIO grew rapidly until 1914. That year, however, the party suffered a major set-back when Jaurès, who had campaigned vigorously against preparations for war, was assassinated on 31 July. Soon party unity was weakened by a militant peace movement which developed within party ranks (though, in fact, the SFIO formed part of the Sacred Union which governed France during the first years of the war). Later, a large influx of new members who had been enthused by the Russian revolution of 1917 and believed that revolutions would follow throughout Western Europe created further division within the party. At its National Congress at Tours in December 1920, a majority of the delegates declared in favour of joining the Third International, directed from Moscow, and later became the French Communist Party, while the minority broke away to reconstruct the SFIO on new foundations.[3]

Under the guidance of Paul Faure, its General Secretary, and of Léon Blum, its parliamentary leader, the new SFIO gradually rebuilt its organizational and electoral strength throughout the 1920s. During this period of reconstruction, it maintained its independence; it often came into bitter conflict with the Communist Party in working-class areas such as the northern industrial suburbs of Paris and the textile manufacturing and coal-mining regions of north-eastern France, and had frequent clashes with the Radical Socialists as it attempted to extend its electoral strength into country regions.[4] After a swing to the left in the general elections of 1924, its parliamentary group refused several opportunities to join with the Radicals in forming coalition governments, a strategy criticized by some Socialist deputies. In response to their query as to whether the party would ever participate in a government unless it were heading for a political revolution, Blum made a distinction between the conquest of power in a revolutionary situation, and the exercise of power within the existing parliamentary framework. He considered that the latter course could be justified under certain circumstances,[5] but differences of opinion about the wisdom and terms of such participation continued to cause division within the party.

A particularly serious conflict began early in 1933, when a majority of the party's representatives in the Chamber of Deputies decided to offer consistent support to the Radical Government headed by Edouard Daladier and voted for the ministry's general budget to confirm their commitment. An extraordinary National Congress of the party which met in April 1933 took the view that this constituted a breach of discipline, and adopted a resolution reaffirming the principle that the parliamentary group should oppose the budget, along with estimates of expenditure for military and colonial purposes. Despite this, a majority of the Socialist deputies voted for the budget when it was again presented to the Chamber. They were duly censured for doing so by the party's regular National Congress in July, and the SFIO's National Council subsequently expelled six of the leading rebels, who later formed a new party which included a small number of former Socialists from the Chamber and the Senate. The dissidents were described as neo-Socialists, and the moral outrage generated by the affair tended to strengthen support for those who had adopted an anti-participationist position within the party.[6]

From a theoretical point of view, the interest of this case lies in the rapidity with which the conflict changed its form. At the outset, in the early months of 1933, that form was basically sectarian; the dissidents were not only asserting that the party should abandon its ritual of voting against budgets, but were raising fundamental issues about the nature of the party's mission and the extent of its commitment to the Republican form of government. This was the time when Hitler was taking power in Germany and dismantling all that remained of the Weimar Republic, the disintegration of which had been blamed in part on the failure of the German Social Democratic Party to take its full part in governing the country in the 1920s. The neo-Socialists could claim that they were reminding the SFIO of its obligations to the Third Republic at a time when National Socialism was in the ascendant in Germany. However, by July 1933 when the National Congress met, the conflict within the party had deteriorated into a clash between personalities. In this clash, Blum and

Faure were at odds with Adrien Marquet and Marcel Déat, the neo-Socialist leaders, who were now accused of having ulterior motives in making support for the budget a matter of principle. From this point onwards, the factional aspect of the confrontation became increasingly important and, by the stage of the final expulsions, the neo-Socialists had been reduced to a small number of intransigent members. In party mythology, they were represented as a mixture of the conspiratorial and the misguided, the original issues having been quietly ignored.

It may seem surprising that three years later, in 1936, the SFIO should show no hesitation about taking power as the leading party in a Popular Front coalition. The origins of the Popular Front lie in the reactions of left-wing groups to the Parisian street riots of 6 February 1934, which were taken to signify that a fascist insurrection was about to overthrow the Republic. By the end of 1934, the Socialist and Communist Parties had formed an alliance with the double aim of resisting fascism and of taking power to carry out a limited programme of economic and social reforms. The Radical Socialists joined this alliance in 1935, and together the three parties won a decisive victory in the general elections of 26 April and 3 May 1936. Blum then formed a Government consisting of Socialists and Radicals, the Communists having decided to offer support to the government in Parliament but not to participate in the ministry.[7] The Blum Government then introduced a number of reforms, including agreements about wage increases and collective bargaining, a forty-hour working week, paid holidays, a system of conciliation and arbitration in labour disputes, and the establishment of a national wheat board. However, Blum continually stressed to his party that this was a Popular Front rather than a Socialist administration. In the following year when financial and economic difficulties obliged the Government to ask Parliament for special powers and these were refused by the Senate, Blum resigned office on 21 June 1937.[8]

By this stage, opposition to Blum within his own party was being organized by two dissident groups, the Bataille Socialiste and the Gauche Révolutionnaire, whose respective leaders were Jean Zyromski and Marceau Pivert. The first of these, the Bataille Socialiste, had been formed in 1927, and although it had originally opposed the idea of the SFIO's participation in government, it was now strongly in favour of the Popular Front and co-operation with the Communists. One of the most prominent figures in the group in the early 1930s, Marceau Pivert had broken away from it in October 1935 to form the Gauche Révolutionnaire to express the views of those in the party who believed that the Popular Front could be turned into a revolutionary movement.[9] Such intra-party groups were described as *tendances* (which in this context means 'organized persuasions'). They were allowed by convention to publish their own periodicals for circulation within the party, they could form clubs for the readers of their periodicals, and could circulate lengthy policy resolutions for consideration by party members prior to meetings of the party's National Council and the National Congress. When such resolutions were discussed at congresses of the departmental federations, delegates from these federations were usually instructed to assign their votes (or mandates) in agreed proportions to the various texts when these were considered by either the National Council or a national congress. At meetings of these bodies, a resolutions committee was supposed to produce a single motion to express a common view. In practice, however, the *tendances* would often insist upon putting their texts to the vote, knowing that at the national congress the allocation of places on the party's executive, the Permanent Administrative Committee (CAP), would take account of the proportion of the total vote obtained by 'loyalist' or 'official' resolutions and by the texts of the *tendances*.

The conflict between the *tendances* themselves and the clashes between individual *tendances* and the party's central leaders became particularly acute in the early months of 1938, by which time the declining momentum of the Popular Front had further increased the anti-participationist sentiment within the party. Each of the *tendances* was exploiting particular themes within the SFIO's traditions and, in the large Seine Federation enclosing Paris, and in a number of provincial federations, they succeeded in forming what were predominantly sectarian followings. Each was addressing a different audience: whereas the Gauche Révolutionnaire appealed to the romantic revolutionary sentiment in the party and praised the virtues of voluntarism and activism in organizational work, the Bataille Socialiste appealed to Guesdist ideas and to the view that the SFIO should remain closely in touch with the Communists at both the national and international level, given the seriousness of the threat from fascism.

The terms of participation in government were still the cause of dissension. The Socialists had held posts in the Popular Front Government headed by Camille Chautemps, a Radical Socialist, between June 1937 and January 1938, but they had left the ministry in the latter month, whereupon Chautemps had formed a purely Radical Government. He resigned early in March 1938, however, and Blum, who had been commissioned by the President to form the new ministry, outraged the leaders of the Gauche Révolutionnaire by obtaining from the SFIO's National Council on 12 March a vote of confidence for his plan to form a broad coalition. This was essentially a proposal to construct an alliance consisting of a Popular Front core and an outer circle of right-wing groups (the rally of all Republicans around the Popular Front[10]), with the aim of giving France a strong government to deal with the international crisis caused by Germany's occupation of Austria. In the event, Blum was unable to persuade the conservative groups to join such a ministry, and he was forced to form another Popular Front coalition consisting of Socialists and Radical Socialists. In spite of this, the Gauche Révolutionnaire insisted on debating his attempt to form a broad-based government, claiming that it would have constituted a national union – in other words, a general alliance of the kind which the SFIO had always condemned in the past. The group had just taken control of the party's Seine Federation and was obviously gaining in strength and confidence, when suddenly it became involved in a legal dispute.

Paul Faure, the party's General Secretary, learned that the Seine Federation, whose Secretary was now Marceau Pivert, had, on its own authority, issued a tract attacking the National Council for its decision of 12 March in support of Blum's planned coalition. This was clearly a breach of the party's rules, a federation usurping the role of the executive, and Faure promptly referred the matter to the party's administrative and disciplinary bodies. It and another complaint were upheld, and Pivert and other leaders of the Seine Federation were banned from party office, for three years in Pivert's case and two in the case of the others. Refusing to accept this decision, Pivert then led the Seine Federation into rebellion, with the result that the party's authorities established a new federation to take its place.

Now the Seine rebels and the Gauche Révolutionnaire found themselves engaged in two parallel campaigns – to obtain the lifting of the sanctions against the rebel federation and its leaders and to persuade the party to condemn the principle of a national union. Both campaigns had a factional aspect; that for the annulment of sanctions entailed a direct attack on the integrity of the General Secretary, while that against a national union was widely seen as criticism of Léon Blum rather than as an exercise in doctrinal clarification. The last phase in this confrontation was played out at the Royan National Congress of June 1938, which upheld the sanctions and approved a compromise (basically 'loyalist') resolution on policy, in preference to the rival texts put forward by the Bataille Socialiste and the Gauche Révolutionnaire. At the end of the congress, Marceau Pivert and some of his followers left the SFIO to form a new party, the Parti Socialiste Ouvrier et Paysan (PSOP).[11] The attempt by the Gauche Révolutionnaire to intensify a sectarian conflict and to commit the party to a revised doctrinal position had failed, having lost momentum once Pivert had committed the group to a confrontation with the party's authorities. By its attack on Faure's integrity and Blum's judgement, it had virtually given the conflict a factional dimension but it lacked the broad backing which it would have required were it to mount a successful attack on the leadership.

In the two crises reviewed above, the party's central authorities had retained the support of their loyalist majority, despite the strain which certain phases in each cycle of conflict had placed upon party unity. However, the fierce dispute over the SFIO's international policy which broke out at the end of 1938 split the governing group in two and created new patterns of alignment. After the Munich Agreement of September 1938, the main issue for the Socialists was whether Western liberal democracies should build up their military resources and join with the Soviet Union in a defensive alliance against Germany and Italy, or whether France should refuse to take part in a new European war under any circumstances. Blum and his supporters made common cause with Zyromski and the Bataille Socialiste in favour of resistance to the fascist powers, while Paul Faure and a large proportion of the former loyalist majority adopted a strictly pacifist position. In December 1938, a special National Congress at Montrouge endorsed Blum's views, but the pacifists continued to stand their ground, with the result that a compromise resolution was adopted at the Nantes National Congress of May 1939.[12] Bitter conflict over the issue continued until the armistice of June 1940 and the establishment of the Vichy regime, and it seriously damaged the authority of the party's central officers and institutions.

Open party politics came to an end in France during the years of military occupation and Vichy rule, and could be resumed only in the closing months of 1944, after the liberation of most of the country from the Germans. The SFIO now had a new leadership, formed during the wartime resistance and anxious to see the party make a new beginning. Many former Socialist parliamentarians were expelled for not having opposed the granting of full powers to Marshal Pétain at the National Assembly on 10 July 1940; the party's rules were amended to give more authority to the central executive, which was now to be known as the Comité Directeur; steps were to be taken to discourage the formation of *tendances* (in particular, by ending the use of proportional representation in elections to the executive and other central bodies); and Blum, who had returned to France from captivity in Germany, was asked to draft a new declaration of principles to replace the Charter of 1905. Within the provisional Government which ruled France after its liberation, the SFIO found itself at the centre of a three-party alliance of the Communists, Socialists and the Mouvement Républicain Populaire (MRP), a newly created Christian Democratic Party, which formed the basis for a series of coalition Governments, first under General de Gaulle and later, after his resignation in January 1946, under two successive party leaders, Félix Gouin, a Socialist, and Georges Bidault, a Christian Democrat. The party also played a leading role in the affairs of the first Constituent Assembly, elected on 21 October 1945, and, after the rejection of the first constitutional proposal by referendum, in the second Constituent Assembly, elected on 2 June 1946. The Constitution prepared by the latter body was approved by referendum on 13 October 1946, and the institutions of the Fourth Republic were then set in place.

In these two general elections of 21 October 1945 and 2 June 1946, the party had not polled as well as it had expected to and many members blamed the central leaders for what were considered to be mistakes in strategy. They therefore supported a revolt headed by Guy Mollet, a deputy from the Pas-de-Calais Department, who, on the opening day of the party's 38th National Congress held between 29 August and 1 September 1946, led an attack against the executive's annual report. The report was rejected, whereupon Daniel Mayer, the incumbent General Secretary, at once announced that he and his fellow officers would not seek further terms in their respective posts. Mollet was then appointed as the new General Secretary by the incoming executive on 4 September.[13] From the beginning of the campaign, he and his group had stressed the need for the *redressement* (rectification) of the party's doctrine and strategy on neo-Guesdist lines, thereby giving the conflict a sectarian content. However, they did not propose a complete transformation of the SFIO as the Gauche Révolutionnaire had done, implying that a change in leadership was all that was required. What had begun as a sectarian dispute had rapidly developed factional characteristics.

Guy Mollet remained General Secretary of the SFIO until 1969, that is, throughout the whole period of the Fourth Republic (1946–58) and for the first decade of the Fifth, which was established in 1958. Backed from the beginning of his period in office by the powerful Pas-de-Calais Federation and, after 1947, by the equally powerful Nord Federation, he maintained a firm control over the Parliamentary group and the party organization and successfully countered several challenges to his position. In the early 1950s there was fierce controversy in the party over the issue of German rearmament and matters came to a head on 30 August 1954 when the National Assembly voted against the proposal for a European Defence Community (EDC). Amongst the deputies who had rejected the idea of an EDC were fifty-three Socialists, who included Daniel Mayer, Jules Moch and others of the party's former resistance leaders, but SFIO policy was to support the EDC as a logical step towards European integration. In spite of the emotive nature of the issue, Mollet and his executive were in a strong enough position to take disciplinary action against the rebels. A later source of dissension within the party was French policy towards the Algerian war. Mollet had become Prime Minister on 1 February 1956 and held office until 21 May 1957, during which time his Government was pursuing a policy aimed at achieving a cease-fire so that elections could be held in the territory and negotiations for a political settlement set in train. The prior importance attached to a cease-fire implied a reliance on military action which disturbed a substantial minority within the SFIO, who favoured a greater use of political methods to solve the problem. This group, led by Édouard Depreux, was conducting a systematic campaign aimed at building up a strong opposition to Mollet within the party, The critical point came at the SFIO's 50th National Congress in September 1958 when the Depreux group's motion calling for a 'No' vote in the Constitutional Referendum was defeated. Once again, Mollet had been able to disarm the revolt, and after the Congress Depreux and his main supporters left the party to form the Autonomous Socialist Party (PSA). After his departure, opposition to Mollet within the SFIO was concentrated within two groups, one headed by Albert Gazier and another led by Gaston Defferre, the Mayor of Marseille, who was to make an unsuccessful bid to become a candidate for the French presidential election of December 1965.[14] All these conflicts had factional overtones but in every case Mollet was able to contain the dissident group and prevent a return to the pre-war system of *tendances*.

By 1969, the non-Communist left consisted of a diversity of organizations and personal followings, but it was generally agreed that a unified party should be constructed. Congresses in May and July 1969 resulted in the absorption of the SFIO and some other groups into a new Parti Socialiste (PS) which was remodelled at the Epinay Congress of June 1971.[15] François Mitterrand, who then became its First Secretary, immediately set to work to improve the party's electoral position; as the main candidate of the left, he had come close to defeating de Gaulle in the presidential elections of December 1965 and was widely expected to run for the presidency on some future occasion. His basic strategy for winning power was to work with the Communists, and in June 1972 a common programme was agreed upon by these two parties and a group of left-wing Radicals. At first, progress was rapid: the PS and the left as a whole made gains in the National Assembly elections of March 1973, Mitterrand almost succeeded in defeating Giscard d'Estaing, the liberal candidate, in the presidential elections of May 1974, and the left-wing alliance captured further ground in the municipal elections of March 1977. Then came a series of set-backs: negotiations to revise the common programme of 1972 finally broke down in September 1977 and dissensions between the Socialists and the Communists contributed to the defeat of the left in the National Assembly elections of March 1978. However, the PS continued to gather support on its own terms, and, in the presidential elections of April–May 1981, Mitterrand finally succeeded in his bid for the highest office in the Republic. He then appointed another Socialist, Pierre Mauroy, as Prime Minister and a Socialist Government was formed in May 1981, It was confirmed in office when the PS won an absolute majority of the seats in the National Assembly elections of 14 and 21 June 1981.

The internal politics of the PS during its rapid rise to power had been lively and complicated. As we have seen, the SFIO had taken immediate steps in 1946 to prevent any return to the system of *tendances* which had caused so much dissension in the late 1930s, and Mollet had managed to restrict the scope for organized dissent during his period as General Secretary. To take account of the continued existence of the various groups which had combined to form the PS between 1969 and 1971, the new organization's rules restored proportional representation as the means of choosing members for the party's executive bodies. Under this system, the congresses of the departmental federations were required to share out their votes between various policy resolutions and on the occasion of the National Congress the proportion of the total vote attracted by each resolution was to determine the proportion of places on the Comité Directeur and the Executive Bureau to which its sponsors were entitled. While this arrangement encouraged the growth of a number of groups, known as *courants d'opinion*, the system of *courants* which obtained in the PS differed from the system of *tendances* which had existed in the pre-war SFIO in important respects. Firstly, Mitterrand's personal following in the party was quite small at that stage, and his control of the party depended upon his ability to form alliances between his group and other *courants* rather than on a stable loyalist majority of the kind which had proved so valuable to Blum and Faure until it split into two at the end of 1938. Secondly, the leaders of the *courants* in the PS (men such as Pierre Mauroy, Gaston Defferre and Michel Rocard) were not outsiders, but rather members of the party's established elite. Finally, with the notable exception of the Centre d'Études, de Recherches et d'Éducation Socialistes (CERES) which had begun life in the SFIO under the leadership of Jean-Pierre Chevènement and which was generally in favour of class action and of co-operation with the Communists, very much in the style of the Bataille Socialiste, the *courants* of the 1970s were far less disposed to promote sectarian conflict than their pre-war counterparts had been. Throughout the party congresses of the 1970s, they changed their alignments frequently and usually formed loyalist and opposition blocs in the crucial elections to the Comité Directeur, but at the Valence Congress of October 1981, the first to be held after the party's return to power, they formed a united front.[16]

After 1981, the PS gradually come to terms with its role as a party of government and its internal politics changed accordingly. The Mauroy Government, which included four Communist ministers, attempted to carry out an ambitious policy of nationalization and, by means of a series of social reforms, to bring about economic growth by stimulating consumption, but it soon found itself dealing with relatively high rates of inflation and a worsening balance of trade. In June 1982 the Government was forced to introduce wage and price controls and to prepare for reductions in public expenditure. Further deflationary measures followed, and the policy of financial restraint was continued by Laurent Fabius, the Socialist appointed to succeed Mauroy as Prime Minister in July 1984. Fabius included no Communists in his Government, and when the Socialists lost their majority in the National Assembly after the general elections of March 1986, Mitterrand had no option but to invite the Gaullist leader, Jacques Chirac, to form a conservative ministry.[17] However, Mitterrand's own re-election for a second seven-year term in the presidential ballots of 24 April and 8 May 1988 provided him with a further opportunity to bring his party back to power, and he chose Michel Rocard to head a Socialist Government, which took office on 13 May 1988. Although the Socialists failed to win a clear majority in the National Assembly polls of 5 and 12 June 1988, their position in the legislature was sufficiently strong to justify their remaining in power and Mitterrand again invited Rocard to form a Government. This took office on 28 June 1988 and continued the policies of restraint and financial prudence which had been initiated under Mauroy and Fabius earlier in the decade, the cautious nature of which was causing some dissatisfaction within the ranks of the PS. Partly in response to this, Mitterrand removed Rocard from the premiership in May 1991 and replaced him with the more flamboyant Edith Cresson. She in her turn was replaced in April 1992 by Pierre Bérégovoy, who persevered with cautious financial and economic policies in a period of severe recession until, in the National Assembly elections of 21 and 28 March 1993, his party was voted out of power.

Apart from the two years of the Chirac ministry (1986–8), the Socialists had charge of the national Government in France for over a decade, from 1981 until 1993, and for much of that time the party's *courants* came under heavy pressure to avoid excessive criticism of the administration. Even though he was President, Mitterrand continued to take a direct interest in the party's affairs, maintaining his influence upon it through what was effectively a court of party notables built around the Élysée Palace. The obligation to exercise constraint was felt even by the CERES group (which adopted the title Socialisme et République in 1986), which moderated its position after its failure to win support for an alternative economic policy at the party's Bourg-en-Bresse Congress of 1983. The subsequent Congresses of Toulouse (1985) and Lille (1987) were relatively uneventful affairs. Meanwhile, the factional aspect of the competition between the *courants* had become more evident: each of the party's notables (nicknamed 'the elephants') had recruited a core group of secondary leaders to provide support in the battles for position. The attenuation of the doctrinal content of their competition was revealed by the nature of the policy resolutions circulated in advance of the Rennes Congress of March 1990. According to one commentator:

> Each of these motions is presented as a kind of general platform dealing at one and the same time with international, economic and social questions, as well as with political problems and the internal problems of the PS. Fundamentally there are few major differences between most of them, which explains particularly why so many alliances can be arranged at the congress.[18]

When the seven motions in contention were considered by the congresses of the departmental federations, most attention was given to the text sponsored by Laurent Fabius and his group and to a rival motion associated with Pierre Mauroy (who was then First Secretary) and his two chief allies, Louis Mermaz and Lionel Jospin. This state of affairs prompted the comment from Chevènement that the party had become 'less a place for debating ideas, less an "intellectual collectivity" . . . than a machine for selecting candidates for the presidential elections'.[19] At the Rennes Congress itself the party notables were unable to reach agreement on the usual joint motion and Mitterrand was forced to intervene several days after the close of proceedings to obtain a settlement which cleared the way for appointments to the Executive Bureau and the National Secretariat.[20]

A new and more moderate programme was adopted at a Congress held in Paris between 13 and 15 December 1991[21] and in the following year the party's leadership once more assumed a settled pattern: in January 1992 Laurent Fabius succeeded Pierre Mauroy as First Secretary[22] and Michel Rocard established himself as the person most likely to be the Socialist candidate in the next presidential elections. However Rocard faced the problem that the Socialist Party itself was in electoral decline and he saw the solution as being its transformation into a broader and more inclusive party representing the whole of the French Left – much as Mitterrand had enlarged the scope of the original party in the 1970s. In a speech which he made on 17 February 1993, he criticized his own party and called for the creation of a movement in which Socialists would be joined by ecologists, centrists, Communists and those concerned with human rights.

> There are men and women in this grouping who have always fought alongside us. Today many of them are without a cause but they are still prepared to commit themselves anew for something worth the trouble.

He warned that the existing party could not remain 'a closed society tolerating disputes between cliques and conflicts between *courants* while claiming to present a monolithic statement to the outside world . . . and accepting as allies only those who consent to submission'.[23] Implicit in his remarks was a rejection of the idea that democracy within a party necessarily entailed the organized expression of doctrinal differences: Rocard's notion of his transformed party was much closer to the Gaullist idea of a rally of diverse opinions than to the Guesdist idea of a party representing in a coherent, disciplined way the aspirations of a single sector of French society.

II

The presence of such a complexity of elements within the French Socialist tradition has given rise in the past to particularly intense debates about doctrine and strategy, as this brief survey has tried to show, and those debates are likely to be renewed as the party adapts itself to an opposition role following its 1993 defeat at the polls. On the one hand, that tradition has always held fast to the belief that Socialist ideas are produced by systematic enquiry within an avant-garde of intellectuals engaged in a perpetual search for enlightenment, and on the other, the idea that demands for policies arise from ordinary men and women and constitute an expression of the collective will.

The fact that the party's tradition still encloses such contradictions provides considerable scope for special pleading when groups engage in internal conflict. The basic pragmatic rule for driving a dispute in a sectarian direction is to take a premise which is open to discussion and present it as the unambiguous statement of a truth which has been either ignored or consciously misrepresented by the central leadership. Most of the dissident leaders in the past have applied this rule to some effect: Marceau Pivert stressed the values of activism and voluntarism as if they were the essential elements of revolutionary theory; Mollet, during the 1946 revolt, emphasized the importance of the class struggle for the neo-Guesdist version of Marxism while making light of the significance of the party's humanist inheritance; and in the late 1970s, Rocard affirmed his belief in the value of decentralization, playing down the emphasis on the reforming power of a centralized state which has always been so important an element in French Socialism.

Another feature that we have noted is how quickly sectarian conflict within the SFIO can shift towards factionalism. This was particularly evident in the neo-Socialist crisis of 1933 and in the crisis caused by the rebellion of the Seine Federation in the spring of 1938. The rapidity of such change reflects the inherent difficulty of sustaining a sectarian conflict without reference to personalities; for example, it is not easy for a central leader to resist a call for doctrinal reorientation without also questioning the wisdom or integrity of those who have made the call, and it is equally hard for a sectarian leader to reply to such criticism without impugning the motives of the central leader, in his turn. Given the high seriousness of disputes about doctrine, the charges made by each side are likely to be very emotive and the question as to who should be in authority is almost bound to be raised. If a dissident group calls for the removal of the central leaders on the ground that they lack integrity, the latter are bound to claim that the dissidents are interested in power for its own sake, and are simply raising matters of principle in order to further their selfish ambition.

Sectarian conflicts in both the SFIO and the PS would probably have been less intense and more stable had these bodies been subject to stronger sectional pressures. When the SFIO was formed in 1905, the central trade-union organization in France, the Confédération Générale du Travail (CGT) was still very much under the influence of revolutionary syndicalism and reluctant to become involved in party or parliamentary politics, with the result that it did not develop close relations with the Socialist Party. After 1921, when the CGT split into Communist and non-Communist units (the Confédération Générale du Travail Unitaire (CGTU) and the new CGT respectively), the CGT did become more interested in policy matters than its pre-war equivalent had been, but it still remained apart from the SFIO. The two trade-union bodies merged in 1936 and the unified CGT grew steadily in size and influence, adopting a pro-Communist stance after the Second World War. A Socialist-leaning CGT–Force Ouvrière was established in December 1947 but its ties with the SFIO have remained weak and indirect. Under the Fifth Republic, the CGT has retained its close connection with the Communist Party but its main rival, the Confédération Française Démocratique du Travail (CFDT, known as the Confédération Française des Travailleurs Chrétiens until 1964) has remained politically independent. Although the PS has developed some ties with the CFDT, these have been neither as systematic nor as strong as those which have existed between, say, the trade unions and the Labour Party in Britain or between the trade unions and the Social Democratic Party in Germany. The same relative weakness of sectional ties has been evident in relations between the French Socialist Parties and other sectors of the French economy, from agriculture to small industry. Only through its control of specific departments of state or of ministries when it held or shared office has the SFIO and later the PS come to know at first hand the detailed concerns of particular sections of the population. French Socialists have always been sensitive to the interests of some social groups such as the coalminers and ironworkers of the north-east, the white-collar workers in the public services, the schoolteachers, and the small farmers, but the influence of these groups upon the party has been diffuse rather than specific.

Had sectional interests been represented directly in the annual congresses and other plenary sessions of the party, it might have led to some degree of sectional conflict from time to time, but the intra-party groups thus formed would almost certainly have moderated the intensity of the sectarian conflict. In particular, they could have challenged the abstract anti-participationism – that refusal to join coalition governments and thereby gain access to crucial ministries – which had such a strong influence on the SFIO through its entire history. Sectional groups concerned to increase the party's influence on legislation and government policy could have aligned themselves with the loyalist majority during flares of sectarian conflict, thus greatly strengthening the position of the central leaders. The long period of office enjoyed by the PS between 1981 and 1993 brought Socialist ministers into much more direct contact with interest groups and increased the party's knowledge about their detailed policy requirements, but there was little sign that the party organization itself was concerned to harness and express the energies of such groups. In any case, the party's activists were still attached to the idea that French Socialism entailed the pursuit of a generalized ideal of a reformed society rather than a style of enlightened administration of the kind exemplified by the Mollet Government of 1956–7 and those of Rocard, Cresson and Bérégovoy during the period 1988–93. In August 1991, when Edith Cresson was Prime Minister, one Socialist deputy claimed that 'many activists and sympathisers today feel wounded in their commitment. They did not expect to find the PS being drawn into "Molletism".[24] The implied contrast between Socialism and Molletism indicates the continuing importance of differences of opinion about organizational ethics within the party. The libertarian ethic has always been a very powerful influence, especially on those PS units located in the Paris region. It was this ethic, which prescribes that the party should encourage all sectors of opinion within its membership to explore the abstract areas of party doctrine and to concentrate on the prospects for reforming society, by revolutionary means or otherwise, which provided the normative justification for the system of *tendances* in the 1920s and 1930s. While the revival of the system by the PS was justified on similar grounds, it was essentially atavistic, an attempt to return to a relatively esoteric form of internal politics with its own complicated rituals. Conversely, the disciplinarian ethic developed by the SFIO's strong northern federations in the Nord and Pas-de-Calais reflects the sternness and puritanism of northern Guesdism. It prescribes that once a plenary session has discussed a subject, the delegates should reach agreement and that, subsequently, they should respect the result of that agreement in the interest of party unity and for the sake of the party's ordinary members. Within these northern departments, where the Socialists have long controlled important municipalities such as Lille, they learned from experience the value of catering for the concrete needs of the local people and of managing social services, especially in the fields of education, health and housing, for their benefit. Molletism, which libertarians derided as a form of pragmatism covered by Leftist rhetoric, represented an attempt to project into national politics some elements of the disciplinarian ethic of these northern federations. By treating it as being of no account or best forgotten, a section of the PS was refusing to consider on its merits an ethic which has formed a major part of its inheritance.

One of the ironies of the history of the PS is that the revival within the party of a libertarian ethic has been associated with much greater competition for office and status than would ever have been tolerated by the SFIO, in whatever incarnation. For most of its history, the SFIO was strongly disposed to remain in opposition at the national level; the only major offices for which there was any competition were those of the parliamentary leader and General Secretary, although ministerial posts were also objects of controlled competition during the party's participation in the Popular Front coalitions of 1936–7 and 1938, and in those of the post-war and Fourth Republican periods. There has been nothing in the past to compare with the tremendous tidal pull which the institutions of the Fifth Republic have exerted upon the PS. Since 1981 when it acquired the status of a party of government, its notables have begun to compete not only for the office of First Secretary and other posts within the party organization, but for the privilege of being the Socialist candidate in the next presidential elections or for advantageous positions in the hierarchy of deputies and senators from which future Prime Ministers are drawn.

Notes

1 For a detailed history, see Daniel Ligou, *Histoire du Socialisme en France (1871–1961)* (Presses Universitaires de France, Paris, 1962), and for the philosophical background, see Tony Judt, *Marxism and the French Left: Studies in labour and politics in France, 1830–1981* (Clarendon Press, Oxford, 1986). For recent developments, see D. S. Bell and Byron Criddle, *The French Socialist Party: The Emergence of a Party of Government* (Clarendon Press, Oxford, Second Edition, 1988).

2 On the background to this document, see Aaron Noland, *The Founding of the French Socialist Party (1893–1905)* (Harvard University Press, Cambridge, Mass., 1956), pp. 165–87.

3 On the Tours congress, see Jean Lacouture, *Léon Blum* (Seuil, Paris, 1977), pp. 163–76.

4 See Tony Judt, *La reconstruction du Parti Socialiste 1921–1926* (Presses de la Fondation Nationale des Sciences Politiques, Paris, 1976).

5 See Joel Colton, 'Léon Blum and the French Socialists as a Government Party', *The Journal of Politics*, XV, 4 (November 1953), pp. 517–43.

6 See Joel Colton, *Léon Blum: Humanist in Politics* (Alfred A. Knopf, New York, 1966), pp. 80–8; John T. Marcus, *French Socialism in the Crisis Years 1933–1936: Fascism and the French Left* (Frederick A. Praeger, New York, 1958), pp. 7–40.

7 See James Joll, 'The Making of the Popular Front', in Joll (ed.),

The Decline of the Third Republic, St. Antony's Papers, Number 5 (Chatto and Windus, London, 1959), pp. 36–66; Nathanael Greene, *Crisis and Decline: The French Socialist Party in the Popular Front Era* (Cornell University Press, Ithaca, New York, 1969), pp. 71–106; Julian Jackson, *The Popular Front in France: defending democracy, 1934–38* (Cambridge University Press, Cambridge, 1988), pp. 17–81.

8　See Irwin M. Wall, 'The Resignation of the First Popular Front Government of Léon Blum, June 1937', *French Historical Studies*, VI, 4 (Fall 1970), pp. 538–54; Greene, *Crisis and Decline*, pp. 102–6. See also, Jackson, *The Popular Front in France*, pp. 271–87.

9　See D. N. Baker, 'The Politics of Socialist Protest in France: The Left Wing of the Socialist Party, 1921–39', *The Journal of Modern History*, XLIII, 1 (March 1971), pp. 2–41.

10　See above, pp. 94–5.

11　On this period of internal conflict, see Greene, *Crisis and Decline*, pp. 185–224; Jean-Paul Joubert, *Marceau Pivert et le pivertisme: Révolutionnaires de la S.F.I.O.* (Presses de la Fondation Nationale des Sciences Politiques, Paris, 1977); Daniel Guérin, *Front populaire: Révolution manquée: Témoignage militant* (François Maspero, Paris, Second Edition, 1976).

12　See Greene, *Crisis and Decline*, pp. 225–77.

13　On the post-war conflict, see Jérôme Jaffré, 'Guy Mollet et la conquête de la SFIO en 1946', in Bernard Ménager *et al.*, *Guy Mollet: Un Camarade en République* (Presses Universitaires de Lille, Lille, 1987), pp. 17–32; B. D. Graham, 'The play of tendencies: internal politics in the SFIO before and after the Second World War', in David S. Bell (ed.), *Contemporary French Political Parties* (Croom Helm, London, 1982), pp. 138–64; Graham, *The French Socialists and Tripartisme 1944–1947* (The Australian National University Press, Canberra, 1965), pp. 197–219.

14　On this period, see Harvey G. Simmons, *French Socialists in Search of a Role 1956–1967* (Cornell University Press, Ithaca, New York, 1970); Frank L. Wilson, *The French Democratic Left 1963–1969: Toward a Modern Party System* (Stanford University Press, Stanford, California, 1971); Serge Hurtig, 'La S.F.I.O. face à la Vᵉ République: Majorité et minorités', *Revue Française de Science Politique*, XIV, 3 (June 1964), pp. 526–56.

15　See Bell and Criddle, *The French Socialist Party*, pp. 42–66.

16　See ibid., pp. 66–115.

17　On the period 1981–6, see ibid., pp. 114–25.

18　*Le Figaro* (Paris), 13 March 1990, p. 7.

19   In an interview with Jacques Fleury and J. Macé-Scaron, ibid., 9 March 1990, p. 6.
20   *La Monde* (Paris), 23 March 1990, p. 7.
21   See *Le Figaro*, 14–15 December 1991, p. 6; 16 December 1991, p. 6; 17 December 1991, p. 9.
22   See ibid., 8 January 1992, pp. 1 and 6; 10 January 1992, pp. 1 and 6.
23   Ibid., 19 February 1993, p. 7.
24   Jean-Marc Ayrault (Loire Atlantique), in ibid., 22 August 1991, p. 13.

10

Conflict in the Congress Party
of Uttar Pradesh

Although factionalism, as an ideal type of intra-party conflict, is a transient phenomenon given its association with bids for high office, groups with factional characteristics can sustain themselves for relatively long periods of time if they employ the techniques of clientelism to build up support inside and outside the party. In the discussion of politics within the Uttar Pradesh unit of the Indian National Congress between 1948 and 1970 which follows, we shall examine how such a combination provided the ingredients for a severe round of conflict. We shall also see how the fact that the state of Uttar Pradesh is part of a federation, the Union of India, and therefore subject to strong constitutional and political controls from the capital, New Delhi, affected the outcome of this conflict.

I

Under the Constitution adopted in 1950, independent India established a robust system of parliamentary democracy within a federal structure. At the level of the Indian Union, the central Council of Ministers is responsible to a popular assembly, the Lok Sabha, which is balanced within the Union Parliament by an upper house, the Rajya Sabha. The executive power of the Union is vested in the President of India, who is elected by the members of the central parliament and those of the lower houses of the state legislatures. Each constituent state of the Union has its own Council of Ministers responsible to a popular assembly, known as the Vidhan Sabha, and in some states this house is associated with an upper chamber, the Vidhan Parishad. The executive power of each state is vested in a Governor appointed by the

President of India. Elections to both the Lok Sabha and the Vidhan Sabhas are conducted on the basis of universal adult suffrage under the simple-majority, single-ballot voting method. Electoral constituencies are single-member (although between 1951 and 1961 a proportion were either double-member or triple-member to provide reserved seats for special groups) and Vidhan Sabha (or assembly) seats are usually geographical sub-divisions of the Lok Sabha (or parliamentary) seats.[1]

For a number of years, the Indian National Congress won large electoral majorities and was able to maintain sufficient discipline over its groups in the central Parliament and the state legislatures to form secure Governments. Under the leadership of Jawaharlal Nehru, who was Prime Minister from 1947 until his death in 1964, the Congress Party appeared to have established an unassailable position at the heart of the party system. However it lost some ground in the fourth general elections of 1967 when, although it retained control of the Lok Sabha, it failed to secure an absolute majority of the seats in eight of the sixteen states. In 1969, a worsening of the conflict between Nehru's daughter, Indira Gandhi, who had become Prime Minister in 1966, and a group of established Congress leaders led to a division of the party into two units. Mrs Gandhi took her section of the Congress to a convincing victory in the Lok Sabha elections of 1971 and in the subsequent state elections of 1972, but an agitational movement launched by some of the opposition parties and an adverse court decision on an electoral matter persuaded her to impose a state of emergency on the country in June 1975. When this came to an end early in 1977, the main opposition groups combined to form a Janata Party which won power through elections at the centre and in a number of states. The disintegration of Janata in 1979 led eventually to the dissolution of the Lok Sabha and, when elections were held in January 1980, Indira Gandhi's Congress Party (now known as Congress I, for Indira) was able to form a new Government. Mrs Gandhi's assassination on 31 October 1984 shocked the whole country, and the leadership of the party was assumed by her son, Rajiv Gandhi. He also succeeded his mother as Prime Minister and led Congress to victory in the Lok Sabha elections of December 1984.

This second period of Congress ascendancy was brought to an

end in November 1989, when the party was defeated at the polls and a non-Congress ministry formed under the leadership of Vishwanath Pratap Singh, of the Janata Dal. Resignations from his parliamentary majority later forced him to resign, and he was succeeded by the leader of another section of the Janata Dal, Chandra Shekhar, who had been promised the support of Congress I. When this support was withdrawn, Chandra Shekhar resigned as Prime Minister on 6 March 1991. The President then dissolved the Lok Sabha, but before the elections for the new house could be completed, Rajiv Gandhi was assassinated on 21 May 1991. When the elections were finally completed in June 1991, Congress I found itself with sufficient seats in the new Lok Sabha to take power under the Prime Ministership of one of its veteran leaders, P. V. Narasimha Rao. It is interesting to note that some members of the Congress had become so accustomed to leadership by members of the Nehru family that they made a great effort to persuade Rajiv Gandhi's widow, Sonia, who is an Italian by birth, to take over the party leadership in his stead.

The above narrative highlights the way that the Congress Party, which had such an ascendancy over its rivals in the 1950s, has found it increasingly difficult to hold its own within the Indian party system. Its first period of central rule from New Delhi came to an end in 1977, when it lost the federal elections held in the wake of a two-year period of emergency; the second lasted from 1980 until another electoral defeat in 1989; and the third began in 1991. By that stage, Congress had become heavily centralized and oligarchic and its membership at the local level had not been called upon to participate in the choice of delegates since the holding of organizational elections in 1972. Although in the early 1990s Congress can still attract considerable support, as it did in the Lok Sabha elections of 1991, it lacks a firm social base in Indian society, having relied too heavily on the rallies built up around the personality of its leaders and the inability of the other parties to form stable governing coalitions. There are elements of tragedy in this history. Why has a party which embodied so much of the idealism of the nationalist movement lost so much of its vitality? Part of the explanation lies in the fact that the non-Congress parties have grown in stature and effectiveness since the late 1970s. Nevertheless, attempts to answer these questions always take the analyst back to the division of the party in 1969, when Mrs Gandhi finally broke with the Congress leaders of her father's generation. For all their failings, they had respected the regional sources of the party's strength and had tried to establish a collective style of leadership. Mrs Gandhi, on the other hand, was wary of regional chieftains and adopted a highly personal style of leadership, relying for advice on a small group of advisers. There is no denying the importance of this break, but there are also grounds for arguing that the weakening of the party's state units had begun much earlier during the golden days of Nehru's premiership. To explore the problem, we must examine the history of the Congress unit in India's largest state, Uttar Pradesh (UP), with special reference to the patterns and sources of its internal conflicts.

II

UP is situated in northern India at the upper reaches of the Ganges valley. From 63 million in 1951, the population of the state had grown to 111 million at the time of the 1981 census. Its level of urbanization is low by Indian standards: according to the census only 17.95 per cent of its population were city or town dwellers in 1981, compared with the All-India figure of 23.31 per cent. The UP economy is heavily dependent on agriculture and, within this sector, on food crops such as wheat, millet, rice and pulses, with sugarcane as the main commercial crop. Peasant farming is the norm; the 1981 census found that 58.02 per cent of the workers in the state were cultivators, 16.32 per cent were agricultural labourers, 4.39 per cent were employed in household industry, and the remaining 21.27 per cent in other occupations. There are considerable regional contrasts within this huge state, which consisted of fifty-one administrative districts until 1960, when the total was increased to fifty-four.

Politically, the UP appeared to be one of the most reliable of the Congress Party's strongholds in the post-independence period. In the assembly elections of 1952, Congress candidates won 47.93 per cent of the votes and 390 of the 430 seats in the state's Vidhan Sabha. However, at that stage the party's social base was still undefined and it was by no means clear what interests would find expression in the Congress Legislature Party

(CLP), the state unit of the party's organizational structure. A great deal depended on how the society would develop in the years ahead and what sections of the population would form associations to advance their interests.

The state's peasantry was cut through by a number of economic and social divisions, any of which could have formed the basis for political conflict. The issue of land tenure was one of the main sources of tension in the years immediately following independence. Under British rule, agrarian society in UP (which was then known as the United Provinces) had been dominated by an upper stratum of landlords, the *zamindars*, who, while letting out most of their holdings to tenants and acting as intermediaries in the collection of land revenue for the state, were entitled to keep some of the proceeds for themselves. The Congress Government which took office in UP after the 1946 general elections was determined to break the social and political power of the *zamindars* and to give their tenants the ownership of the holdings for which they were paying rent. On the basis of a far-reaching enquiry, it secured the approval of the provincial legislature for the Zamindari Abolition and Land Reforms Act of 1950, which abolished tenancy and ended the *zamindars'* rights over land revenue collection. Most of the former landlords became *bhumidhars*, having retained their home farms and the land which they had cultivated themselves, and most of their former tenants became *sirdars*. (A *sirdar* was expected to pay a higher level of land revenue to the state than the *bhumidhar* and was not entitled either to transfer his interest or to use his land for non-agricultural purposes.) Thus, although the reform converted large numbers of tenant cultivators into peasant proprietors and ended landlordism, it created a new legal distinction between landholders and left unsolved the problem of the land requirements of the many agricultural labourers and poor peasants who still formed the base of the agricultural pyramid.[2] It was conceivable that the different strata of landholders might become sectional groups under certain circumstances, for example if the *sirdars* sought easier access to *bhumidhari* status or called for reductions or remissions in the payment of land revenue.

In agrarian society in UP at this time there were three other potential lines of horizontal division. Firstly, it was possible that broad caste strata might form throughout certain regions of the

state. There were marked social and ritual differences between
the upper castes such as the Brahmans and Rajputs, and the
middle castes such as the Ahirs, Kurmis and Yadavas, strongly
represented amongst the mass of peasant cultivators; equally
marked was the distinction between these two strata as a whole
(composed as they were of ritually 'clean' castes) and the lower
castes, who enclosed most of the agricultural labourers and had
in the past been treated as ritually impure, or 'untouchable'.[3]
Secondly, it was conceivable that, under certain circumstances,
perhaps as a result of the impoverishment of marginal producers
arising from an unregulated land market, or because of intense
competition between different groups of the peasantry, a fusion
of caste, legal and economic categories could lead to a tripartite
class division between rich peasants, middle peasants and agricultural labourers. Thirdly, although most agricultural regions
in the state were multi-crop in character, producing a variety of
fine grains for the urban market, some cash crops, and coarse
grain for the regional markets, the spread of commercial practices in agriculture was increasing the extent of crop specialization and, consequently, the sensitivity of producers to policies
affecting price levels, storage and transport facilities, and marketing institutions; from there it could have been but a short
step to the emergence of specialized associations representing the
interests of particular sectors of the agrarian economy.

In other words, rural society in UP in the early 1950s could
be considered to be, to use Landé's terminology, a bewildering
kaleidoscope of trait groups, some of which were expressing a
land interest, some a caste interest, some a class interest, and
some a sectional interest. Were these trait groups to consolidate
and define their particular objectives, it was by no means clear
how the different parties would react to them. Would the Congress try to base itself on selected groups such as the broad
middle strata (whether conceived in legal, caste or class terms),
or would it try to remain detached from social competition,
maintaining a generalized and diffuse relationship with the social
changes which were in train? Its response would be of particular
importance.

Religious differences constituted another potential source of
political division. In the closing stages of British rule there had
been a good deal of tension between the Muslim and Hindu

communities of UP, and the Muslim League had claimed to
represent the interests of the Muslim minority against Congress
(and indirectly Hindu) domination. Although some UP Muslims
had moved to the territory which was to become West Pakistan
at the time of the partition of India in 1947, the great majority
had remained. According to the 1951 census, there were 9 million Muslims in UP at that time, concentrated mainly in the
western and central districts of the state, and constituting 14.3
per cent of its total population. Their attachment to the *shari'at*,
the system of Islamic personal law, and their pride in the Urdu
language and its literature had aroused the hostility of Hindu
nationalists in such parties as the Hindu Mahasabha (the Hindu Congress) and the newly formed Bharatiya Jana Sangh
(Indian People's Party).[4] Although at the national level Nehru
was advocating the need for social and religious pluralism in the
new India, the UP Congress had decided that Hindi should
be the state's official language and that Urdu should not even be
afforded the status of a second or minority language.

Besides the bewildering range of interests with which the UP
Congress was faced within its own territory, it had also to take
account of policy decisions made at the national level of government. Under the Constitution of India, legislation affecting industry was under the control of the central Parliament, while
agricultural policy was controlled by the state legislatures. The
central Government was concerned to co-ordinate the planning
of the national economy through such institutions as the Planning Commission, established in March 1950, and the National
Development Council, formed in 1952, which included among its
members the Prime Minister, all the Chief Ministers of the
states, and the members of the Planning Commission. These
bodies played a leading role in the framing of the First and
Second Five Year Plans, covering the periods 1951–6 and 1956–
61 respectively, and were at the centre of debates about whether
the Indian economy should be organized on liberal lines, with a
strong private sector, or on social democratic lines, with the
balance in favour of the public sector. The merits of these rival
approaches were discussed mainly at the national level but the
debate took place at the state level also. There was still talk in
New Delhi of the need for collective farming and for the state
control of produce marketing and rural credit, and any concrete

proposals for policies directed towards such goals were bound to produce divisions of opinion amongst the UP peasantry and within the ranks of the UP Congress Party itself.

A sequence of Congress Governments held power in Lucknow, the state capital of UP, from 1946 until April 1967, having won solid majorities in the elections of 1952, 1957 and 1962, and a comfortable plurality in that of February 1967. In the section which follows we shall see that, in spite of this, the institutions of the UP Congress Party itself were often in turmoil during this period because of intense and prolonged group conflicts, and we shall examine how and to what extent these conflicts were affected by the sectional and sectarian issues mentioned above.

III

A convenient starting point for our enquiry[5] is a conflict which occurred in 1948 shortly after India became independent, when the country was still governed according to the provisions of the Government of India Act of 1935, with a central Government in New Delhi and provincial rather than state Governments at the regional level. The leading figure of the UP Congress in 1947 was Govind Ballabh Pant, a lawyer who had played an important role in the national affairs of the party in the inter-war period and had been Premier of the province between 1937 and 1939 and again from April 1946 onwards. He had relied heavily on his Revenue Minister, Rafi Ahmed Kidwai, to manage the party's internal organization, but when Kidwai was called to New Delhi to join the central Cabinet, that responsibility fell to Chandra Bhanu Gupta, who became the Minister for Food and Civil Supplies in September 1947. Kidwai remained in close touch with the network of his supporters within the UP Congress, however; known as 'the Rafians', they formed a rival force to Gupta's own group of followers. The two men came from quite different backgrounds. Kidwai, a Muslim, had been active as a student in the non-co-operation movement in the early 1920s, had become secretary to Nehru's father, Motilal, and a close personal friend of Nehru. Closely identified with the Congress Party in UP at a time when many Muslims were allying themselves with the Muslim League, he was renowned for his ability as an organizer and was elected in 1946 to the Constituent Assembly of India. Gupta, a Hindu, belonged to the Bania (or merchant) caste, and after studying law at Lucknow University he had made Lucknow his political base. Unlike Kidwai, who had made his mark at the national level, Gupta had devoted himself almost exclusively to provincial Congress affairs.

The relative power of Kidwai and Gupta within the party was affected to some extent by a number of sectarian conflicts which flared up from time to time within the Congress Legislature Party (CLP) and the Provincial Congress Committee (PCC). These conflicts had not led to the formation of particular groups but they had created overlapping fields of opinion amongst the party's members and thus formed a diffuse doctrinal context for group competition within the party. First of these was the tension between Hindus and Muslims which existed in the province. Some of the leaders of the UP Congress were in favour of making Hindi the official language and denying Urdu even a subordinate status. They were also concerned to preserve Hindu conventions and practices and though they did not go to the length of proposing that India should be a Hindu state, their resistance to Muslim pleas for an assured place for Urdu speakers in the administration, the law courts and the schools placed them at odds with Muslim opinion in the province. They were opposed within the party by those liberals, Kidwai included, who agreed with Nehru that India should be a plural society in which the state was not identified with any particular religious or cultural tradition and who, in the name of secularism, championed the cause of Urdu and the right of Muslims to preserve the *Shari'at*.

This line of conflict cut across another division amongst Congressmen, a division between those who placed a particular interpretation on Gandhi's doctrines and those who disagreed with that interpretation. Gandhi, who had been assassinated on 30 January 1948, had won the affection and admiration of everyone in the party, but there were those who were less than happy about some of his ideas. The strict Gandhians were pressing at this time for an essentially rural, village-based programme of economic and social development, for the conversion of Congress into an organization devoted to social service rather than to routine politics, and for maintaining Gandhi's creed of nonviolence as the means of promoting change. There were, of course, no 'anti-Gandhians' in the party, but many felt that Congress should maintain its established organization and its role as a party of government; moreover, many Congressmen considered that India's future depended on her pursuing industrial rather than agricultural development.

A third line of division within the Congress in UP, as in the national party as a whole, was that between the Socialists and the liberals. Many young Congressmen had been drawn into the Congress Socialist Party (CSP) after it was formed in 1934 as a defined sub-group within the national organization; strongly influenced by Marxist ideas, the Congress Socialists favoured land reforms and the 'socialization' of basic industries and public utilities.[6] The Socialists constituted a strong network within the UP Congress and many were committed to the view that, now its anti-imperialist mission had been completed, Congress should develop a programme of economic and social reforms. Their opponents, the liberals, lacked organization with the result that their resistance to the 'progressive' ideas of the Socialists largely took the form of isolated and low-key objections to specific proposals on the grounds that these were impractical or divisive, or that they would be too costly. However, the CSP was to face a major set-back at the beginning of 1948. Although before independence the Indian National Congress had tolerated a diversity of views within its ranks, it was now confonted with the task of converting itself from a broad and inclusive nationalist association into a disciplined and unified party of government. Towards this end, the All-India Congress Committee adopted, in February 1948, the basic framework of a new party constitution, which included the provision that no member of any elective committee in the party could be a member of another political party 'which has a separate membership, constitution and programme'.[7] As the most organized of all the party's sub-groups, the CSP was directly affected by this ruling; it meant in effect that the Socialists had either to disband the CSP or to resign from it if they wished to hold any office within the Congress. In the event, the sixth Socialist conference at Nasik in March 1948 called upon members of the group to leave the Congress,[8] and in UP, the main Socialist leader, Acharya Narendra Dev, resigned both his membership of the Congress and his seat in the Provincial Legislative Assembly.[9] His example was followed by other

Socialists, including Damodar Swarup Seth, the President of the PCC.[10] The departure of the Socialists produced a number of vacancies in the membership of the Legislative Assembly and the PCC, and the by-elections to fill these places, along with the parallel elections to the District Boards of the province, became something of a plebiscite on whether the Socialists were justified in offering themselves as a progressive alternative to the Congress. Considerable moral pressure was put on secularists and Gandhians to follow Narendra Dev in his revolt, and many who resisted this pressure justified their choice as being one of means rather than of ends. For example, Sampurnanand, the Minister of Education and Labour in the provincial Government and one of the founders of the CSP, tried to argue that the departure was premature:

> We . . . know that dark forces are at work within [the Congress], they may now make an attempt to curb, if not suppress, the expression of any but a prescribed set of opinions. Central and provincial Governments may be forced to adopt policies and programmes which no Socialist can honestly support and the sphere of provincial autonomy may be seriously encroached upon, better to serve the ends of authoritarianism. The danger of all this happening is real. Let us hope that it will not materialise but, if it does, then it will be time for some of us to go out of the Congress in defence of those very principles for which the Congress has stood all these years.[11]

Kidwai's reaction was more direct: in an obvious attempt to rally socialist, secularist and progressive opinion generally against the Gupta group, he came forward to compete with the 'official' candidate, Purushottamdas Tandon, a Hindu traditionalist, in the contest for the vacant post of PCC President. The combined challenges of Narendra Dev and of Kidwai brought the UP Congress close to an open and damaging sectarian conflict, but in the end the party's state leaders were able to win the decisive electoral contests and to demonstrate their control over the organization. Congress had no difficulty in carrying the day in the poll for the District Boards; its candidates were returned in all but one of the fifteen by-elections to the Legislative Assembly,[12] and it successfully managed the plenary meeting of the

PCC in Lucknow on 4 and 5 July, when Kidwai agreed to withdraw his nomination so that Tandon could be elected to the organizational presidency without opposition.[13]

The sectarian overtones which had coloured this conflict were surprisingly absent from the party's next major internal crisis, which occurred in the period between 1957 and 1960.[14] Immediately before this, at the end of 1956, the informal structure of the party still remained as it had been during the earlier crisis of 1948. Pant had been reappointed as Chief Minister after the party's victory in the 1952 Vidhan Sabha elections but had resigned office in December 1954 in order to join the central Government in New Delhi. Sampurnanand had then been appointed as Chief Minister in his stead. Like Pant before him, Sampurnanand had continued to rely for the management of the party on Gupta, who held the important post of Minister for Planning, Health, Industries and Civil Supplies, rather than on the PCC President, who was then Munishwar Datt Upadhyaya. In spite of the fact that the Hindu traditionalists, with whom Sampurnanand had some sympathy, remained an important force (especially as Kidwai's death in October 1954 had removed the mainstay of their secularist opponents), and although some Socialists remained in the party despite the existence of the Praja Socialist Party (PSP) and the Socialist Party, the party appeared to be stable and unified under the control of Sampurnand and Gupta.

The first signs of a break in this pattern appeared in the weeks following the second general elections, held in March 1957. Although the UP Congress was returned to power with a secure majority in the Vidhan Sabha, Gupta suffered the humiliation of being defeated in his own constituency. A leader of his stature could have been given a place in the upper house, the Vidhan Parishad, in order to qualify him for inclusion in the new Council of Ministers, or he could have expected to return to the assembly in a by-election, but the Central Parliamentary Board at national level, taking a hard line on ministers who had been defeated at the polls, ruled out both such options. Sampurnanand was therefore prevented from providing Gupta with a place in the Council of Ministers, and although Gupta remained the Treasurer of the PCC, he was now in a weak position. By December 1957, three important members of the new Council of

Ministers – Charan Singh, the Minister of Revenue, Kamalapati Tripathi, the Minister for Home, Education and Information, and Mohanlal Gautam, the Minister for Co-operation and Forests – had combined their personal followings to form an alliance against him. Together they sponsored a list of nominees for the offices and executive places of the PCC and for the places on the State Parliamentary Board, the body responsible for the selection of election candidates and the regulation of the affairs of the CLP. Gupta promptly prepared an alternative list of nominees, challenging his rivals to a trial of strength at the plenary meeting of the PCC, which was authorized to make the appointments. A confrontation was avoided by the transference of the right of appointment from this plenum to Pant (still a central minister) and Sampurnanand, who were to act as arbiters. When they announced their decisions on 7 March 1958, Gupta found that his power within the organization had been further weakened: Tripathi was to replace him as party Treasurer, the number of his followers on the executive had been reduced, and an independent figure, Chaturbhuj Sharma, had become the PCC President.

Up to this point, conflicts between the party's internal groups had been fought out within a set of restrictive informal rules, but Gupta now began to organize his group openly and to break these rules with impunity. One of his lieutenants proposed to the PCC plenum which met on 18 and 19 October 1958 that exceptional elections should be held to replace the PCC Executive Committee and the Parliamentary Board appointments which had been made by Pant and Sampurnanand, and when the latter decided to make the matter one of confidence, insisting that all his ministers support him in his stand, nine pro-Gupta members of the Council of Ministers refused to do so. Having made his point, Gupta withdrew the group's proposal but in November 1958 the nine ministers who had supported him resigned from the Government in a further challenge to the authority of the Chief Minister. In the following year, a minority of pro-Gupta members of the CLP began to harass the ministry in the Vidhan Sabha; and in August 1959, during a censure debate in the house, ninety-eight Congress members, while not supporting the opposition motion, put their names to a statement expressing a lack of confidence in their own ministry.

The Gupta group was now concentrating its energies on

winning a majority on the PCC plenum, which consisted of over 600 delegates elected from single-member constituencies and a number of *ex officio* members, including the presidents of the sixty-seven District and City Congress Committees (DCCs and CCCs) in the state. The first meeting of the plenum, at which new members were to be appointed to the executive bodies, was eventually arranged for 4 October 1960 and was generally ex-pected to be a trial of strength between the rival groups. When the elections were held, Gupta was elected as PCC President by 363 votes to his rival's 300; Charan Singh (who had switched from the ministerialist side to Gupta's following his resignation from the Government in April 1959) was chosen as Treasurer; all four of the vice-presidencies were won by Gupta's lieutenants; and his group took thirteen of the twenty-one places on the executive. Gupta was then called to Delhi by the Prime Minister, who asked him to take over from Sampurnanand as Chief Min-ister; he was elected as leader of the CLP on 1 December 1960, and took office at the head of the Council of Ministers on 7 December. All that remained of the bloc which had opposed him was a fragile alignment of the Tripathi and Gautam groups. However they had sufficient influence in New Delhi to be able to secure a reasonable share of the party's nominations for the third general elections of March 1962 and to obtain some im-portant portfolios in the Cabinet which Gupta formed after this poll, which was won by Congress.

A surprising feature of this protracted struggle was its almost complete lack of sectarian content. The normative factors which had affected the 1948 crisis were still present but they were largely ignored by the two sides in the dispute: Sampurnanand claimed merely to be defending the authority of the Chief Min-istership just as Gupta declared that he was upholding that of the PCC Presidency. Nor did the rival groups take up opposed positions over the major sectional debates of this period. Charan Singh, for example, was strongly opposed to Nehru's proposals for joint co-operative farming, but he did not raise this question in the arena of the organizational elections. Both sides owed their coherence to patronage, but whereas the ministerialists had been able to strengthen their support through their control of key ministries, Gupta's followers had only the prospect of future benefits to be enjoyed if and when their group took power.

Gupta's victory did not restore to the UP Congress the degree of unity which it had enjoyed in 1956, when the Chief Minister had been the undisputed leader of the party by virtue of good management and secure majorities on both the CLP and the PCC plenum. In his long march back to power, Gupta had built up an extensive system of alliances between his own state-level 'machine' and various groups which had gained control of the Congress organization at district and city level. Had Uttar Pradesh been a unitary state rather than a segment within a federal state, he would have been in an excellent position to gather support for his administration by responding selectively to demands for basic services. Elements of clientelism were already a feature of Congress rule and had they been developed, could eventually have produced systems of patronage extending from Lucknow through the districts and cities right down to the local level, systems very like those which had existed in many American states in the nineteenth century. Like his American counterparts of that period, Gupta knew his state well, was more interested in local than in national politics, and was wary of doctrinal issues which he could not resolve with the resources at his disposal. By New Delhi standards, however, he was considered to be a provincial and unprogressive politician, interested in power for its own sake, and this attitude helps to explain why the Congress High Command went to great lengths to support the man who had succeeded Sampurnanand as Gupta's main rival within the UP Congress, Kamalapati Tripathi.

An opportunity to remove Gupta and place Tripathi at the head of the state Congress appeared to have come in 1963 when the Congress Working Committee adopted the scheme known as the Kamaraj Plan. As we have seen,[15] this was the scheme for releasing a certain number of central ministers and chief ministers from office so that they could devote themselves entirely to work for the party. Gupta was one of those whom Nehru ruled should resign and the High Command clearly expected that his place as Chief Minister would be taken by Tripathi. Instead, Gupta and his group were strong enough to secure the election of Gupta's protégé, Mrs Sucheta Kripalani, who defeated Tripathi in the ballot for the leadership of the CLP on 21 September 1963. Mrs Kripalani's Council of Ministers was strongly weighted towards the Gupta group and in the organizational elections of the following year, Gupta narrowly defeated Tripathi in the ballot for PCC President. However, an appeal to the national Congress President led to a recount of the votes and to a reversal of the result in Tripathi's favour. Thus, by successive interventions, the Congress High Command had prevented Gupta from establishing his pre-eminence in the party in UP and had virtually created a balance of power between the two groups which was both stultifying and destructive.[16]

Time had now run out for the UP Congress Party. Although it emerged from the elections of February 1967 as the largest unit in the Vidhan Sabha, enabling Gupta to form yet another Government, the defection of Charan Singh and his supporters from the party led to the installation of a non-Congress Government, with Charan Singh as Chief Minister, in April 1967. A long period in opposition helped to mend the differences between the rival Congress groups and, after the Charan Singh ministry had fallen and a period of direct rule from New Delhi had intervened, the party won the mid-term elections of February 1969. Gupta once more took power as Chief Minister and appointed Tripathi as one of his ministers. This settlement was destroyed by the split which spread throughout the national Congress Party in the closing months of 1969. On 20 November, Tripathi and seven of his colleagues resigned from the UP Government (an eighth did so the following day) and the party subsequently divided into two practically identical units, each with its own CLP and its own PCC organization. Tripathi's group became the state unit of Indira Gandhi's Congress and Gupta's the local unit of the rival Congress, whose leaders were known as 'the Syndicate'. The *National Herald*, the Lucknow newspaper which had been founded by Nehru and which now supported Indira Gandhi, gave the following version of events:

> Mr. Gupta, with his Bonapartist baton and Little Napoleon demeanour, has proclaimed that the Syndicate is the Congress and he is the Congress in U.P. This is both Bourbonism and Bonapartism, for the Syndicate stands for all that is bad in the Congress, and as a part of the Syndicate, he has added to the political and economic consequence of his long regime of casteism and power politics a last chapter of factionalism and power lust.[17]

This was a caricature of Gupta, but it does reveal the kind of attitude which had prompted the central Congress leaders to restrict and humiliate a man whose political and administrative abilities could well have served to make the UP Congress a stable and robust party with fair prospects for developing the economy of the state.

IV

Why did this protracted period of group conflict do so little to create connections between the UP Congress and the society on which it was based? Part of the explanation, as we have seen, lies in the fact that the central Congress leadership in New Delhi continually tried to manipulate events in Lucknow without having the means to impose their will completely. The attempt by Pant and Sampurnanand to exclude Gupta from he PCC in 1958 was ultimately frustrated; although Nehru agreed that Gupta should replace Sampurnanand as Chief Minister in December 1960, he refused to give him a free hand and eventually removed him from office by means of the Kamaraj Plan in 1963; even so, New Delhi was unable to control the succession and Mrs Kripalani rather than Tripathi took over from Gupta as Chief Minister. All that the High Command had achieved through acts of arbitration and by supporting Tripathi had been to create sufficient opposition to Gupta to ensure that the party in UP would be debilitated by a wasteful and inconclusive series of confrontations. This, though, is not the whole explanation, for the conflict might have taken a different form had either one or both of the groups drawn strength and power from the underlying society. One reason that the UP Congress was so little affected by the sectarian and sectional pressures in its own environment lay in the fact that the Congress Party's style of electioneering militated against stable patterns of representation either of interests or of constituencies. With substantial financial resources at its disposal, the party was able to provide its candidates with more workers, better transport and more publicity material than rival parties were able to muster. However, instead of defining certain constituencies as safe, others as marginal and others still as unlikely to be won, Congress blanketed the whole state with candidates and resources, assuming that the pattern of gains and losses would work to its advantage. It knew that even if a high proportion of its sitting members were defeated, it could still expect to gain a substantial number of seats from other parties and maintain its position.[18] Enmeshed in such a mechanical system, Congress candidates tended to rely heavily on the Congress organization itself and on powerful patrons within that organization rather than on the structured support they might have obtained from particular social groups. Insecure, they looked to the party's power-brokers to provide them with packages of votes instead of mobilising support themselves, and the end result was a legislature group which lacked systematic links with definable electoral regions and social constituencies.

In the same way, the UP PCC was isolated from the people it was supposed to represent because, although the Congress Party's constitution contained many democratic elements, it conspicuously lacked provision for a stable system of branches capable of sustaining an informed and active local membership. Instead, the party recruited a nominal and unorganized membership whose numbers fluctuated wildly under the tidal pulls of the party's internal elections and its preparation for general election campaigns. Under revised rules which came into effect in 1951, all that a person aged eighteen years or over had to do to become a primary member of Congress was to sign a form accepting the party's general statement of objectives and pay a small fee; to become an active member, a primary member had to be over twenty-one years of age and give proofs of commitment to the party; and primary members of two years' standing were eligible to vote in the election of delegates to the PCC plenum in their state.[19] An individual PCC was entitled to frame its own constitution and, as we have seen, the UP unit had provided that its President, Vice-Presidents, Treasurer and members of its Executive Committee should be elected by the PCC plenum. With such important posts at stake, the biennial election of delegates was preceded by an unseemly competition between party notables to enrol as many primary members as possible throughout the state, which was divided for this poll into single-member constituencies, each of about 100,000 people. As only active members could be delegates, they too were recruited in large numbers before these elections. In addition, both primary and active members were recruited to augment the pool of party workers who helped during the general election campaigns.

Reliable figures for the 1950s are difficult to obtain, but it is instructive to compare the enrolments for the UP Congress organizational elections of 1952 – 1,716,426 primary and 4,369 active members[20] – with those reported for the contest of 1959–60 between the Gupta group and the ministerialists – 2,432,000 primary and 24,413 active members.[21] The corresponding figures for the 1960s are set out in table 1.

Table 1 Indian National Congress: membership figures of Uttar Pradesh unit, 1961–1966

Year:	Category of member:	
	Primary	Active
1961[1]	1,700,925	19,111
1962	131,488	4,100
1963	144,005	5,972
1964[2]	1,174,326	11,666
1965[3]	5,476,708	106,474
1966[4]	1,350,113	26,776

Notes:
[1] Year preceding the general elections of 1962.
[2] The organizational elections of 1964 were held on the basis of a revised version of the 1961 membership roll.
[3] A fresh membership roll was prepared for further organizational elections but these were postponed following the outbreak of war with Pakistan.
[4] Year preceding the general elections of 1967.
Sources: All India Congress Committee, *Report of the General Secretaries* (New Delhi), for 1962–3, p. 70; for 1964, p. 68; for 1965–6, p. 90; for 1966–8, pp. 86–7.

Local groups of committed activists would have been completely swamped in such an open recruitment process and it was quite impossible for an adequate system of representation to develop when delegates were elected under these conditions. In any case, it was unusual for PCC plenums to discuss policy matters; delegates were usually assembled to take part in the election of PCC officers and executive bodies and were then sent back to their homes.

When two such important channels for interest representation were so constricted, both the CLP and the PCC remained in a closed universe unless the state was shaken by a major crisis such as the food shortages of 1958 or the protest against the Government's attempt to increase land revenue rates in 1962. This is not to say that either the members of the CLP or the delegates to the PCC lacked opinions of their own; however, they had not been elected because they represented particular values or policies except in the very general sense that they were members of the Congress, and they had nothing either to gain or to lose by trying to invest the group conflict with sectarian or sectional overtones.

It is possible that pressure groups representing social segments could have pushed the conflict in UP in a sectional direction but at this time there were none in a position to do so. The All-India Kisan [Peasant] Congress, formed in 1936 and renamed as the All-India Kisan Sabha in 1937, had had some support in UP but by the post-war period it had come under Communist control and was no longer a factor in Congress politics.[22] Although Congress itself had not sponsored a peasants' union or an agricultural labourers' union, it had established its own association for urban workers, the Indian National Trade Union Congress (INTUC), which was in a position to influence party policy in states with large concentrations of industry. However, in UP the only major industrial city was Kanpur. INTUC certainly had a presence there, but it was not strongly placed to exert subtantial or direct pressure on the UP Congress.

Clientelism remained the essential binding force for groups within the party and until 1956 the line of development within the Congress in UP had been towards a unified system of patronage at the disposal of the leadership. However, that leadership was by no means a closed and tightly controlled oligarchy and there were several courses of action open to those individuals who wished to strengthen their own position. They could exploit the patronage resources of key ministries such as Industries, Civil Supplies, Co-operation, Public Works and Irrigation to establish their own following; they could maintain connections with important figures in the High Command in New Delhi; and they could keep in touch with the local power brokers in their home cities and districts. The attempt to remove Gupta from the reckoning in 1957 and 1958 was in one sense an offensive by an alliance of minor oligarchs, including Tripathi, Charan Singh and Mohanlal Gautam, against the unified system of patronage and control. In April 1958, immediately after Gupta had failed to win the assembly by-election which was intended to restore him to the state legislature and to power, that offensive appeared to have succeeded but, as one observer implied, the nature of the Congress Party itself had not been changed.

> What will be the political consequences of Mr Gupta's defeat? One need not be an astrologer to predict that Mr Gupta's group, now rudderless, will drift for a while. Groups or factions in the Congress camp here have no ideological roots. A faction is like a cluster of bees round a queen bee. If the queen is damaged they quickly find another to cluster round.
>
> It might be laid down as a law that groups are held together by the cementing force of 'power' and he is the most successful leader of them all who can share the fruits of office with the largest number of party men. A group disperses when circumstances dislodge a leader.
>
> According to Congress dialectics, when a group fades away, it does not necessarily follow that groupism decays. It is in the nature of a group to find a new leader. One may emerge from among its members or they may join the existing rival groups. It works out quite smoothly in the end.[23]

The strength of Gupta's subsequent counter-offensive was in fact almost overwhelming, but it is important to recognize that the organizational principle for which he was fighting was that the Congress machine should be unitary and that the principle of a pluralistic oligarchy should be rejected. He could probably have established such a machine in the early 1960s but for the steps taken by the High Command in New Delhi to sustain the group which opposed him. In consequence, the party's energies were absorbed in a bitter and continuous group conflict until it lost power in April 1967. The final division of the Congress into separate parties in November 1969 was the last act in this ruinous civil war.

Notes

1   For the general political background to India in the period covered by this case study, see W. H. Morris-Jones, *The Government and*

Politics of India (Hutchinson, London, Third Edition, 1971). For a more recent survey, see Paul R. Brass, *The politics of India since Independence* (*The New Cambridge History of India*, vol. IV.1) (Cambridge University Press, Cambridge, 1990).

2　On the abolition of the Zamindari system, see Peter Reeves, *Landlords and Governments in Uttar Pradesh: A Study of Their Relations until Zamindari Abolition* (Oxford University Press, Bombay, 1991), pp. 264–317. See also Walter C. Neale, *Economic Change in Rural India: Land Tenure and Reform in Uttar Pradesh 1800–1955* (Yale University Press, New Haven, 1962), especially pp. 211–58.

3　On castes in Uttar Pradesh, see Paul R. Brass, *Factional Politics in an Indian State: The Congress Party in Uttar Pradesh* (University of California Press, Berkeley, 1965), pp. 16–18; Angela Sutherland Burger, *Opposition in a Dominant-Party System: A Study of the Jan Sangh, the Praja Socialist Party, and the Socialist Party in Uttar Pradesh, India* (University of California Press, Berkeley, 1969), pp. 24–9.

4　On the interests of Muslims in Uttar Pradesh, see Paul R. Brass, *Language, Religion and Politics in North India* (Cambridge University Press, Cambridge, 1974), pp. 119–274.

5　On the internal politics of the Uttar Pradesh Congress Party in the 1950s and 1960s, see Brass, *Factional Politics in an Indian State*, pp. 33–61; B. D. Graham, 'The Succession of Factional Systems in the Uttar Pradesh Congress Party, 1937–66', in Marc J. Swartz (ed.), *Local-Level Politics: Social and Cultural Perspectives* (Aldine, Chicago, 1968), pp. 323–60; K. P. Misra, 'Factionalism in U.P. Congress', in Iqbal Narain (ed.), *State Politics in India* (Meenakshi Prakashan, Meerut, 1967), pp. 511–34. On the question of ministerial instability, see Subrata Kumar Mitra, *Governmental Instability in Indian States: West Bengal, Bihar, Uttar Pradesh and Punjab* (Ajanta, Delhi, 1978).

6　See Hari Kishore Singh, *A History of The Praja Socialist Party* [1934–59] (Narendra Prakashan, Lucknow, 1959), pp. 26–51.

7　*Congress Bulletin* (Allahabad), No. 7 (15 March 1948), p. 17.

8　See Socialist Party, *Report of the Sixth Annual Conference held at Kotwalnagar, Nasik, March 19th to March 21st, 1948* (Socialist Party, Bombay, 1948), pp. 39–40.

9　*National Herald* (Lucknow), 29 March 1948, p. 1.

10　Ibid., 2 April 1948, p. 1.

11　Ibid., 31 March 1948, p. 3.

12　P. D. Reeves et al., *A Handbook to Elections in Uttar Pradesh 1920–1951* (Manohar, Delhi, 1975), pp. 363 and 368–72.

13 *National Herald*, 6 July 1948, p. 1.
14 See Graham, 'The Succession of Factional Systems', pp. 331–44; Brass, *Factional Politics*, pp. 43–50; Misra, 'Factionalism in U.P. Congress', pp. 517–31.
15 See above, pp. 106–7.
16 On this period of conflict, see Graham, 'The Succession of Factional Systems', pp. 344–56; Brass, *Factional Politics*, pp. 51–4; Misra, 'Factionalism in U.P. Congress', pp. 513–4.
17 Editorial, 'Gupta Must Go', *National Herald*, 21 November 1969, p. 5.
18 See B. D. Graham, 'The Candidate-selection Policies of the Indian National Congress, 1952–69', *The Journal of Commonwealth and Comparative Politics*, XXIV, 2 (July 1986), pp. 197–218.
19 For the Congress constitutions of the 1950s, see M. V. Ramana Rao, *Development of the Congress Constitution* (All India Congress Committee, New Delhi, 1958), pp. 104–22 (January 1951), 126–43 (September 1952), 168–89 (January 1957) and 208–28 (September 1957). See also Stanley A. Kochanek, *The Congress Party of India: The Dynamics of One-Party Democracy* (Princeton University Press, Princeton, NJ, 1968).
20 *Pioneer* (Lucknow), 22 November 1952, p. 1. These figures do not include those enrolled by the Tehri Garhwal District Congress Committee and by the Dehra Dun City Congress Committee.
21 *Hindustan Times* (Delhi), 15 October 1959, p. 1.
22 See Myron Weiner, *The Politics of Scarcity: Public Pressure and Political Response in India* (University of Chicago Press, Chicago, 1962), pp. 132–5.
23 *Statesman* (Delhi), 14 April 1958, p. 7.

11

Sectionalism and Intra-party Conflict

In a liberal democracy there are often large and relatively cohesive social categories which identify themselves with certain broad sectors of the economy, bringing strong sectional pressures to bear upon the party system. Where this occurs, and parties become dependent on the sectional groups associated with them, they are often unable to prevent conflict within these groups from spreading throughout their own membership. In this chapter we shall consider two cases of this kind in the context of the political history of Australia, whose party system was strongly affected by sectional activity in the first half of this century. We shall then turn to consider briefly the importance of agrarian and trade-union sectionalism in American party politics, and the extent to which trade unions have played a part in the affairs of the British Labour Party and of French left-wing parties.

I

In Australia, the system of responsible government, in which ministries are accountable to local legislatures, was instituted in the colonies of New South Wales, Victoria, South Australia, Tasmania and Queensland in the 1850s and in Western Australia in 1890. These colonies became the constituent states of the Commonwealth of Australia when the federal system came into being in 1901 and the present constitutional arrangements assumed their basic form. The Commonwealth Parliament was to consist of a House of Representatives whose members were elected from single-member constituencies, and a Senate containing an equal number of members from each state. The executive power of the Commonwealth was vested in the monarch, who was at that time Queen Victoria, but she was to be represented by a Governor-General, who had the authority to summon and to prorogue the two houses and to dissolve the House of Representatives. There was also provision for a Federal Executive Council to advise the Governor-General, but in practice the ministers constituted a Cabinet, headed by a Prime Minister. Within the Federation, the six states retained their original constitutional forms; their parliaments were bicameral, each containing a lower and an upper house (although Queensland abolished its Legislative Council in 1922); their chief executive officers were known as Governors and their heads of Cabinet as Premiers.

The economies of the Australian colonies in the late nineteenth century depended to a large extent on the export of primary products to the rapidly expanding British and European markets. Exports of wool formed the early basis for a thriving pastoral industry but by 1900 the demand for meat, dairy produce and wheat was steadily increasing and stimulating the use of specialized commercial farming methods by Australian farmers. The development of service industries, public administration, commerce and industry conditioned the expansion of the capital cities of the colonies and the growth of a number of large country towns. The major policy issue affecting this largely urban sector of the economy was whether Australian industry should be given the shelter of tariff protection or whether free trade, so strongly supported by pastoral interests, was more advantageous. Although Victoria had adopted a protectionist tariff as early as 1864, the other colonies tended to favour free trade. With the establishment of the federation, when 'the collection and control of duties of customs and of excise' became the responsibility of the Commonwealth, the centre of the debate between free traders and protectionists shifted to the federal parliament. The first Commonwealth Customs Tariff of 1902 was a relatively mild measure but the second, adopted in 1908, substantially raised the degree of protection afforded to Australian industries.[1] Australian trade unionists at first differed in their attitude towards the tariff issue, despite its obvious links with employment policy, but they were of one mind where industrial relations were concerned. The hardships caused by the depression of the 1890s, and the failure of strike action in that decade, had impressed them with the need for parliamentary action to improve working conditions in factories and to settle industrial disputes by means of a judicial system of conciliation and arbitration.

The early Australian party system was strongly influenced by this sectional pattern. The complicated order of colonial politics, characterized by localism, disputes over land policy and, in the legislatures, by unstable group alliances built around prominent party leaders, gave way in the period 1890–1910 to a regular system of parties. In reaction to the rise of the Labor Party, the various non-Labor groups, including protectionists and free traders, came to accept the need for a unified Liberal Party and by 1910 a two-party system had taken shape.[2] This system was subsequently modified by the formation of the Country Parties, the first in Western Australia in 1914 being followed by others in the eastern states between 1917 and 1920. Seen from the angle of sectional politics, this tripartite structure was functional, with the Labor Party representing the interests of the organized working class, the Country Party those of the farmers, the graziers (landholders who raised cattle and sheep besides growing wheat) and the country townspeople, while the National Party (formed in 1917 by the fusion of the former Liberals with a breakaway Labor group) represented the interests of commercial and industrial concerns along with those of the pastoralists (owners of large estates devoted mainly to the merino wool industry). Seen from the angle of general policy, however, the division was a binary one between the Labor Party, standing for a strong public sector with a mixed economy, and the combination of the two non-Labor parties, standing for economic liberalism.

Since the 1920s, this system has changed in some respects. In 1931, the National Party became the United Australia Party, which in its turn became the Liberal Party in 1944. The Labor Party has been shaken from time to time by serious internal disputes and by the formation of rival groups, such as the Democratic Labor Party, which was established in the 1955–7 period to express an anti-Communist objection to various aspects of Labor's defence and foreign policies. The Country Party, which changed its name to the National Country Party in 1975 and became simply the National Party prior to the 1983 federal elections, now works closely with the Liberals. Thus, the Australian party system has conformed since the Second World War to the dualist model of two units alternating in the roles of government and opposition.[3]

For our purpose, the most interesting period remains the 1920s, when there were continuous sectional pressures on the party system and when intra-party conflicts were strongly influenced by those pressures. We shall look at two such conflicts, one affecting the Victorian Country Party and the other the New South Wales Labor Party, and discuss the historical background to each in turn.

At the end of the nineteenth century, agrarian politics in Australia had been dominated by land-tenure issues which stemmed mainly from the subdivision of large holdings for closer settlement, from disputes about tariff policy, and from endless lobbying for preferential road, bridge or rail construction. However, the pressure groups which were largely responsible for establishing the Country Parties in the 1914–20 period were acting not only from an interest in these older issues but from a concern with more pressing questions about the regulation of markets and produce prices, the terms of trade between town and country, and the provision of credit for farmers.[4] The Victorian Country Party has always been more affected by the problems of the wheat industry than its counterparts in other states and when it was first formed it was very preoccupied with policies regarding the sale of Australian wheat on the international market. Victoria was an exporter of wheat by the closing decades of the nineteenth century, and before the First World War it was selling about half of its wheat crop abroad. Until that time, wheat marketing had been handled by a mixture of Australian and overseas firms but during the war an Australian Wheat Board was established to arrange for the compulsory purchase and then for the export and sale of the wheat crop. Although farmers made many complaints about the administrative efficiency (or lack of it) evinced by the Board and its agencies, they also came to appreciate the advantages it brought them in the way of payment at agreed rates, the acceptance of all wheat supplied without regard for demand, and the scope for the representation of producers on its policy-making bodies.[5]

The Victorian Farmers' Union (VFU) was formed in 1916 when interest in the Board's operations was at its height, and it quickly developed political ambitions. From 1917 onwards it was returning to the state's Legislative Assembly small numbers of members who constituted a Country Party, but it soon became clear that its supporters were divided in their views about policy. The conferences of the VFU saw frequent clashes between radical delegates from the Mallee, a region in the far north-western part of the state where wheat-farming was difficult to sustain, and delegates from other regions such as the Wimmera, situated to the south of the Mallee, and the Goulburn Valley, in the north-central area. Whereas the radicals wanted the newly-formed Country Party to remain neutral in the competition between the large Labor and National Parties in the Legislative Assembly, offering support to whichever of the two was willing to make the most concessions to the farmers, other delegates became increasingly receptive to the idea that the Country Party had more to gain from joining with the National Party in electoral pacts and coalition governments. These differences over strategy coincided to some extent with differences over economic policies, particularly where produce marketing was concerned. As the extension into peacetime conditions of a compulsory wheat pool did not seem possible, the Victorian government had established the Victorian Wheat-Growers' Corporation Ltd in 1921 to operate as a voluntary pool in the wheat market, alongside private firms. However, fluctuations in wheat prices later in the 1920s led many farmers to demand the reintroduction of a compulsory pool. Matters came to a head at the VFU conference in March 1926. Both the Federal and the Victorian Country Parties were in coalition Governments with their National Party allies at the time, and the radicals took the line that their representatives should leave both ministries on the grounds that neither had reduced protectionist tariffs or formed a rural bank or established a compulsory wheat pool. When the radicals found themselves being outvoted at the conference, they decided to withdraw from the VFU and to found a new association, the Primary Producers' Union (PPU).[6]

The PPU then set out to persuade the farmers who had remained with the VFU (which adopted the title of Victorian Country Party (VCP) in March 1927) that they should accept the radicals' views concerning compulsory pooling, rural banking and the conditional-support strategy. It returned four representatives to the sixty-five-member Legislative Assembly in the state elections of April 1927 and, in return for a number of concessions, supported a minority Labor Government in power from May 1927 until November 1928. Then, after a defeat in the house, the Labor Premier resigned office and a minority Nationalist ministry held power until the elections of November 1929. The Labor Party formed another Government in December 1929 and again attracted support from the Country Progressive Party (CPP), as the PPU's representatives were called. Meanwhile, the PPU was succeeding in its attempts to persuade the members of the VCP to accept its views on party strategy. Although the VCP was increasing its branch strength at this time, its members were becoming more and more convinced of the value of the conditional-support strategy and of the need to reunite the rival groups, and the fusion of the two parties finally took place at a conference held in September 1930. There exacting conditions for a coalition were agreed upon: no parliamentarian could be a member of the party's Central Council, nor could that body approve a coalition unless the proposal received a two-thirds majority and the Country Party were allocated six portfolios (including the Premiership) in the coalition Cabinet.[7]

This was not the end of the dispute about strategy, which flared up again when the reunited Country Party joined a coalition with the UAP in May 1932 on terms which were much less demanding than those set out in 1930, but later events do not alter the significance of that settlement. The merger of the PPU with the VCP marked a return to the original idea that the conditional-support strategy was the most effective means of influencing government policy for the benefit of farmers and of country people generally. According to the theory behind this strategy, Australian society consisted of a limited number of large social groups – chiefly the working class, the farmers, the graziers, the pastoralists, and businessmen engaged in commerce and industry – and it was the Country Party's role to represent its two main supporting sections, the farmers and the graziers, in a bargaining process within the state and federal Parliaments, just as the Labor Party represented the interests of the workers and the National Party (and subsequently the UAP) those of the businessmen and pastoralists. Implicit in this theory was the notion that farmers and graziers constituted a distinctive culture within Australian society and that the Country Parties which represented them were essentially projections into the field of government of an underlying social force. As a result, Members of Parliament representing these parties were expected by their supporters to act as delegates bound to pursue predetermined policies rather than merely as representatives possessing scope for independent action. The opposition to the conditional-support strategy came from those Country Party leaders who considered that the conflict between Labor and non-Labor transcended sectional boundaries, and that the Country Party shared with the Nationalists an obligation to uphold the values of economic liberalism and individualism against the collectivist policies of the Labor Parties.

The clash between the PPU and the VCP also reflected a degree of factional conflict. The leader of the Victorian Country Party, John Allan (1866–1936), was very popular with country people and, before the break with the radicals in 1926, had been firmly in command of the parliamentary party and of its leadership hierarchy. A wheat and dairy farmer from Wyuna South in the Goulburn Valley area, he belonged to a generation which had been mainly concerned with building up communications and services in rural areas, and in resisting the extension of administrative control from Melbourne, the state capital. Having been a member of one coalition Government between September 1923 and March 1924 and Premier of another between November 1924 and May 1927, he knew at first hand what could be achieved through the control of government departments and the statutory bodies responsible to ministers and he was therefore sceptical about the value of conditional support. In May 1928, he spoke of his opposition to the Labor Party and said that, although when he had first been associated with the Country Party he had been 'inclined to sit on a rail' he would never do so again.[8] His challenger, Albert Dunstan (1882–1950), had grown up in rural Victoria and was living in the Bendigo district in the 1920s. Using the agrarian radicalism of the Mallee farmers and the bargaining power of the Country Progressive Party he had conducted a series of attacks against Allan's position as the leader of the Country Party and, after the settlement of 1930 had been reached on his terms, he had claimed a senior position in the reunited party and succeeded Allan as its leader in 1933. Dunstan was later Premier of Victoria from April 1935 to September 1943 at the head of a purely Country Party Government,

and from September 1943 until October 1945 he led the Country Party-UAP coalition ministry.[9]

The predominantly sectional character of this conflict helps to
explain why the separation of the PPU from the VFU in 1926
was so orderly, and why the two organizations and their respective parties formed such a relatively stable binary system until
their reunification in 1930. At the local level, the issues of strategy and economic policy were discussed within a basically sectional context and it was agreement at this level that prepared
the way for agreement at the level of the parliamentary parties.
The strength of sectional feeling, and the spurious practicality
of the solutions offered (support in return for concessions and
a compulsory wheat pool), ensured that the debate did not
become one about high moral principle or one about the personal merits of Allan or Dunstan.

The close connection between the Labor Parties and the trade
unions in Australia resembles the relationship between the early
Country Parties and their supporting organizations. Except
in Tasmania (where the Labor Party began as a parliamentary
group) it was the leading trade unions which formed and sustained the Labor Parties in the colonies in the 1890s. As a result,
all these parties possessed very similar organizational arrangements: parallel systems of affiliated trade unions and locality
branches were linked through a layer of constituency councils
with an annual conference which, while it constituted the supreme authority in the party, delegated its powers to an elected
executive between sessions. The whole purpose of this structure
was to create strong parliamentary groups, but elaborate pre-
cautions were taken to ensure, firstly, that Labor candidates
were pledged to support agreed policies and to observe voting
discipline in parliament; secondly, that in each colony, the Parliamentary group (or 'caucus') was responsive to the outside organization; and thirdly, that any Labor Government was
subject to strong influence from the caucus and, more indirectly, from the annual conference. These provisions were justified by a characteristic organizational ethic which stressed the
primacy of the trade-union (or 'industrial') as distinct from the
branch (or 'political') wing of the party and the collective rights
of the membership (referred to as the 'rank and file').[10]

In Australia, as elsewhere, the Labor Parties have always been concerned about policies affecting wage levels, conditions of work, and industrial conciliation and arbitration, an interest which stems naturally from their relationship with the trade unions,[11] but at the parties' federal conference of 1905 it was decided that their objective was to achieve 'the collective ownership of monopolies and the extension of the industrial and economic function of the State and the municipality' and the conference of 1921 approved the explicitly Marxist aim of the 'Socialization of Industry, Production, Distribution and Exchange'.[12] There were some in the party of that time who interpreted this objective to mean that Australia should have an economic system in which public rather than private ownership of industry was the norm, but most Labor leaders and members favoured a mixed economy in which the state would play an important role in developing and managing the economy. In general, the Labor Party has been pragmatic in judging the suitability of economic strategies for Australian conditions; it was as responsive to neo-Keynsian ideas in the 1950s and 1960s as it was to liberal notions of monetary and financial regulation which were applied by the federal government when Bob Hawke was Prime Minister (March 1983–December 1991), and continued by Paul Keating, who succeeded him. The connection between the unions and the party has remained strong despite such shifts in policy; as late as 1975, about two-thirds of Australia's 2.5 million unionists belonged to trade unions which were affiliated to the Australian Labor Party.[13]

Conflict within the Labor Party has often been bitter, especially when it has been generated by divisions within the underlying layer of trade unions. One of the most spectacular of the party's crises in the inter-war period was that which affected the New South Wales unit in 1926 and 1927, during the first Premiership of John Lang (1876–1975).[14] This developed after the state elections of 30 May 1925, when the New South Wales Labor Party found itself with forty-six seats in the ninety-member Legislative Assembly and therefore in a position to take power. Its parliamentary group (or 'caucus') re-elected Lang as its leader and he was commissioned by the Governor to form a Government, his ministry (whose members had also been chosen by the caucus) taking office on 17 June 1925. Labor had been in power between October 1910 and November 1916 and, with one

brief interruption, between April 1920 and April 1922, so it did
not lack ministerial experience. A radical legislative programme
was set in train but an attempt to abolish the Legislative Council
failed early in 1926.

One of Lang's main problems was the instability of his own
party, which had suffered from prolonged bouts of internal conflict since as far back as 1916. The source of this conflict was
the rivalry which existed between powerful trade-union leaders
and, at a further remove, between different sectors of the trade-
union organization in the state, in which the largest and most
influential central bodies were the Australasian Coal and Shale
Employees' Federation (the Miners' Federation), the Australian
Workers' Union (AWU) and the Labor Council of Sydney. The
Miners' Federation was firmly rooted in the coal-mining regions
surrounding Sydney, in the districts of Newcastle, Lithgow and
Wollongong; it was led by Albert C. Willis, a Welshman who
had arrived in Sydney in 1911 and who was the organization's
Secretary from 1916 until 1925. Its main rival was the AWU,
which drew the bulk of its membership from shearers, station
hands, and the railway and construction workers in the country
areas of the state; it represented the tough-minded practicality of
the native Australian tradition of union practice personified by
the President of its Central Branch, John Bailey. Although the
AWU was affiliated to the Sydney Labor Council, the latter body
was based mainly on the large number of craft and general
unions (such as the Waterside Workers' Federation) which
flourished in the Sydney metropolitan area. The Labor Council's Secretary from 1918, John S. Garden, a Scot, was one of
the founders of the Communist Party of Australia, though he
resigned from that body in 1926.

By that date, these three men and their organizations had
become deeply involved in the politics of the New South Wales
Labor Party. Bailey and his allies had virtually taken charge of
the party's organization in 1916 when they had opposed the
principle of conscription for overseas military service in the referendum on that issue, and had led the attack which forced the
then Labor Premier, W. A. Holman, one of the supporters of
conscription, to leave the party and form a non-Labor Government.[15] The AWU was deriving full advantage from a Labor
constitution which made the party organization susceptible to

trade-union domination. Formally known as the New South Wales Branch of the Australian Labor Party (ALP), the party was therefore subordinate to the institutions of the Federal Labor Party, but in practice it enjoyed a considerable degree of autonomy. Its most important plenary body was its annual conference, which was empowered to elect a thirty-two-member executive headed by a president and two vice-presidents. The delegates to this conference were chosen by two means; one group was appointed by the party's electorate councils, representing the party's local branches (or 'leagues') and a second group was chosen by the affiliated unions on the basis of one delegate for each 1,000 members or part thereof. Union delegates were usually in the majority under this system; at the state conference of April 1924, for example, the league membership of 35,000 was represented by 111 delegates and the union membership of 100,000 by 185 delegates.[16] Furthermore, under rules 6 (a) and 6 (b), an affiliated union could purchase party membership for each of its adult members by the payment of a nominal fee and thus acquire for them the right to join their local branch or league and to stand or vote in the election of conference delegates. It was therefore possible for unions such as the AWU and the Miners' Federation to place large numbers of their members in the local leagues and thus to participate in the choice of delegates through the non-union channel.[17]

Between 1916 and 1923, the AWU was generally able to sway the party's annual conferences and to secure an impressive number of places on the executive. At the 1919 conference, Willis and Garden led their supporters in an attempt to win support for the principle of the One Big Union, a revolutionary doctrine, but they were defeated and expelled from the party. Willis was readmitted in 1922 and was therefore able to take advantage of a weakening in the position of the AWU, which had clashed with the state parliamentary group and the party's federal leadership, and to form a winning coalition at the conference of June 1923, when he was elected President of the party. Bailey had been accused of complicity in the use of ballot boxes with sliding panels and, when a committee found him guilty of the charges, he was expelled from the party. Having won power within the organization, Willis had then to defend his administration against the AWU on the one hand and, on the other, against

Garden's phalanx of radical unions. Garden had also been read-mitted to the party and was a member of its executive, but his position became untenable in October 1923 when the executive decreed that no member of the Communist Party could be a member of the ALP; he was removed from membership in the following month.[18] Willis had an additional advantage in that he controlled the only daily newspaper associated with the Labor Party in New South Wales. This was the *Labor Daily*, which had begun publication in January 1924 with financial support from the Miners' Federation.[19]

Lang, who had been elected leader of the parliamentary Labor group on 31 July 1923, worked closely with Willis and shared with him an interest in controlling the Members of the Legislative Assembly (MLAs) belonging to that group. The most effective sanction against a sitting MLA was the threat to withdraw organizational backing in the pre-selection ballot for nomination as a Labor candidate at the next election. Many MLAs kept in touch with those unions which were strongest in their constituencies and were sensitive to shifts in the balance of forces in the party's internal conflicts. In theory, individual MLAs and the parliamentary group as a whole could have cultivated the electorate councils and the local leagues as a structure of support capable of resisting trade-union pressure, but in practice these were under the influence of the AWU in many rural areas, of the Miners' Federation in mining seats, and of the unions affiliated with the Labor Council in the Sydney metropolitan area. Yet the powers of the parliamentary group (or caucus) were considerable; it was entitled to elect its leader annually, and whenever that leader was commissioned to form a government, the caucus also selected the members of his cabinet, although their portfolios were allocated by the Premier.[20] This was the system which applied when Lang formed his first Government in June 1925.

Lang appointed Willis as Vice-President of the Executive Council and nominated him for membership of the Legislative Council to provide leadership for the Labor group in that house; Willis then resigned as President of the party, and was succeeded in this post by a moderate unionist, E. C. Magrath.[21] No conference was held in 1925, but that which took place in April 1926 proved to be both eventful and turbulent, with groups manoeuvring for position in a bewildering series of alignments.

The decisive (though unnatural) alliance formed between the AWU group and a group of union delegates led by Magrath and T. J. Tyrrell ensured the election of W. H. Seale of the Waterside Workers' Federation as President of an executive which was reported to contain fifteen supporters of the AWU (including officials) and seventeen of the Magrath-Tyrrell group.[22]

With this background information, we are now in a position to follow the course of the conflict which waged so fiercely throughout the first seven months of 1927. A convenient starting point is the situation which obtained in the middle of September 1926, at which time the Labor Party still had a majority in the Legislative Assembly, and Lang's thirteen-member ministry appeared to be relatively secure after fifteen months in office. The senior members of the team were Lang himself (Premier and Treasurer), Peter F. Loughlin (Secretary for Land and Minister for Forests), John M. Baddeley (Secretary for Mines and Minister for Labour and Industry), Edward A. McTiernan (Attorney-General), William F. Dunn (Minister for Agriculture) and Willis (Vice-President of the Executive Council). As we have noted, Seale had become president of the party in April 1926 and the members of his executive included a substantial number with AWU affiliations.

Lang was an enigma. He had shown himself to be an able administrator, a robust debater and a skilled politician but it was difficult to judge how his public personality would develop when subjected to continuous stress. Born into a Catholic family in Sydney in 1876, he had been an estate agent before becoming involved in local politics in the Auburn area of the city. First elected to the Legislative Assembly in 1913, he had served as Treasurer in three ministries between 1920 and 1922 and had been elected leader of the parliamentary group in 1923. His political instincts were those of a populist and he took pride in the number of radical measures which his Government had carried into effect in 1925 and during the first half of 1926; these included the restoration of the 44-hour working week, a Rural Workers' Accommodation Act, a Workers' Compensation Act and an Industrial Arbitration Act designed to replace the State's Arbitration Court with an Industrial Commission. Such achievements, along with his attempt to abolish the Legislative Council, had increased his support amongst ordinary unionists, party

members and Labor voters and had thus given him enough
standing to allow him to appeal for direct popular backing.
Despite this, he remained an insecure individual, uncertain of the
range of his formal authority as Premier and reluctant to free
himself from the personal and group connections which he had
formed during his rise to power.

He faced his first serious challenge when his deputy, Peter
Loughlin, announced on 13 September that he had submitted
his resignation from the ministry to the Secretary of the parliamentary party so that he would be free to challenge Lang in the
annual contest for the leadership of the party to be held at an
impending meeting of caucus. Loughlin justified his decision on
several grounds, referring to allegations of attempts to bribe
Labor MLAs which had not been investigated by the executive,
and to threats to hold a special conference 'which . . . would
modify the control of the movement, and, incidentally, pave the
way for Communist control of the organisation'.[23] Loughlin
was one of the representatives of the rural constituency of
Cootamundra and, as Secretary for Lands, had taken a keen
interest in the reaction of rural groups to the Government's programme. When the caucus met on 14 September, he and Lang
each received twenty-three votes and on the following day the
chairman of the meeting ruled that, as neither had obtained a
majority, Lang should continue as leader. As Loughlin's resignation had not been sent to the Governor but had remained a
matter for caucus, it was a simple matter to reinstate him as a
member of the Cabinet with his former portfolio.[24]

Having found that his position inside the parliamentary party
was so weak, Lang had necessarily to look for support amongst
the trade unions in order to redress the balance. His reputation
as a reformer with their interests at heart now worked to his
advantage, and he found himself being supported by Willis and
the Miners' Federation and also by Garden (who had resigned
from the Communist Party but had not yet been readmitted to
the Labor Party), who was able to command the allegiance of a
substantial number of unions affiliated to the Labor Council.
This new coalition was intended to protect Lang from his opponents in the parliamentary party and, indirectly, from Bailey and
the AWU. Lang's supporters dominated a special conference of
the party held on 12–13 November 1926 and persuaded the

delegates to accept a motion which not only expressed confidence in Lang's leadership but also confirmed him as leader of the parliamentary party for the remainder of the parliamentary term of three years, contravening the rule that caucus should hold an annual election for the post. They then proceeded to grant him special powers in the following terms:

> recognising that unity is essential to the successful carrying out of the platform and policy of the Labour party, the Premier is hereby authorised in the event of circumstances arising which, in his opinion, imperil the unity to do all things and exercise such powers as he deems necessary in the interests of the movement.[25]

What made this decision all the more extraordinary was Lang's acceptance of it, given that it was bound to upset many of his parliamentary colleagues. He had been drawn several steps down the road towards a plebiscitary democracy. Commenting upon the resolution, the AWU's journal suggested that:

> Mussolini himself could wish for nothing more than that. But Mussolini has an army of blackshirted ruffians to back up the power reposed in him, while the dictator of the New South Wales Labor Movement has nothing of the kind to make his dictatorship real. It may come yet, of course, with red shirts instead of black, and Jock Garden as Generalissimo of the forces, but 'The Worker' doubts it.[26]

Resistance to Lang was still evident at the parliamentary level and on 18 November Loughlin submitted his resignation from the ministry. On this occasion it was sent directly to the Governor and took effect on 19 November. Speaking in the assembly on that day, Loughlin referred to 'efforts being made by outsiders to control this Parliament'. He maintained that:

> persons who are outside have to-day instituted what is termed a dictatorship. That dictatorship is supposed to be exercised by the Premier. My belief is that dictatorship will not be exercised by the Premier. It will be exercised through the Premier by men who are outside.[27]

The open support which Loughlin was receiving from two other country MLAs, V. W. E. Goodin and R. T. Gillies, made it

likely that the Government would lose its majority in the Legislative Assembly, thereby clearing the way for the opposition to
win a vote on a censure motion. Intensive negotiations took
place in the Labor camp in an effort to avoid this outcome, with
the result that the three defectors did not vote in the division
when the censure motion was put to the house on 22 November,
and it was defeated by forty-four votes to forty-two. In December, a delegation from the federal executive persuaded Goodin to
return to the party and Gillies to give an undertaking that he
would support the Government, which was thus given the numbers to remain in office.

Seven months later, Goodin revealed that he and Gillies had
received separate undertakings from the Cabinet, the Treasurer
(Lang) and party representatives as the price for their co-
operation; these included not only several specific policy concessions for rural interests but also agreements that an earlier
decision to remove Willis from the Cabinet and the leadership of
the upper house should be implemented, that the motion dealing
with Lang's leadership which had been adopted at the special
conference would be referred to the party's forthcoming federal
conference, that the caucus should endorse a statement by Lang
repudiating the powers given him by the special conference, and
that the caucus should be invited by the state executive to co-
operate with the committee which the latter had appointed to
revise the party's rules.[28] Had they been put into effect, these
concessions would have forced Lang to accept that his position
depended on caucus approval rather than on that of the organization. However, he behaved as though he were not a party to
the agreement, claiming much later that, although he knew that
'some compromise had been reached', he had not seen what
became known as the Goodin–Gillies pact.[29]

Lang's ability to maintain his position as party leader now
depended on whether or not the coalition of union forces which
had backed him in November 1926 could dominate proceedings
at the party's next annual conference (due to take place in Easter week in April 1927) and, moreover, on whether or not it
could go further and change the party's constitution in order to
strengthen the position of the metropolitan unions relative to
that of the AWU and the country branches. As we have seen,
the existing rules favoured the AWU (and also the Miners'

Federation), but the conference of April 1926 had appointed a small committee under the chairmanship of Willis to prepare a new set of rules. It soon became known that this committee's proposals, which were nicknamed the 'Red Rules', would, if applied, work to the advantage of the metropolitan unions associated with the Labor Council to the disadvantage of the AWU. In line with the existing rules, the new scheme envisaged the election of the party President and two Vice-Presidents by the annual conference, but it specified new methods for the election of the other members of the executive and for the appointment of conference delegates. Executive members were to be chosen by one electoral council representing the metropolitan area, entitled to four representatives; three country electoral councils, each entitled to two representatives; and eleven groups of trade unions (with the AWU confined to one group) entitled to return members on the basis of one for every 7,000 members (with a maximum of three per group). Conference delegates were also to be selected within the three-sector framework – a metropolitan division with a minimum of fifteen delegates, three country divisions each with eight delegates, and the trade-union groups with varying numbers, on the basis of one delegate for every 1,500 members. In this case too, the AWU was to be confined to a group of its own. In addition to the party's annual conference, there was also provision for the holding of separate country, metropolitan and union conferences.[30] These provisions threatened not only to restrict the AWU (directly, by placing it in a single group in the trade-union sector of representation and indirectly, by imposing low ceilings on the numbers of executive members and delegates to be chosen in country areas), but also to reduce the representation of the leagues and to increase that of the unions in the metropolitan area.

A section of the parliamentary group combined with the AWU section and other moderate members of the party's executive in a determined bid to prevent the adoption of these rules. Using the pretext that the reversion to single-member constituencies (brought in the previous year to replace the multi-member constituencies which had functioned under proportional representation) for elections to the Legislative Assembly required the formation of a new set of Labor electorate councils for the appointment of conference delegates, a majority on the executive decided on 28 January 1927 to postpone the annual conference until June.[31] This was intended to give more time for opponents of the 'Red Rules' to rally support, and also to provide an opportunity for the party's federal conference, meeting in Canberra in May, to express its views on the proposed changes. Meanwhile, committees of the parliamentary group and the executive had prepared a revised version of the old rules, which was adopted by the caucus on 14 February and by the executive on 18 February.[32] The party's President, Seale, who had tried to resist the executive's decisions to postpone the conference and to work with the caucus in preparing an alternative set of new rules, finally took the drastic step of instructing the party's Secretary to convene the conference for Easter instead of June.[33] On 6 March, the executive suspended him from office for having defied its decisions and appointed F. Conroy to serve as acting president.[34] Lang's supporters then rallied behind Seale and went ahead with preparations for an Easter conference.

The existence of two executives – one official and the other unofficial – presented Lang with a dilemma. Under normal circumstances a party leader would have been expected to stand by the formally constituted, duly elected executive of his party, but Lang let it be known that he would attend the Easter conference. To justify his decision he said:

> If the differences that exist are to be finally and satisfactorily settled, the Easter conference, representing the rank and file, is manifestly the proper place to thrash out all points of contention. To call a few leaders of factions together, and invite them to come to terms, would be futile, and give satisfaction to no one.[35]

In other words, he was equating the formal heads of his organization with the leaders of what was in fact a dissident group, as if there were nothing to distinguish between the official executive and its rebel counterpart. At the Easter gathering, addressing the large number of delegates who had attended, he said:

> This great conference is manifestly representative of the organised Labour party in this State, and I regret that a minority, however sincere and well meaning, should continue to take up an exclusive attitude towards the rank and file.[36]

The conference, acting as if it possessed full plenary powers, suspended Conroy and several other members of the official executive from party membership for three years, expelled Loughlin, Goodin and Gillies from the party, repudiated the Goodin–Gillies pact, approved the new rules, and confirmed the decision of the special conference to increase Lang's powers as leader, adding the additional instruction that he should reconstruct his Cabinet. It also elected a provisional executive with Seale as President.[37] Then, on 19 April, while the conference was still in session, Lang was taken to task by a group of ministers for associating himself with the conference. He subsequently persuaded the delegates to agree that the new rules should include a provision that no member of the Communist Party could be a member of the New South Wales branch of the ALP[38] but that was the extent of his intervention. Subsequently, on 26 April, the caucus decided by twenty-five votes to eighteen to pass a motion declaring that Goodin and Gillies were still members of the parliamentary group[39] but making no reference to Loughlin, whose resignation from the party had been accepted in February.

The triennial conference of the Federal Labor Party, which met in Canberra between 11 and 16 May, could have provided the official state (or Conroy) executive and the caucus majority with much needed support, but its anxiety to avoid an open break with Lang and the rebels, who could easily have formed their own party, was only too evident. Although the conference allowed the official delegates from New South Wales to take their seats, and recognized that the Conroy executive had been duly constituted, it did nothing to encourage that body to proceed with the plans for a June conference, nor did it seek to impose sanctions on the rebels. Instead, it announced that the federal executive would arrange for a unity conference to be held under its own auspices.[40]

The rebels exploited this indecision to the full. The Seale executive decided to put forward its own candidate, A. A. L. O'Gorman, for the by-election for the federal seat of Warringah despite the fact that an official Labor candidate, T. P. Conway, was already in the field. Lang gave his support to O'Gorman, who lost the contest when polling took place on 21 May, but who obtained 4,285 votes to Conway's 3,159. Lang was now ready to renew his attack on his opponents in the parliamentary group. On 26 May he resigned his commission and received a new one from the Governor, who imposed only one condition upon him, namely, that he would request a dissolution of the assembly 'at the earliest possible time' after the enrolment of electors had been completed.[41] He then formed a new Cabinet consisting entirely of his own supporters, while his rivals formed a separate parliamentary group under the leadership of Thomas D. Mutch. Giving way to pressure from the rebels, the federal executive eventually agreed that the unity conference, which was held in Sydney over the weekend of 23–4 July, could approve the new 'Red Rules' by a simple rather than a two-thirds majority.[42] This conference, dominated by Lang's supporters, confirmed the key decisions of the Easter conference to approve the 'Red Rules', to exclude Loughlin, Goodin and Gillies from the party, to extend Lang's powers as leader and to suspend from office the members of the official (Conroy) executive.[43] The AWU group and their parliamentary allies had been completely defeated.

Although the Labor Party lost the state elections of October 1927, it managed to win those of October 1930, enabling Lang to form another Government. He clashed over financial policy with the federal Labor ministry headed by J. H. Scullin and subsequently the state executive of the New South Wales party was expelled from the ALP in March 1931. In May 1932, by which time another non-Labor Government was in power in Canberra, Lang again came into conflict with the federal authorities and was dismissed from office by the Governor. His own party was reinstated as the New South Wales branch of the ALP in February 1936 but in 1939 the familiar sequence of a rebellion and a so-called unity conference led to his removal from the leadership. He was expelled from the ALP in 1943 and was not restored to membership until 1971, four years before his death.[44]

In some respects his role in the events of 1926 and 1927 is obscure for two things remain unclear – whether or not he was a full party to the Goodin–Gillies pact, and the extent of his dealings with Willis and Garden. Although by the early 1930s he was working through an inner circle to manage the party's affairs,[45] his behaviour in the 1926–7 crisis appears to be that of a man who was improvising his tactics as he went along, uncertain of the strength of the opposing sides. He later expressed the view that politics have 'much in common with the law of the jungle. 'Always be with the strength' is the advice usually tendered to a young politician.'[46] One of the most interesting features of this period of conflict is the way that Lang's readiness to turn for aid to his supporting coalition amongst the unions and to appeal for rank-and-file approval not only gave him considerable room for manoeuvre but also allowed him to flout the party's formal rules and procedures. There were attempts to bind him down and embarrass him; Loughlin challenged him to a contest in September 1926 and, less openly, in November 1926, but once he had retired from the scene, no one was willing to risk open confrontation with Lang.

Both this and the Victorian case suggest that economic sectionalism creates activists whose primary loyalties lie not with the party organization itself but with the underlying pressure groups. The activist's complaint that institutions corrupt the people's representatives was here directed not only against Parliament but against the central bodies of the parties themselves. Both Lang and Dunstan in their respective parties were exploiting the belief that only in the local community, where ordinary people lived and worked together, could politics acquire a moral dimension. From such a perspective, the groups fighting for power within the party organizations and assemblies in Sydney and Melbourne were 'factions', taking on meaning only if caught and swept along by a current of popular demand from the grass roots. It was difficult for their opponents to resist this kind of attack: neither the VFU nor the New South Wales Labor Party of this time contained a solid majority of activists whose loyalties – or career expectations – were invested in the party organization itself, and the underlying sectional conflicts, having once broken into the plenary institutions of these organizations, became pervasive and all-absorbing.

The sectarianism generated under these conditions was quite distinctive. In situations where loyalty is strong, competing groups tend to find normative justification for their positions within the party's own tradition and culture, whereas in cases such as these in which sectional loyalty is much stronger than party loyalty, there is a much greater tendency to portray the underlying interest group as a community threatened from beyond its boundaries and dependent on its leaders for protection. In the New South Wales conflict, for example, Lang's opponents worked outwards from the Australian nativism of the AWU with its themes of mateship and pragmatic collectivism, to claims that strangers were importing alien ideas such as Communism into the Labor movement; for their part, Lang and his supporters were playing upon the populist strain in the Labor tradition and implying that he, Lang, the only leader who cared for 'the little people', was seeking out and destroying those who would betray them to the capitalists.

Both these Australian cases illustrate the situation which arises when broadly based interest groups consider themselves to be corporate entities within the political system, possessed of their own identities and their own ethical standards. Such groups tend to see the electoral system not as a means of representing the general will but as a means of placing envoys in Parliament to defend collective rights. The parties created to achieve this result are treated as agencies of the interest groups concerned and are not expected to develop broad programmes; their aim in participating in government is to obtain 'concessions' which can be translated into particular legislation. Particularly in New South Wales and at the federal level until 1908, the early parliamentary Labor Parties would occasionally offer conditional support to ministries in return for measures which would benefit the trade unions or specific groups of workers, and the attitudes formed in that early period carried over into the internal debates of the much stronger Labor Parties of the inter-war period. For many trade unions, the formation of a Labor Government was still hailed as an opportunity to pass a series of particularistic laws rather than as a means of broadening the party's base beyond its sectional limits. The conditional-support strategy was valued by the VFU for similar reasons, and the difference between Dunstan and Allan in the late 1920s was very largely that between an agrarian leader who represented a restricted and sectional definition of the Country Party's constituency and one who, while proclaiming his party's attachment to economic liberalism, was aware that it must broaden its scope to appeal not only to all categories of farmers but to country townsmen as well. The dialogue between the political and industrial wings of the early Labor Parties and that between the agrarian radical and the conservative wings of the early Country Parties was more concerned with the legitimacy of economic sectionalism as a philosophy of politics than with a choice of strategies.

II

The 1920s and 1930s marked the high point of economic sectionalism within the Australian party system, and in the same period, Canada and New Zealand, with similar economies, were also affected by this style of politics, though not to the same extent. In other countries such as the United States, Britain and France, the relationship between organized interests and political parties took significantly different forms, and it is to these that we must now turn.

To look first at the USA, there were indications in the early 1890s that years of agrarian discontent might be leading to the formation of a farmers' party. The wheatfarmers of several midwestern states including North Dakota, South Dakota, Nebraska and Kansas, felt that they were being exploited by the land and railway companies, by the Chicago grain dealers and, at a further remove, by the powerful economic interests situated on the eastern seaboard; at the same time, cotton farmers in a number of southern states were being gradually impoverished by the crop lien system under which they were obliged to make over their crops to local merchants, and were being frequently reduced to the status of tenants. The grievances of the wheat and cotton farmers provided the fuel for a Farmers' Alliance movement and for the People's (Populist) Parties which contested the elections of 1890. The Populists then formed a national party and their candidate for the presidential election of 1892 won more than one million votes and twenty-two electoral votes. There were plans to put forward another Populist nominee in the presidential election of 1896 but, much to the annoyance of the 'midroaders' amongst them, the Populists eventually decided to support the Democratic candidate, William Jennings Bryan.[47]

Compared with the Australian Country Parties, the American Populist Parties of the 1890s were more disposed to express a generalized anti-urban, agrarian revivalist philosophy than to pursue the specific interests of particular groups of producers. In this century, however, the majority of American farmers have moved in the opposite direction, relying more on pressure groups than on political parties to influence government policy in their favour. At one level, they have built up a number of specialized groups identified with particular fields of production, such as the American Livestock Association and the National Wool Growers' Association, while depending on large and well-established general organizations, such as the American Farm Bureau Federation, the National Farmers' Union and the National Grange, to ensure that Congress responds to their demands. The Farm Bureau, for example, was instrumental in forming a farm bloc composed of Senators and Representatives from both the Democratic and Republican Parties in Congress in 1921 and 1922 and has played a prominent part in influencing the farm and produce price policies of a succession of federal administrations from the 1920s onwards. Agrarian sectionalism in the American party system, therefore, has been converted into a refined form of pressure group activity, aimed partly at administrative agencies and partly at the parties themselves, and its impact on intra-party affairs has been specific and precisely calculated.[48]

The politics of labour in America also contrasts with the Australian experience. The American Federation of Labor (AFL), the largest general organization of trade unions in the United States at the turn of the century, represented unions of skilled workers and did not build up a following amongst the masses of unskilled workers who were pouring into American cities from the rural areas and from Europe. It was very much concerned with issues affecting wages, hours of work and factory conditions, and also with procedures for collective bargaining and with the defence of the legal rights of the trade unions. In many industrial cities, the material needs of unskilled workers were met by the political machines and it was these, rather than politically motivated trade unions, which provided the urban basis for the Democratic Party in the late nineteenth and early twentieth centuries. The trade-union movement was greatly strengthened during the period of the New Deal, when the formation of the Congress of Industrial Organizations (CIO) between 1935 and 1938 coincided with the growth of class feeling amongst American industrial workers and with the weakening of the ethnic and religious divisions within their ranks. However, despite its association with the Democratic Party in the 1930s, the CIO chose to remain within the tradition of non-partisan trade unionism and finally merged with its older rival to form the AFL–CIO combination in 1955.[49]

Like their agrarian counterparts, American trade-union federations, whether specialized or generalized in form, have sought to represent the concrete interests of their members and have developed specific lobbying techniques to that end. The reason for their relative lack of interest in the idea of forming a socialist or labour party has often been explored;[50] essentially it seems to stem from the fact that they have been able to defend their legal status and to pursue their sectional objectives quite effectively by lobbying the administration and by placing pressure on the parties. During the New Deal, when they were concerned about the need for welfare policies and social reform, they found that the Democratic Party was generally sympathetic to their views. In the late 1960s and early 1970s, the unions' affinity with the Democrats was weakened to some extent as a rising generation of intellectuals and activists, interested in the 'new liberalism' rather than in the values of the New Deal, gained influence within the party.[51] In any case, the unions themselves were losing some of their organizational force; the percentage of non-agricultural workers contained in their membership fell from 33.2 in 1955 to 26.1 in 1974,[52] a trend which threatened to undermine their ability to represent the interests of the workforce as a whole.

In Britain, on the other hand, the close ties between the Labour Party and the trade unions have attracted attention as an example of interest group intrusion into party politics. The Trades Union Congress (TUC), founded in 1868, sustained the Labour Representation Committee in its efforts to establish a group of members in the House of Commons in the first decade of this century, and the unions were given a commanding position in the Labour Party when it adopted its modern Constitution in 1918. The relationship between the party and the trade unions changed in some respects in the inter-war period but a reasonably stable balance of power had been established between the two bodies by the 1950s. The TUC was then completely dominant in the trade union field; in 1951 it contained 183 unions with a total membership of 8,020,079, which constituted

84.6 per cent of all trade unionists (9,480,000) in the country.[53] Its annual conference, the Trades Union Congress, was the main policy making body in the organization, and executive work was delegated to the General Council and to its principal officer, the General Secretary. The General Council served as the main intermediary between the trade unions and individual ministers and government departments.[54] The TUC had earned a reputation as a competent and professional pressure group but, even so, it preferred to maintain its powerful position within the Labour Party rather than adopt a non-partisan approach.

The Labour Party's organization in the 1950s combined the social democratic practice of branch representation at a national conference with the principle of 'industrial' participation of the kind accepted by the Labor Parties in Australia. The party's membership consisted mainly of two large categories, those recruited on an individual basis to local constituency branches, and those for whom named organizations (mainly trade unions) had paid an affiliation fee. Using the latter method freely, the trade unions regularly converted a high proportion of their own membership into affiliated membership of the Labour Party; in 1951, for example, eighty-two unions established an affiliated Labour membership of 4,937,427 which constituted 84.4 per cent of the party's total membership of 5,849,002, the remaining components being 876,275 individual members, 28,000 members representing Co-operative Societies, and 7,300 representing Socialist societies and other bodies. This share of the total membership entitled the trade unions to 82.2 per cent of the votes at the party's annual conference and to representation at that conference at the rate of one delegate for every 5,000 votes.[55] The trade unions also held a commanding position on the party's National Executive Committee (NEC), which after 1953 consisted of twenty-eight members, recruited as follows:

1 *ex officio*, the leader and deputy leader of the Parliamentary Labour Party (PLP)
2 twelve members directly elected by the affiliated trade unions
3 one member elected by the Socialist, Co-operative and other bodies affiliated to the party
4 seven members representing constituency branches, chosen by the delegates from those branches at the conference

5   five women members elected by the conference as a whole
6   one treasurer elected by the conference as a whole

Thus, not only did the trade unions have the right to choose twelve of the twenty-eight members on their own account, but they were in a position, with four-fifths of the votes at the conference, to determine the outcome of the ballots for the five women members and for the treasurer.[56]

In the 1950s, the Labour Party was heavily dependent on the trade unions for financial support. Between 1951 and 1958 the proportion of central Labour Party funds provided by trade-union contributions came to an annual average of 81.75 per cent[57] and trade-union donations to Labour's national general election fund constituted 84.9 per cent of the total in 1951, 95.2 per cent in 1955 and some 94.2 per cent in 1959.[58] To form a complete picture of the party's accounts, some estimate has to be made of income and expenditure at the regional and constituency levels as well as at the national level, and a careful study of the whole picture found that in 1957, for example, 50 to 55 per cent of the party's total income had been contributed by the trade unions. If the latters' outlay on administration and participation in party activities is taken into account, the unions' contribution to combined party income and union expenditure comes to almost 70 per cent.[59] Trade unionists also formed an important proportion of the Labour Party's team of election candidates and parliamentary members. In the 1951 general elections, for example, the trade unions sponsored 137 Labour candidates, of whom 104 were returned to the new house[60] in a total Labour contingent of 295 members.

The unions have often influenced the course of the Labour Party's internal politics in the period since the Second World War. In the early 1950s when Aneurin Bevan was leading a left-wing group in an attack on the party's established policies, Clement Attlee and the party's central leaders were supported by the heads of some of the biggest unions – the Transport and General Workers' Union, the National Union of Mineworkers and the National Union of General and Municipal Workers – but in the crucial conference decisions of the period both the loyalist majorities and the dissenting minorities were composed of varying proportions of trade-union and constituency-branch votes.[61]

Later in the 1950s, Frank Cousins, as General Secretary of the Transport and General Workers' Union, played a leading role in the campaign for unilateral nuclear disarmament; he was also one of those who opposed the attempt of the new party leader, Hugh Gaitskell, to revise clause four of the party's constitution, which stated the commitment to 'the common ownership of the means of production, distribution, and exchange',[62] and thus presented a ready target for those who claimed that the party was still committed to extensive public control of the economy. In 1960 sufficient trade unions had been influenced by the Campaign for Nuclear Disarmament to provide majorities for unilateralist motions at the party's Scarborough conference but Gaitskell's policy of remaining within NATO gained increased support at the party's Blackpool conference of October 1961, which adopted a resolution in line with his views.[63] The most sensitive issues for the unions were those affecting industrial relations and they therefore came into direct conflict with Harold Wilson's Labour Government in 1969 over its proposal to pass legislation to deal with the problem of unofficial strikes. The proposal was shelved on the understanding that the TUC General Council would apply its own rules more strictly in handling unofficial strikes.[64] The party and the unions joined forces in their opposition to the Heath Government's Industrial Relations Act of 1971, at which time there was an increasing tendency for some unions to align themselves with the left wing of the party,[65] but in general the trade unions offered Labour's central leaders their sympathetic support in NEC and conference affairs.

In the 1980s, the party's connection with the unions came under increased scrutiny. When the party decided that the leader of the PLP should be chosen by an electoral college, a special conference in January 1981 agreed to restrict the unions' share of the votes to 40 per cent, and in June 1990 the NEC adopted a proposal that the proportion of union votes at party conferences should be cut down from 90 to 70 per cent after the next general elections, with the prospect of a further reduction to 40 per cent at a later stage.[66] Although the TUC's membership fell from 12.2 million in 1979 to 8.15 million in 1991,[67] the unions still provided about 75 per cent of the party's funds, they still retained their commanding position on the NEC, and they still sponsored a large number (140) of the party's MPs.[68] However

John Smith, who succeeded Neil Kinnock as Labour leader in July 1992, has put forward in February 1993 proposals intended to reduce further the power of the unions, as organizations, within the party's institutions. He has suggested that parliamentary candidates and sitting Members should be pre-selected by party members in their constituencies without the unions having 40 per cent of the vote, as in the past; that in future the trade unions should not take part in the election of the leader and deputy leader of the party, who should be chosen by an electoral college consisting of Members of Parliament and party members, each group having 50 per cent of the votes; and that the union block vote at party conferences should be reduced from 70 to 50 per cent of the total vote.[69]

The TUC's attachment to the Labour Party is governed by its continuing belief that a Labour government provides it with a greater influence on policy than a Conservative administration and that it has a direct interest in the Labour Party's improving its chances of taking office. For the most part, therefore, it has accepted the necessity of the Party's moderating its policies and granting more power to membership in the constituencies in order to broaden its electoral appeal. The unions remember with bitterness the industrial legislation brought into effect by the Thatcher Government in the 1980s and resent the loss of the extensive rights of consultation which they enjoyed under the Labour administrations of the 1974–9 period.

In France, trade unions are less involved in party politics than they are in Britain. The Confédération Générale du Travail (CGT) has aligned itself with the French Communist Party but has sufficient organizational autonomy to stand on its own feet as that party continues to decline in strength. The Confédération Générale du Travail–Force Ouvrière (CGT–FO), although founded in December 1947 with leanings towards the then Socialist Party, the SFIO, has remained separate from the new Socialist Party. Following the division of the original Confédération Française des Travailleurs Chrétiens (CFTC) in 1964, two Catholic trade unions were established – a new, more secular organization known as the Confédération Française Démocratique du Travail (CFDT) and a smaller CFTC, which has maintained close ties with the Roman Catholic Church. On the right flank of this range of unions is the Confédération Générale des Cadres (CGC), which was formed immediately after the Second World War to represent managerial staff and which is, in economic terms, more liberal in outlook than the other peak organizations.[70] Party feeling is strong amongst the membership of the trade unions but the alignments between parties and unions are not symmetrical: whereas Communist trade unionists are to be found mainly in the CGT, Socialist trade unionists are located in several organizations – they are well represented in the teachers' union, the Fédération de l'Education Nationale, and others are to be found in the CFDT and the CGT–FO as well as in the CGT.[71] There have been times when the Socialist Party would have benefited from a direct trade-union connection of the kind which exists between the Labour Party and the unions in Britain but on the whole its relative independence from organized interests has enabled it to adapt itself much more quickly and more fully to changes in policy ideas and in public opinion in Western Europe than its British counterpart has done.

It has always been much easier to gather information about the political influence wielded by trade unions and by farmers' organizations than about the corresponding influence exercised by business interests on (mainly conservative and centre) parties. In discussing the part played by 'external organizations' in forming political parties, Duverger referred to 'the action of industrial and commercial groups: banks, big companies, industrial combines, employers' federations, and so on. Unfortunately here it is extremely difficult to pass beyond the bounds of generalizations and hypotheses, for such action is always cloaked in great discretion'.[72] Whereas specific business organizations openly lobby members of the legislature in their efforts to influence bills affecting their own particular industries, and while large generalized associations such as the Confederation of British Industries or the Conseil National du Patronat Français or the National Association of Manufacturers and the Chamber of Commerce of the United States all participate in policy debates in the hope of having some effect on party programmes, business interests are very reluctant to discuss the role they play in funding parties sympathetic to their cause. Even when they have a fee-paying membership, however, conservative and centre parties usually rely for a substantial part of their finance on donations from business concerns,[73] but both sides to such transactions are at pains to stress that such financial support does not entail any policy commitments.

Modern liberal democracies accept that the activities of pressure groups overlap to some extent the activities of political parties but they prescribe both formal and informal rules to maintain proper boundaries between the two phenomena. It is generally recognized that some sections of society will choose to align themselves with particular parties and that, in some cases, the relationship may take an organizational form. Provided that the boundary conditions are respected, no problems need arise. However, if a particular pressure group sets out to subvert or to dominate a party or if a particular party tries to convert a pressure group into a 'front' organization, sanctions against rule-breaking may be called for. In either case, the most effective sanctions will be those exercised by a well-informed voting public prepared to ostracize the offender.

Notes

1 See *The Australian Tariff: An Economic Enquiry* (Melbourne University Press, Melbourne, 1929), pp. 147–9; Geoffrey Sawer, *Australian Federal Politics and Law 1901–1929* (Melbourne University Press, Melbourne, 1956), pp. 70–1.

2 See P. Loveday, A. W. Martin and R. S. Parker (eds), *The Emergence of the Australian Party System* (Hale and Iremonger, Sydney, 1977).

3 On the problems of interpretation, see L. C. Webb, 'The Australian Party System', in S. R. Davis et al., *The Australian Political Party System* (Angus and Robertson, Sydney, 1954), pp. 84–117; Henry Mayer, 'Some Conceptions of the Australian Party System 1910–1950', in Margot Beever and F. B. Smith (compilers), *Historical Studies, Selected Articles, Second Series* (Melbourne University Press, Melbourne, 1967), pp. 217–40; Don Aitkin and Brian Jinks, *Australian Political Institutions* (Pitman, Carlton, Victoria, 1980), pp. 141–58. On the sectional aspect of the system, see Hugh V. Emy, *The Politics of Australian Democracy: An Introduction to Political Science* (Macmillan, Melbourne, 1974), pp. 389–96.

4 On the development of the Australian Country Parties, see Ulrich Ellis, *A History of the Australian Country Party* (Melbourne University Press, Melbourne, 1963), and on the New South Wales party, see Ellis, *The Country Party: A Political and Social History*

of the Party in New South Wales (Cheshire, Melbourne, 1958);
Don Aitkin, *The Country Party in New South Wales: A Study of
Organisation and Survival* (Australian National University Press,
Canberra, 1972).

5   B. D. Graham, *The Formation of the Australian Country Parties*
(Australian National University Press, Canberra, 1966), pp. 96–103.

6   Ibid., pp. 110–13, 125–6, 157–66, 198–205 and 249–54.

7   Ibid., pp. 254–65.

8   *Argus* (Melbourne), 8 May 1928. See also the biography of Allan
by J. B. Paul, in Bede Nairn and Geoffrey Serle (eds), *Australian
Dictionary of Biography* (Melbourne University Press, Melbourne),
vol. VII (1979), pp. 34–6.

9   See the biography of Dunstan by Paul in Nairn and Serle (eds),
Australian Dictionary of Biography, vol. VIII (1981), pp. 376–9.

10 On the formation of the early Labor Parties, see Robin Gollan,
*Radical and Working Class Politics: A Study of Eastern Australia,
1850–1910* (Melbourne University Press, Melbourne, 1960), pp.
69–213, and accounts contained in the chapters written by D. W.
Rawson (Victoria), R. B. Joyce (Queensland), Loveday, Martin and
Patrick Weller (New South Wales), D. Jaensch (South Australia),
B. de Garis (Western Australia), Weller (Tasmania) and Loveday
(the Commonwealth) in Loveday, Martin and Parker (eds), *The
Emergence of the Australian Party System.* For revealing pictures of
the Labor Parties in the inter-war period, see Maurice Blackburn,
'The Historical Development of Australian Political Parties', in W.
G. K. Duncan (ed.), *Trends in Australian Politics* (Angus and
Robertson, Sydney, 1935), pp. 1–15; and J. A. McCallum, 'The
Economic Bases of Australia Politics', in ibid., pp. 44–71. See also
D. W. Rawson, *Australia Votes: The 1958 Federal Election* (Mel-
bourne University Press, Melbourne, 1961), pp. 11–21; James Jupp,
Australian Party Politics (Melbourne University Press, Melbourne,
1964), pp. 53–73; D. W. Rawson, *Labor in Vain? A Survey of the
Australian Labor Party* (Longmans, Croydon, Victoria, 1966); Emy,
The Politics of Australian Democracy, pp. 372–414.

11 See D. W. Rawson, 'The Paradox of Partisan Trade Unionism: The
Australian Case', *British Journal of Political Science*, IV, Part 4
(October 1974), pp. 399–418; Rawson, *Unions and Unionists in
Australia* (Allen and Unwin, Sydney, 1986), pp. 46–74; P. M.
Martin, 'Trade Unions and Labour Governments in Australia: A
Study of the Relation between Supporting Interests and Party
Policy', *Journal of Commonwealth Political Studies*, II (1963–4),
pp. 59–78.

12   L. F. Crisp, *The Parliamentary Government of the Commonwealth of Australia* (Longmans, London, 1949), pp. 78–9.

13   D. W. Rawson, 'The Labor Campaign', in Howard R. Penniman (ed.), *Australia at the Polls: The National Elections of 1975* (American Enterprise Institute for Public Policy Research, Washington, DC, 1977), p. 82.

14   For an authoritative account of Lang's career, see Bede Nairn, *The 'Big Fella': Jack Lang and the Australian Labor Party 1891–1949* (Melbourne University Press, Melbourne, 1986). On the conflicts within the New South Wales Labor Party in 1926–7, see also D. W. Rawson, *The Organisation of the Australian Labor Party* (D. Phil. Thesis, University of Melbourne, 1954), pp. 103–30; I. E. Young, *Conflict within the N.S.W. Labor Party, 1919–1932* (M. A. Thesis, University of Sydney, 1961), pp. 174–263; James Hagan, 'Lang and the Unions, 1923–32', in Heather Radi and Peter Spearritt (eds), *Jack Lang* (Hale and Iremonger, Neutral Bay, New South Wales, 1977), pp. 38–48, and Frank Farrell, 'Dealing with the Communists, 1923–36', in ibid., pp. 49–68; Louise Overacker, *The Australian Party System* (Yale University Press, New Haven, 1952), pp. 134–44; S. Encel, *Cabinet Government in Australia* (Melbourne University Press, Melbourne, 1962), pp. 156–60; Jim Hagan and Ken Turner, *A History of the Labor Party in New South Wales 1891–1991* (Longman Cheshire, Melbourne, 1991), pp. 68–81 and 121–7. On background issues, see D. W. Rawson, 'Politics and "Responsibility" in Australian Trade Unions', *The Australian Journal of Politics and History*, IV, 2 (November 1958), pp. 231–3; I. Young, 'The impact of J. T. Lang on the N.S.W. Labor Party', *APSA News*, VIII, 1 (May 1963), pp. 19–30. See also, J. T. Lang, *I Remember* (Invincible Press, Sydney, 1956); Lang, *The Great Bust: The Depression of the Thirties* (Angus and Robertson, Sydney, 1962); and the following biographies: of John Bailey by Martha Rutledge, in Nairn and Serle (eds), *Australian Dictionary of Biography*, vol. VII (1979), pp. 136–7; of John S. Garden by Nairn, in ibid., vol. VIII (1981), pp. 614–17; of J. T. Lang by Nairn, in ibid., vol. IX (1983), pp. 661–6; of Peter F. Loughlin by Nairn, in ibid., vol. X (1986), pp. 148–9; of Albert C. Willis by Frank Farrell, in John Ritchie (ed.), ibid., vol. XII (1990), pp. 509–11.

15   See H. V. Evatt, *Australian Labour Leader: The Story of W. A. Holman and the Labour Movement* (Angus and Robertson, Sydney, Abridged Edition, 1954), pp. 289–93 and 300–24; Nairn, *The 'Big Fella'*, pp. 15–21; Robin Gollan, *The Coalminers of New South*

Wales: A History of the Union, 1860–1960 (Melbourne University Press, Melbourne, 1963), pp. 144–5.

16 Nairn, *The 'Big Fella'*, p. 66.

17 Hagan, 'Lang and the Unions', in Radi and Spearritt (eds), *Jack Lang*, pp. 38–9.

18 Nairn, *The 'Big Fella'*, pp. 62–3.

19 Ibid., p. 65.

20 See R. S. Parker, 'The Government of New South Wales', in S. R. Davis (ed.), *The Government of the Australian States* (Longmans, London, 1960), pp. 139–41; Parker, *The Government of New South Wales* (University of Queensland Press, St Lucia, Queensland, 1978), pp. 246–7.

21 Nairn, *The 'Big Fella'*, p. 96.

22 Ibid., pp. 116–17, citing *The Australian Worker* (Sydney), 14 April 1926, p. 18, regarding the composition of the executive.

23 *Sydney Morning Herald*, 14 September 1926, p. 9; Nairn, *The 'Big Fella'*, p. 126.

24 *Sydney Morning Herald*, 15 September 1926, p. 16; 16 September 1926, p. 11.

25 Ibid., 13 November 1926, p. 18.

26 *The Australian Worker*, 17 November 1926, p. 3.

27 *New South Wales Parliamentary Debates*, vol. 108, 19 November 1926, p. 1321.

28 *Sydney Morning Herald*, 23 July 1927, p. 15. See also Nairn, *The 'Big Fella'*, pp. 142–3.

29 Lang, *I Remember*, p. 318.

30 Nairn, *The 'Big Fella'*, pp. 154–5. See also Rawson, *The Organisation of the Australian Labor Party*, pp. 115–19; *Sydney Morning Herald*, 18 April 1927, p. 8. For an interpretation of the version of the rules current in 1930–3, see Robert Cooksey, *Lang and Socialism: A Study in the Great Depression* (Australian National University Press, Canberra, 1971), pp. 12–14.

31 Nairn, *The 'Big Fella'*, p. 142; *Sydney Morning Herald*, 29 January 1927, p. 15.

32 *Sydney Morning Herald*, 15 February 1927, p. 11; 19 February 1927, p. 16. This was the rules revision procedure envisaged by the Goodin–Gillies pact.

33 Ibid., 4 March 1927, p. 12.

34 Ibid., 7 March 1927, p. 11.

35 Ibid., 7 April 1927, p. 9.

36 Ibid., 16 April 1927, p. 11.

37 Ibid., 16 April 1927, pp. 11 and 12; 18 April 1927, pp. 7 and

8; 19 April 1927, p. 9; 22 April 1927, p. 12; 23 April 1927, p. 15.

38   Ibid., 20 April 1927, p. 13.
39   Ibid., 27 April 1927, p. 13.
40   Ibid., 13 May 1927, p. 11; 14 May 1927, p. 15.
41   Ibid., 27 May 1927, p. 11; Encel, *Cabinet Government in Australia*, pp. 81–3.
42   *Sydney Morning Herald*, 27 June 1927, p. 11.
43   Ibid., 25 July 1927, pp. 11–12.
44   Nairn, *The 'Big Fella'*, pp. 163–317.
45   Ibid., pp. 190 and 256. See also Cooksey, *Lang and Socialism*, pp. 12–16 and 86–9; Farrell, 'Dealing with the Communists', in Radi and Spearritt (eds), *Jack Lang*, pp. 63–4.
46   Lang, *I Remember*, p. 327.
47   On the events of 1896, see Lawrence Goodwyn, *Democratic Promise: The Populist Movement in America* (Oxford University Press, New York, 1976), pp. 470–92.
48   See V. O. Key, *Politics, Parties, and Pressure Groups* (Crowell, New York, Fifth Edition, 1964), pp. 20–43.
49   See ibid., pp. 44–71. On the growth of class feeling in the New Deal period, see Samuel Lubell, *The Future of American Politics* (Doubleday, New York, Revised Second Edition, 1956), pp. 29–60.
50   For an excellent statement of the problem, and for a review of the main political factors inhibiting the growth of an American Socialist Party in the early years of this century, see Werner Sombart, *Why is There No Socialism in the United States?* ed. C. T. Husbands, tr. Patricia M. Hocking and Husbands (Macmillan, London, 1976), pp. 3–58. See also Leon D. Epstein, *Political Parties in Western Democracies* (Pall Mall, London, 1967), pp. 130–66; G.-E. Lavau, *Partis Politiques et Réalités Sociales: Contribution à une étude Réaliste des Partis Politiques* (Armand Colin, Paris, 1953), pp. 76–9.
51   See Everett Carll Ladd with Charles D. Hadley, *Transformations of the American Party System: Political Coalitions from the New Deal to the 1970s* (Norton, New York, Second Edition, 1978), pp. 385–6; Seymour Martin Lipset, *Political Man: The Social Bases of Politics* (Heinemann, London, Second Edition, 1983), pp. 503–15.
52   Ladd with Hadley, *Transformations of the American Party System*, p. 192.
53   Bernard Hennessy, 'Trade Unions and the British Labor Party', *American Political Science Review*, XLIX, 4 (December 1955), p. 1050, n. 4.

54 See Ross M. Martin, *TUC: The Growth of a Pressure Group 1868–1976* (Clarendon Press, Oxford, 1980), pp. 286–324.

55 Hennessy, 'Trade Unions and the British Labor Party', pp. 1054–5 (membership figures are from Appendix A of Henry Pelling, *A Short History of the Labour Party* (Macmillan, London, Eighth Edition, 1985), p. 194).

56 R. T. McKenzie, *British Political Parties: The Distribution of Power within the Conservative and Labour Parties* (Heinemann, London, Second Edition, 1963, reprinted 1964), pp. 516–18; Hennessy, 'Trade Unions and the British Labor Party', p. 1057.

57 Calculated from data given in table 13 in Martin Harrison, *Trade Unions and the Labour Party since 1945* (Allen and Unwin, London, 1960), p. 72.

58 Calculated from data given in table 11 in ibid., p. 66.

59 Ibid., pp. 99–100.

60 Hennessy, 'Trade Unions and the British Labor Party', p. 1061.

61 See Samuel H. Beer, *Modern British Politics: Parties and Pressure Groups in the Collectivist Age* (Faber and Faber, London, New Edition, 1982), pp. 217–42; Harrison, *Trade Unions and the Labour Party since 1945*, pp. 224–32; Pelling, *A Short History of the Labour Party*, pp. 105–23.

62 McKenzie, *British Political Parties*, p. 607.

63 See Philip M. Williams, *Hugh Gaitskell: A Political Biography* (Jonathan Cape, London, 1979), pp. 537–653.

64 See Martin, *TUC*, p. 308; Pelling, *A Short History of the Labour Party*, pp. 144–5.

65 See Lewis Minkin, *The Labour Party Conference: A Study in the Politics of Intra-Party Democracy* (Manchester University Press, Manchester, 1980), pp. 342–5.

66 *The Times* (London), 28 June 1990, pp. 1 and 22; and 13. On the background to these proposals, see Lewis Minkin, *The Contentious Alliance: Trade Unions and the Labour Party* (Edinburgh University Press, Edinburgh, 1991), pp. 362–74.

67 *The Times* (London), 24 June 1991, p. 4; the *Sunday Times* (London), 2 September 1990, p. 7.

68 *The Times*, 31 May 1991, p. 2.

69 See ibid., 25 February 1993, pp. 1 and 2.

70 See René Mouriaux, *Les syndicats dans la société française* (Presses de la Fondation Nationale des Sciences Politiques, Paris, 1983); Vincent Wright, *The Government and Politics of France* (Unwin Hyman, London, Third Edition, 1989), pp. 274–7; D. L. Hanley, A. P. Kerr and N. H. Waites, *Contemporary France: Politics and Society since 1945* (Routledge, London, Revised Edition, 1984,

reprinted 1989), pp. 196–202. On the relationship between trade unions and the French Socialist parties, see above pp. 179–80.

71 D. S. Bell and Byron Criddle, *The French Socialist Party: The Emergence of a Party of Government* (Clarendon Press, Oxford, Second Edition, 1988), p. 149. See also Mouriaux, *Les syndicats dans la société française*, pp. 206–11.

72 Maurice Duverger, *Political Parties: Their Organization and Activity in the Modern State*, tr. Barbara and Robert North (Methuen, London, 1954), p. xxxiv.

73 On this point, see Epstein, *Political Parties in Western Democracies*, pp. 242–50.

12

The Stability of Parties

In modern liberal democracies almost all parties, whatever the size of their permanent establishment, like to claim that they are the agencies of much larger social movements. This claim is put to its most stringent test at the time of a general election when a party must show that it can mobilize an army of voters, but it also has organizational implications, for it imposes on those parties with a social-democratic or liberal-democratic constitution (that is, a constitution which makes provision for open branches at the local level and for plenary conferences at the regional and national levels) the obligation to renew themselves in regular cycles of activity. This whole process, beginning with the choice of delegates by the branches, proceeding to regional meetings and culminating in a national conference where general policy issues are discussed and the party executive chosen, has a ritual aspect. It signifies a reaffirmation not only of faith and fellowship but also of the party's representativeness, its unity of outlook, and the solidarity of its central leadership.

Like any ritual, this cycle of organizational renewal can produce conflict and stress, for it furnishes opportunities for groups among the activists to call the party to account: should they consider that traditional values have been neglected or undermined by the party's officers, or should they have other grievances – the feeling that the party has compromised its principles for the sake of short-term advantage, for example – they are likely to use their influence at branch and regional level to ensure that the issues are raised and discussed at the national conference. The conference period, therefore, can be an awkward time for the central leaders. They recognize that the activists provide the stability which the party needs during its organizational cycle but they have also to ensure that the party maintains any advantages which it has gained at the centre of the political system. All parties rely not only on the services of a selfless group of activists, valuable though their contribution undoubtedly is, but also on the technical professionalism of experts in particular fields of policy – economists, and those with special knowledge of the detailed legal, administrative and legislative procedures within which the party must operate at the national level. Running a successful party is essentially a matter of maintaining a balance between these two contrasting areas of support and experience and ensuring that one does not exclude the other.

An established activist culture is both a source of strength for a party, in that it provides a loyalist base for the leadership, and a source of weakness, in that it reduces a party's ability to adapt itself to changing circumstances. Alternative methods of achieving stability at the base of the party organization may seem to have immediate advantages but they can carry with them attendant dangers. The recruiting of large numbers of ordinary members may serve to submerge local activist cultures, but a nominal membership is likely to prove ineffective as a means of sustaining and mobilizing local support, especially at election time. Providing that a party has sufficient resources of its own, or has access through government to public patronage, it is possible for it to construct a network of patron–client systems capable of undermining or displacing a system of activists but the cost of such an operation can be very high and can eventually generate resentment amongst the public. A party may also attempt to achieve organizational stability by basing itself on an organized interest group whose cadres it then borrows, but this exposes it to manipulation and to a loss of electoral support outside the boundaries of the section concerned.

The distinctive leadership structure of parties is another possible source of their weakness. Of course, as in most organizations, advancement within a party depends to some extent upon the possession of certain personal qualities and of the appropriate administrative and management skills, but it tends to be a more open and less regulated process than does advancement in, say, a business corporation, an administrative agency, the army or the police force. Considerations of seniority play a much more prominent part in the selection of a chief of police, for example, than in the choice of a party leader. This difference arises from the fact that a party is looking for someone with the ability to win elections and command support not only amongst its own membership but in the community at large. It must therefore be prepared to reward success by rapid promotion and equally, to discard leaders who have lost their touch and become a liability. A party's leadership team will usually possess some sense of collegiality, particularly if the party is in power or has a reasonable prospect of taking office, but that team will be surrounded by a penumbra of former leaders who have lost their influence and of aspiring leaders anxious to demonstrate their popularity. Challenges to the authority of established leaders and complicated succession crises become almost inescapable elements of intra-party conflict under such conditions.

The fluidity of their leadership means that in some ways parties provide one of the few remaining areas for self-expression and competition in societies whose institutions are increasingly subject to the rational-bureaucratic regulation of social and economic transactions. Unlike most organizations, a party will admit to membership anyone above a certain age who supports its objectives and is willing to pay a nominal fee. From that point on, there are usually no barriers to advancement: a party member can acquire the skills of public speaking, committee politics and self-presentation; he or she can explore areas of expert knowledge in the fields of foreign affairs or public finance, and can challenge specialists' views during conference debates or in the party press; even before becoming a regular delegate, a party member can hold to account the great and the good, questioning motives and searching for hidden interests. In such respects, parties have kept alive the traditions of popular democracy, but their very openness does expose them to subversion from groups searching for a short cut to power or from a pressure group determined to cut a direct path to the party's policy-making bodies.

These special organizational features of parties – the tension between activists and the central leaders, the relative fluidity of the leadership group, and the liberal terms of membership entry – all help to explain the patterns of conflict which occur within them. As we saw earlier, such conflict has three dimensions, namely sectarian, factional and sectional, and the case studies presented in chapters 9–11 are illustrations of what can happen when one of these dimensions becomes predominant. In the case of the French Socialist Parties, which have traditionally placed a high value on the expression of general philosophies, internal conflicts have been marked by sectarianism. We saw that, especially in the pre-war SFIO, a dissenting leader would usually identify himself with an absolute version of one strand in the party's doctrinal tradition. Around him, a group dedicated to the view that respect for that version was all important would call upon the party to free itself from specific policy objectives in contemporary politics and, inspired by doctrines drawn from the past, to strive to realize an ideal future. Such an idea of party action appealed strongly to those activists who, having encountered what they considered to be an insufficient respect for tradition on the part of the central leaders, found in sectarianism a release for their frustration.

A sectarian leader almost invariably finds himself casting doubt on the integrity of the party's official leaders. They stand accused, in the eyes of the sectarians, of having placed more importance on the obtaining of short-term benefits for their supporters than on the realizing of the party's ultimate goals. For this reason, party leaders tend to regard sectarianism as a particularly dangerous form of subversion, capable of undermining the activists' loyalty and sweeping them into a maelstrom of doctrinal fundamentalism. Yet they can do little to deal with such a threat: as the party's formal guardians their own freedom to use traditional themes is subject to ritual restraint, nor can they risk damaging the party's standing by repudiating its external commitments – its membership of a coalition government, for example. Their only effective response is that of counter-attack, accusing the sectarian leader of a deliberate misinterpretation of the party's traditions in an attempt to mislead activists about doctrinal matters. Mutual accusations of bad faith quickly reduce sectarian conflict to a personal dispute between the sectarian leader and the party's duly appointed officers, thus giving it a factional aspect.

In our second study, of group confrontations within the Uttar Pradesh Congress Party, one of the most interesting features was the virtual absence of sectarianism from the conflict. The contrast with the case of the French Socialist Parties is all the more striking because of the number of unresolved normative questions which the Indian National Congress had inherited from past debates – the debate between the Hindu traditionalists and the cultural pluralists (or secularists), that between those who saw the future of Indian agriculture in terms of peasant proprietorship and those who favoured some form of collective farming, and that between Congressmen who were still attached to the Gandhian notion of organic order in society and those who accepted individualism and competition as the inevitable consequences of economic development. Although the discussion of these questions was an integral part of the Congress Party's activist culture, the contingent of activists in the UP Congress was extremely small and was therefore easily outweighed by the large number of primary members deliberately recruited to serve in the party's election armies and swell the ranks of its internal groups. As a result, the clash between C. B. Gupta and his opponents in the late 1950s and early 1960s was almost entirely lacking in policy content; it was ties of alliance and clientelism rather than common conviction that bound each group to its leaders.

As we saw, the early phase of this conflict, between 1957 and 1960, began with a period of confusion following Gupta's exclusion from power and ended in a confrontation between two state-wide groups, each possessing its own structure of subgroups and each determined to control the party organization. Gupta won the crucial encounter of October 1960 and, had the conflict followed its logical course, should then have been able by extensive use of clientelism to have dismantled the opposing group and become the virtual 'boss' of the largest state in India. Faced with such a prospect, the Congress High Command in Delhi stepped in, acting first of all to protect Gupta's opponents and then, in 1963, taking the opportunity offered by the Kamaraj Plan to remove him from office. Had Gupta been permitted to capitalize on his earlier advantage and create a monolithic system of relationships within the party, the UP Congress might well have become an arena for systematic debate about the major social and economic issues facing the state. As it was, the energies of the party were dissipated as the various groups joined in a protracted struggle for power within the informal rules laid down by the High Command.

Finally, the Australian case studies of the Victorian Country Party and the New South Wales Labor Party in the 1920s illustrate what can happen when a party is largely dependent on the support of an organized interest group. In both conflicts, the activists' loyalty to the party's formal authorities was minimal; it was almost as though they considered the party to be merely a derivative of the section which had generated it, and liable to be corrupted by the parliamentary activity in which it was engaged. On the other hand, their allegiance to their respective sections was strong and unqualified. Each group of activists behaved as if it had been delegated to stand vigil over the parliamentary party and to report back to the section if there seemed any likelihood of the latter's interests being neglected or betrayed. In the case of these Australian studies, it is the effect of strong economic sectionalism which we see exemplified, but the same relationship between supporting group and parliamentary party can obtain when parties are bound to sectionalism of a regional, religious or linguistic kind.

A party subject to strong pressure from a single supporting section is vulnerable to particular patterns of internal conflict. As in the Australian cases discussed above, party cohesion becomes a function of cohesion in the underlying group and should that group divide, the fracture runs through the party as well. A party is also vulnerable if it attempts to broaden its electoral base beyond the boundaries of the supporting group and make itself more independent. Such a move will almost certainly produce a reaction from its activists, given their strong sectional ties. One of the points at issue between John Allan and Albert Dunstan in the Victorian conflict was the former's interest in adopting a strategy aimed at giving the Country Party an anti-Labor orientation and at forming coalitions with the Nationalists. In the New South Wales case, Peter Loughlin stood for the principle of freeing the party from external control, whereas John Lang was, for tactical reasons, willing to accept a degree of dependence on the Miners' Federation and the Labor Council.

Whenever a political party enters a period of severe internal conflict, all its energies are absorbed in the processes of containing the spread of disorder and framing the conditions for a settlement. Should the outcome be a radical change in the policies and aims of the party, it may find itself in a limbo, out of touch with its former constituency and struggling to win the attachment of a new one. In the end, the result of intra-party conflict is subject to trial by election, for it is this which provides the basic test of credibility and acceptability. If a party is taken over by a sectarian leadership which ignores the need to offer a broad programme of realistic policy objectives, or if it allows an organized interest group to dominate its affairs at the expense of other interests, or if it is torn apart by a lengthy confrontation between groups which support rival candidates for the leadership, it is likely to find its vote substantially reduced and its position in the political system seriously weakened. However much groups within parties may wish to convince themselves that they alone possess the formula which can determine the party's future success, the ballot box ultimately brings home to them their dependence on external approval.

Conclusion

The liberal democratic model of representative politics is accepted more widely today than it was a century ago, or even fifty years ago, and we now have a great deal more information about how political groups are affected by the conduct of free elections based on universal suffrage. We are also better informed as to how the organization of party systems varies from country to country and from time to time within the same country, and more is known about the relative efficiency of various types of parties in expressing the views of social groups, recruiting leaders and providing a flexible and responsible basis for parliamentary majorities and government. We no longer assume that representative politics can thrive only in relatively urbanized countries with a large middle class and rational-bureaucratic modes of administration; on the contrary, we recognize that representative institutions are quite robust enough to function in a wide range of societies, not least in those which are agrarian and village-based in character.

At the same time, we have become more familiar with the effects which stress can have upon parties and party systems forced to operate under difficult circumstances. Here we have looked in particular at two responses to stress – the first, an accentuation of rally politics in a party system and the second, an intensification of intra-party conflict. These processes are interesting in themselves and pose interesting problems of analysis, but they also enable us to see how parties and party systems protect themselves from a hostile environment while dealing with the problems which it presents. Parties under pressure have shown themselves to be highly adaptable organizations, capable of making significant adjustments in their behaviour within a short space of time. Measured against the liberal ideal which conceives of a party as acting in a rational manner, presenting realistic programmes to obtain a mandate to govern, most actual parties reveal themselves to be complex and versatile associations, driven partly by the need to foster a coalition of economic and social interests, and partly by the desire to convince the community that the state is safe in their hands. They are hybrids, part entrepreneur and part high constable. On the one hand, they engage in politics to manage the bargaining involved in the allocation of scarce resources, and on the other, they offer themselves as a team of men and women capable of taking decisive action to maintain the stability of the state. These two aspects are always in a shifting balance in every party, and the party system as a whole reflects this ambiguity of function. As a polity moves through time, therefore, its representative process may vary, sometimes taking the form of party competition and sometimes the form of a rally movement striving to mobilize the entire community in an endeavour to preserve the state.

We have seen that this duality of form affects the leadership structure of parties, for an individual amply endowed with the personal qualities and experience needed to deal with short-term policy issues and day-to-day bargaining may not necessarily possess those attributes which either the party itself or the community looks for in times of trouble. In such circumstances, someone on the fringe of the party with a reputation for independence and moral probity may find himself called on to become a rally leader. This is not to imply, of course, that a rally leader will always come from outside the party's leadership hierarchy: Nehru is an example of a politician who, in the seventeen years he spent as Prime Minister, never lost his gift for inspiring the Indian people and making them aware of themselves as a collective political force; de Gaulle, on the other hand, exemplifies the way in which an individual of outstanding personal qualities who is outside the formal institutions of government can nevertheless become the centre of a national revival. It is always possible that the shift to rally politics may end badly, that a rally leader may convert his provisional authority into an unregulated dictatorship, and that the form of the state may be changed in consequence. Nevertheless, rally politics should be seen not as a retrograde condition but as an intelligible response to the the threat of breakdown and disorder. Whatever form they may take, rallies are essentially conservative in effect; they provide a means of dealing with a crisis within the framework of the law and presuppose a return to 'normal' politics once the difficulty has been resolved.

In elections and in parliament, parties are constrained to deal with the short-term prospects for implementing policies and framing legislation, and in these contexts they must display the appropriate professionalism, that of reconciling the representation of interests with the making of laws. In the public arena, the credibility of parties depends upon their ability to convince the electorate of their capacity to formulate and carry through policies which will remedy current problems. In their inner working, at branch meetings and at regional and national conferences, they have more scope to consider long-term perspectives, to use imagination, and to discuss what objectives they wish to achieve when in office. Parties cater for quite different expectations: they attract idealists who think of politics in terms of grand designs but equally they draw together those activists who relish the challenge of preparing realistic programmes and working to achieve office. In these ways, they serve as the engines of liberal democracy. They provide a framework within which the ordinary citizen can develop his or her political capacity and test out ideas against the criticism of others who share the same aspirations and goals. Yet, by remaining open and responsive to their constituents, parties run the risk of being overwhelmed by the members they recruit and of being disrupted by unresolved conflict. The dilemma is inescapable: openness is necessary if they are to attract supporters and the ideas, interests and ambitions which they bring with them, but some degree of discipline and control is necessary so that the party may acquire a public personality and the capacity to act as a united force in relation to other parties. If a balance has to be struck, it should be in favour of openness. Although intra-party conflict can be destructive, sometimes to the point of weakening a party beyond remedy, it is more often a sign of vitality, evidence that the party is tapping the raw energy of new generations and new social groups.

As liberal democratic politics comes into play once more in the former Communist states of Eastern Europe and the Soviet Union, we can expect to see the inevitable stresses of this change producing some of the effects – such as frequent bursts of rally politics and periods of severe intra-party conflict – which we have discussed in this book. Some of these effects may be disruptive and some may impede the implementation of urgent programmes of economic and social reform, but only the provision of freedom of discussion and association, free elections, and open parliaments can ensure that the bulk of the people are themselves involved in and engaged by the politics which are being conducted in their name.

Index